PACIFIC AND WORLD STUDIES SERIES

Monographs of the Center for International Studies, Inha University

Series Editors: *Mann-kyu Kim, Hideki Ohata and Stephan Haggard*

This series explores political, economic, social, and strategic issues in the developing world, with particular emphasis on East Asia and the Pacific. Particular volumes will address industrial adjustment and trade conflict; North-South relations; technology transfer and innovation; and trade in food, energy, and strategic minerals.

The series seeks to encourage collaboration among scholars from all countries in the region.

Mann-kyu Kim is the director of the Center for International Studies and Professor of Political Science at Inha University, Korea.

Hideki Ohata is Professor of International Relations at Waseda University, Japan.

Stephan Haggard is Associate Professor of Government and Associate, Center for International Affairs, Harvard University, U.S.A.

PACIFIC AND WORLD STUDIES, NO. 1

Trade and Investment in Services

in the Asia-Pacific Region

Edited by **Chung H. Lee and Seiji Naya**

CIS-Inha University   Westview Press

PACIFIC AND WORLD STUDIES SERIES, NO. 1

Published in 1988 in the Republic of Korea by the **Center for International Studies, Inha University**; 253 Yonghyun-Dong, Nam-ku, Inchon 402-751.

Published in 1988 in the United States of America and distributed exclusively throughout the world excluding Korea, by **Westview Press, Inc.**, 5500 Central Avenue, Boulder, Colorado 80301

Library of Congress Cataloging-in-Publication Data
TRADE AND INVESTMENT IN SERVICES IN THE ASIA-PACIFIC REGION.
(Monographs of the Center for International Studies, Inha University)

Bibliography: p.
Includes index.
1. Service industries—Asia.
2. Service industries—Pacific Area.
3. Asia—Commerce.
4. Pacific Area—Commerce. I. Lee, Chung H. II. Naya, Seiji, III. Series.

HD9987. A2T73 1987 338.4′6′095 87-29597
ISBN 0-8133-0581-0
ISBN 0-8133-0585-3 (pbk.)

Printed and bound in the Republic of Korea by Seoul Computer Press

Contents

Tables

Figures

Introduction

Trade and investment in services such as telecommunications, financial services, insurance, legal services, advertising, shipping, and tourism has become an important issue in trade negotiations between the major economies in recent years. Because the Asia-Pacific region contains some of the most dynamic economies in the world and because its intraregional trade and investment in services is likely to follow its phenomenal growth in trade in manufactured goods, issues in trade and investment in services are of special importance to the region. However, little is known about the patterns and magnitude of trade and investment in services in the region and their economic effects. There is even confusion about what constitutes trade in services and thus about which international forum would be appropriate for dealing with services-related issues.

On 15-19 September 1986 the contracting parties of the General Agreement on Tariffs and Trade (GATT) met in Punta del Este, Uruguay, where the ministers of 92 governments adopted a declaration launching a new round of trade negotiations. The declaration stipulates that negotiations on both goods and services be treated as one policy undertaking and that GATT practices and procedures also apply to the negotiations on services, although they would not be placed within the legal framework of GATT. The aim of the negotiations is thus to establish a multilateral framework of principles and rules for trade in services similar to that for trade in goods.

One of the issues to be resolved in the Uruguay Round is what will be included in the definition of traded services. In pushing for freer trade in services, the United States and other developed countries consider traded services to consist of such services as accounting, banking, insurance, and telecommunications. Certain developing countries—for example, Brazil and India—take the position that construction services should be included as well. Another issue to be resolved is whether direct foreign investment in services and sales of foreign affiliates should be on the agenda for negotiation.

In the past two decades the economies of the Asia-Pacific region have prospered and become highly interdependent. Trade and investment in manufactured goods have played a critical role in this process. As some of the economies in the region become increasingly service oriented, questions have been raised as to whether trade and investment services will be able to play this critical role. What are the patterns of trade and investment in services in the region? How important are they for the region's prosperity? These are some of the questions that need to be addressed now if the region hopes to maintain the momentum it has enjoyed for the past two decades.

Much has been written in recent years on trade and investment in services, and many have advocated freer trade in services as if its benefits to the countries involved are self-evident. Yet there is not a firm consensus on what trade in services includes or whether the principle of comparative advantage—the logical foundation for freer trade—applies to trade in services. This volume addresses some of these issues, beginning with a chapter on conceptual issues relating to trade and investment in services. The inadequacy of data on international transactions in services notwithstanding, several chapters make significant progress toward providing a quantitative picture of the patterns of trade and investment in services as well as describing the salient characteristics of several important service industries. There are, however, too many unanswered questions, and this volume is only the beginning of the arduous work that must be undertaken to answer them.

Chung H. Lee
Seiji Naya

PART I
GENERAL ISSUES IN SERVICES TRADE

OVERVIEW

CHAPTER 1
Stern and Hoekman on Conceptual Issues

Stern and Hoekman investigate some of the conceptual issues relating to international transactions in services. They characterize services as commodities that are intangible and nonstorable and the production and consumption of which normally take place simultaneously. Four types of services are distinguished in terms of the movement of providers and demanders necessary for international transactions in services to take place: case 1, services for which no movement of providers or demanders is needed; case 2, services for which only providers need to move; case 3, services for which only demanders need to move; and case 4, services for which both providers and demanders need to move.

Since they define trade in services as occurring whenever domestic factors of production receive income from nonresidents in exchange for services, wherever the services may be rendered, international transactions involving type 1 and type 3 services constitute trade in services. Even in the case of type 2 and type 4 services, trade in services takes place insofar as domestic factors of production receive payments from nonresidents. It thus follows that trade in services as defined by Stern and Hoekman includes income from direct foreign investment and remittances from expatriate workers. In other words, they make no distinction between trade in nonfactor services and trade in factor services and between the sales of foreign affiliates and trade in services in the narrower and more conventional sense of the term.

On the critical issue of whether the principle of comparative advantage applies to services, Stern and Hoekman argue that it generally holds, with a possible exception in type 2 services. Even in that case they argue that trade will be beneficial to the countries involved. They see no reason why the standard theoretical analysis of distortions and impediments to international trade would not be applicable to services and argue that there is a strong presumption that countries may realize gains from the liberalization of trade in services.

Stern and Hoekman raise the following questions for future research agenda:

1. What is the quantitative magnitude of the four types of services, and what is the importance of traded services relative to factor movements related to services?
2. Given the fact that many services are labor-intensive, will labor-abundant developing countries become major exporters of services?
3. What is the relationship between international trade in goods and trade in services?
4. What is the effect of technological innovations on trade in services?

For the new Uruguay Round, Stern and Hoekman propose the inclusion of issues related to investment, labor mobility (as in construction services), and the linkage between trade in goods and trade in services.

CHAPTER 2
Lee and Naya on Patterns of Trade and Investment

In investigating the patterns of trade and investment in services in the Asia-Pacific region, Lee and Naya differentiate trade in services—defined as transborder transactions between residents and nonresidents involving the output of service industries (i.e., trade in nonfactor services)—from investment in services—defined as direct foreign investment carried out by service industries. The latter results in the establishment of affiliates abroad that provide services to local residents.

Given this definition of trade and investment in services, Lee and Naya see no reason why trade and investment in services should be fundamentally different from trade and investment in goods. They argue that analytically the difference between goods and services in the context of international transactions comes down to a difference in transaction costs. Thus the principle of comparative advantage and the modern theory of multinational corporations should be applicable to services as well.

Data on trade and investment in services are scarcely available, and even those that are available suffer from questionable reliability. The data published by the International Monetary Fund in its *Balance of Payments Statistics* are too aggregated to shed much light on recent developments in the service industries, services there being grouped into shipment; passenger services; other transportation; travel; and other private goods, services, and income. Despite the inadequate data, Lee and Naya have identified the following broad features:

1. The share of services output exported is smaller than the share of merchandise output exported for all the countries in the region, indicating that services are in general less traded than merchandise.
2. Although the United States and Japan—the two largest and most developed economies in the region—export only a relatively small share of the services they produce, they are nonetheless the two largest exporters of services (the Asian newly industrializing countries are also large exporters of services).
3. During the 1976–1983 period all the countries in the region experienced a high rate of growth in the export and import of services; however, the ratio of services trade to merchandise trade over this period remained stable for both exports and imports. This stability in the commodity composition of trade does not lend support to the assertion that U.S. comparative advantage has shifted in recent years to service industries.

Data on direct foreign investment and the sales of foreign service affiliates are even poorer than those on trade in services. Lee and Naya report only on U.S. and Japanese direct foreign investment, although some of the developing countries in the region have also made foreign investments.

It was found that service industries—trade, finance (excluding banking), insurance, and real estate—accounted for about a quarter of the U.S. total direct investment position during the 1977–1983 period. Although direct investment position is not directly comparable with trade in services, this figure nonetheless demonstrates the importance of service industries in U.S. direct foreign investment relative to their importance in the U.S. current account (12 percent for the ratio of services exports to commodity exports for the 1976–1983 period).

The U.S. direct investment position in the Asia-Pacific region has increased in recent years, but it still accounted for no more than 9 percent of the total U.S. investment position in 1983. Lee and Naya estimate the U.S. investment position in services in the region to have been about US$5 billion in 1983—2.3 percent of the total U.S. direct investment position that year.

Although data on the U.S. direct investment position in services for the individual countries are spotty, they nonetheless point to a significant variation from country to country. For instance, in 1983 services accounted for 60 percent of the U.S. investment position in Hong Kong, but they accounted for only 2 percent in Indonesia.

A variable that is more directly comparable with trade in services is the sales of services by foreign affiliates. In 1982 the sales of services by majority-owned U.S. foreign affiliates was 53 billion (US$) SDRs, whereas U.S. export of services was 29 billion (US$) SDRs. These figures, along with the statistics on U.S. trade and investment in services, demonstrate that direct foreign investment, not trade in services, is the major vehicle for the increasing internationalization of U.S. service industries.

CHAPTER 3
Grubel on Direct and Embodied Trade in Services

This chapter stresses that to understand the role of services in international trade, it is necessary to make a distinction between services embodied in merchandise trade and directly traded services. This point is especially important in light of the public concern in Canada that although the service-producing sector there accounts for a rising share of employment, its exports of nonfactor services have been declining relative to its merchandise exports.

Grubel divides services into the following three categories: services for final consumption, consumer services provided by the government, and producer or intermediate services used in further production of goods and services. He found that during the 1976–1985 period, employment expanded most rapidly in the producer services. This is an important finding as the first two categories of services are not, by and large, tradeable. Grubel points out that although direct trade in producer services has not increased as rapidly as Canadian domestic production, these services have been traded in increasing quantities because they are embodied in traded merchandise. His preliminary calculations show that trade in embodied services has in fact expanded more rapidly than merchandise trade for Canada.

If Grubel's calculations are correct, countries such as Canada and the United States need not fear decreasing merchandise trade as their economies become more service-oriented. Since the growth of producer services, which are relatively capital-intensive, is due to increases in various types of capital—physical, human, and knowledge—per worker, and because these countries are well endowed with such capital, they have a comparative advantage in goods that intensively embody the producer services and will expand their exports as capital further accumulates.

CHAPTER 1
Conceptual Issues Relating to Services in the International Economy

Robert M. Stern and Bernard M. Hoekman

Largely as a result of U.S. initiative, issues relating to trade and international factor movements involving services have been given a prominent place on the international policy agenda. This was reinforced by the resolution of the General Agreement on Tariffs and Trade (GATT) member-countries in Punta del Este in September 1986 to include services issues in the new round of multilateral trade negotiations. Although a considerable amount of data and descriptions of individual service sectors and their problems have become available, economists have only recently begun to address the important conceptual issues relating to services. This chapter will review some of these conceptual issues and in the process, it is hoped, stimulate discussion and further analysis of services in the international economy.

Theoretical Considerations

Distinguishing Characteristics of Goods and Services

In his especially insightful paper, Hill (1977:317–18) makes the following distinction between goods and services:

> A good may be defined as a physical object which is appropriable and, therefore, transferable between economic units.
>
> A service may be defined as a change in the conditions of a person, or of a good belonging to some economic unit, which is brought about as the

Helpful comments on an earlier version of the paper were received from the workshop participants and from Alan V. Deardorff. Financial assistance was provided in part by a grant from the Ford Foundation to support a program of research in trade policy at the University of Michigan.

> result of the activity of some other economic unit. This definition . . .is consistent with the underlying idea which is inherent in the concept of a service, namely that one economic unit performs some activity for the benefit of another. . . . Whatever the producer of the service does must impinge directly on the consumer in such a way as to change the condition of the latter. Otherwise no service is actually provided.

It seems clear from the foregoing definitions and from actual experience that service activities are both numerous and diverse in themselves and in the changes they effect in goods and persons.[1] An idea of the range and different types of services that exist is suggested by the following groupings, as noted in Canada (1982:11):[2]

- Services *complementary* to trade in goods (e.g., some forms of transportation, insurance, banking, and advertising)
- Services that *substitute* for trade in goods (e.g., franchising, rental, leasing, and repair)
- Services *unrelated* to goods (e.g., banking, life insurance, professional real estate, telecommunications, data processing and information, and travel)[3]

The preceding definitions, categories, and examples are not exhaustive or mutually exclusive; in fact, it is often difficult to disentangle what constitutes a good or service. Nonetheless, services do have the distinguishing characteristic that their production and consumption generally take place simultaneously and that, as Hill (1977:319) notes, services cannot be stored.[4] In addition, services are intangible.

---

1. In his conception and examples of services to persons, Hill (1977) apparently has households and individual consumers in mind. However, many kinds of services are rendered to businesses that are only indirectly reflected in the goods being produced. Perhaps the entity of a business firm can be considered as a person in this instance.

2. The Government of Canada report includes services embodied in goods as a separate category but with no clear way of distinguishing the services involved. But as Michael Leidy has suggested, by using Lancaster's framework of product attributes, goods can be thought of in terms of the services or attributes they provide.

3. The examples given here relate primarily to traded services, with distinction made between the services provided by private and public enterprise. Hill (1977:311–36) discusses the provision of collective and pure public services (e.g., education, public health, roads, public administration, and national defense), which involve important elements of externalities and can be characterized as "unsolicited" services. By affecting the cost and availability of many private services, the provision of collective and pure public services may have an important bearing on a nation's domestic economy and external trade. This will be the case as well if governments undertake regulatory policies that limit or protect the activities of its service sectors.

4. Although services cannot be stored, Herman and van Holst (1981:9) point out that they can be thought of as a stock of service-rendering capacity that must be available to

Especially in the case of services that are embodied in and thus change the condition of goods, the question naturally arises whether it is analytically meaningful and practical to separate the two. Much will depend here on the nature of technological change and the ways in which the specialized activities of firms are, to use Bhagwati's (1984a) terminology, "splintered" off into services from goods and goods from services.[5] Thus, depending on the level of aggregation for recording transactions, and particularly the time span involved, it may be difficult to distinguish goods from services at the industry level.

This difficulty will become more pronounced if services that previously were purchased at "arm's length" from other firms come to be subsumed within the firm.[6] That is, intrafirm transactions often cannot be measured accurately because there is no direct market analog available to value them. Given the size and complexity of most large corporations, in terms of both their domestic and multinational activities, it seems unlikely it will ever be possible to identify separately the services embodied in goods within the firm. Thus, changes in the relative importance of interfirm and intrafirm transactions will have a major impact on the measurement of the values of goods and services.

As previously mentioned, some services may be supplied by public as well as private enterprises in certain countries; and beyond that a number of collective and "pure" public services are provided by governments. These latter types of services—particularly those involving education, medical care, public administration, and national defense—raise difficult problems of valuation, since, as with intrafirm transactions, there may not be any readily usable direct market analogs. Because of this, input measures are commonly used to represent the

---

meet demand. Hill (1977:318) contends services cannot be analyzed in terms of conventional market exchange because they cannot be transferred physically like goods between buyers and sellers. This may be correct in a literal sense, but the existence of a service-rendering capacity will involve prices in order for the service to be sold. And surely firms and households will be sensitive to price differences among the entities offering services for sale.

5. Bhagwati postulates that as specialization emerges owing to economies of scale, service activities will be splintered off and become part of interfirm transactions—for example, when a firm decides to purchase outside transportation services instead of those supplied internally. He views this as technically progressive. On the other hand, when goods are splintered off from services as a result of technological progress, relatively unprogressive service sectors (as conventionally measured) may be left. An example would be the invention of the phonograph and records and subsequently the development of a "musical services" sector, which now appears technically unprogressive.

6. This point also applies to goods produced within the firm.

value of services in these cases.[7] Thus, services provided by public enterprises and government cannot be measured by the same standards as most private services, and there can be important intertemporal or intercountry differences, depending upon the private–public composition. Finally, governments pursue different regulatory policies regarding services, and the resulting promotion or restriction could result in national differences in the valuation and significance of particular services.

A Typology of Services

As noted previously and in Stern (1985:129–33), there are many different types of services and methods of classifying them for statistical reporting and for analytical purposes. Our interest is to consider services in the context of the theory of international trade; thus we will use a typology of the way services may be provided internationally, based upon consideration of whether the movement of the provider and demander of the service is required between countries. The focus is therefore on mobility or presence considerations. This typology is primarily based on the works of ECS (1982), USTR (1983), Bhagwati (1984a, 1985), and Sampson and Snape (1985). Four types of services are distinguished and each type can be further divided by making a distinction between services related to goods and services that are independent of goods.

Case 1. No movement of providers or demanders: separated services. The term "separated" services is attributable to Sampson and Snape (1985) and is analogous to what Bhagwati (1985) has called "disembodied" or "long distance" services. These can be considered in a sense as pure or independent services since they can in principle be traded just like goods, without any necessity of a foreign presence. Certain of these services can also be thought of as being complementary to trade in goods.

Case 2. Movement of providers only: demander-located services. In this case, physical proximity to the consuming households and firms is a necessary condition for the service, and capital or labor or both must move internationally to provide it. Thus, there may be direct foreign investment (DFI) involving some movement of physical and financial capital as well as skilled and unskilled labor. These international factor movements may provide services in the foreign

7. See Kravis, Heston, and Summers (1982:133 ff) for a careful empirical analysis of alternative measures for these types of services.

production of goods or other services. There need not be complete movement of all factors, however, in providing the services. As Deardorff (1985) has noted, there may be an absent factor—for example, management—that resides in the home country but can supply its services telematically to augment factors of production located abroad. This would be a case of separated factors, as opposed to the separated services discussed in case 1. The separated factors can produce services to be used abroad as inputs for the production of goods or other services. Examples include financial information, product design, and other inputs that can be transmitted electronically.

Case 3. Movement of demanders only: provider-located services. Here, the services are provided in the country in which the providers are physically located. Prime examples would be tourism (including business travel), education, and medical services.

Case 4. Movement of providers and demanders: footloose, non-separated services. This case is included for logical completeness although most instances of trade in service would fall under the previous three cases. It is a situation in which both providers and demanders move to another country where some service is performed and purchased. The services provided by absent factors may also be relevant here.

Whether the movement of providers and demanders of services is required is especially pertinent in analyzing the relation between trade and international factor movements involving the provision of services. Thus, in case 1 (separated services), there can be international trade in services, but there is no need for DFI or movement of labor. In cases 2 and 4, the provision of services requires a foreign presence, and there will be either DFI or the movement of labor internationally or both. In these cases there may also be absent factors that provide inputs telematically for use abroad. In case 3 (only demanders moving), there may, for example, be trade in transportation—a separated service—whereas the foreign expenditure will in general involve purchases of both goods and services.

This discussion suggests a need to clarify what is meant by trade in services. We define it as occurring when domestic factors receive income from nonresidents in exchange for their services. The location where the service is performed is not relevant. Our definition of trade in services thus is much broader than the conventional one, which usually refers only to separated services. In addition to separated services (case 1), we would include provider-located services (case 3) and demander-located services (cases 2 and 4) to the degree that domestic factors receive payments from nonresidents. If demander-located services are provided by a foreign affiliate employing only local factors, trade in services will not have occurred. This seems unlikely, however, since foreign affiliates will usually obtain some inputs from the parent company; therefore, trade in services will occur. How large this trade will be depends on the particular circumstances.[8]

Each of the cases in this typology has unique features with important implications for analysis and policy. From an analytical perspective, it is especially interesting to consider the usefulness of the conceptual framework of comparative advantage when applied to the individual cases included in our typology of services. This is also of interest from the standpoint of policy, since if comparative advantage is applicable to services, it can be argued that all parties gain from the liberalization of the international exchange of services.

Comparative Advantage and International Trade and Factor Mobility Involving Services

The principle of comparative advantage is at the basis of any exchange of goods—and presumably services—across borders. According to this principle, under conditions of competition and abstracting from changes in technology, countries will tend to export those goods and services in which they have a comparative advantage as measured by their relatively low autarky prices. This criterion of comparative advantage can be applied to each of the cases, as follows:

Case 1. (No movement of providers or demanders.) Services that are complementary to goods can be regarded as intermediate goods. Deardorff (1985) has referred to them as "trade services," and he has shown that in a world of *n* countries, *m* goods, and *s* complementary separated services, the value of trade in goods and related services measured in autarky prices is less than or equal to zero. Thus, countries will tend to export those goods and complementary services that are worth less to them in autarky than the goods and complementary services they import.

We have already noted that separated services unrelated to goods can be treated as if they were goods, since they can be traded directly. In principle, autarky prices will exist, and trade in these separated services will be well defined to the degree that there are market transactions across borders. Comparative advantage should therefore

8. There is a difficult empirical issue here, since profit remittances may not be an accurate indication of income accruing to domestic factors because of transfer pricing practices, differential tax rates, exchange restrictions, and variations in reinvested earnings. For further discussion, see Stern and Hoekman (1986).

apply here as it does to trade in goods.

Case 2. (Movement of providers only.) In this case, in which physical movement of factors is a precondition for services to be produced abroad, Deardorff (1985:51) has noted the compatibility with comparative advantage in the sense that both the goods and the factors exported will on average have been cheaper in autarky than those that are imported. This result will hold for both the services related to goods and the services made possible by the factor movements unrelated to transactions involving goods. (A formal treatment of this case is provided in Deardorff [1980] and Ethier and Svensson [1986].)

As previously mentioned, not all factors need to move in this case; that is, there may be absent factors remaining in the parent country and providing their services by electronic means. The most thorough analysis of absent factors is by Deardorff (1985:53–68), who concluded that comparative advantage may not apply in all circumstances. For purposes of analysis, Deardorff used a traditional 2X2X2 Heckscher-Ohlin (H-O) model, with one good and one service being produced and traded and with labor and management being the factors of production. Management has the characteristic of an absent factor, which means it can provide its services without moving abroad. The chief exception to comparative advantage arises in the case of differences in technologies between countries. Thus, if country A has a Hicks-neutral technological advantage for producing services, and services are management-intensive, the return to management in A could be higher than in country B, but by less than the full extent of A's technological advantage. A will then export services in the sense of sending part of its stock of management telematically to B, thus augmenting production there and decreasing it in A. This seems to contradict the principle of comparative advantage, since the autarky price of management is higher in A than in B.

In a comment on Deardorff's paper, Jones (1985:72–76) contended that the foregoing difficulty could be resolved by adjusting the returns to management for differences in quality. However, Deardorff (1985:70–71) in turn has questioned Jones's contention on the grounds that differences in management quality between countries may not be well defined, technological advantage presumably being specific to A's service industry, and that it is not appropriate in a general sense to redefine factors in an effort to salvage the principle of comparative advantage.

Does it make any difference conceptually whether factors physically move between countries? Jones (1985:73) states that the formal structure of models with international factor mobility does not require a factor to move physically. That is, whether or not factors move, there will be an inward shift of the production possibility frontier in one country and an outward shift in the other. There may also be other ramifications arising from the physical movement of a factor that should be taken into account. Thus, situations can exist that violate the principle of comparative advantage. However, even if this happens, trade will still be beneficial to the countries involved.

It is interesting to note that Mundell's (1957) result that factor movements may substitute for trade in goods continues to hold for trade in services. Mundell showed that if the necessary conditions are met, factor mobility will lead to factor price equalization, which in turn leads to equalization of goods prices, even though goods do not move. In this context, factor movements do not substitute for trade in services; instead, they are a necessary condition. Nevertheless, it can be shown—using a standard H-O model with at least one tradeable good, one local (nontraded) service, and one mobile factor—there will be a tendency to equalize unit costs and thus factor rewards. There will accordingly be a tendency for the prices of services to be equalized, as noted by Bhagwati (1984b), which will eventually eliminate trade in services.

Case 3. (Movement of demanders only.) The international movement of demanders of goods or services is not often encountered in economics literature, except perhaps in the case of tourism. Nonetheless, comparative advantage will have to hold almost by definition in this case. That is, in the absence of barriers to mobility and trade, individuals and firms will be motivated to move when there are services that are relatively cheaper abroad than domestically.[9]

Case 4. (Movement of providers and demanders.) This case combines cases 2 and 3. Although the context is more complicated, it seems reasonable to conclude that if comparative advantage applies when providers or demanders are mobile, it should also hold for the two cases combined.

---

9. Care must be taken, however, in specifying what service is actually being provided to demanders. In general, but especially in the case of tourism, a bundle of services will be consumed. This bundle must have a lower average price than in the consumer's home country. As pointed out by Alan Deardorff (personal communication), many, if not most, of the individual services in this bundle will be more expensive than at home (think of the prices of food and lodging at a ski resort), and the services that are appreciably cheaper will often not be measurable (the view, the quality of the skiing). Trivially, prices of these services will be much higher in the consumer's home country if they are available at all. The nonobservability of the (autarky) prices of these services may thus pose some difficulty in determining comparative advantage.

This discussion was premised on the traditional theory of comparative advantage, with the usual assumptions of competition, given technology, and absence of distortions. In addition to distortions, we have yet to consider impediments to trade and factor movements. Different qualifications apply when these matters are taken into account.

Distortions and Impediments to Comparative Advantage

The major kinds of economic distortions, which have been analyzed at length in the literature, include the exploitation of national monopoly power by means of the optimal tariff, production and consumption externalities, operation off of the efficient production possibility frontier due to wage rigidities or other types of factor market imperfections, and such dynamic considerations as the realization of the infant-industry benefits of learning-by-doing and improvements in technology. Policies to implement various kinds of noneconomic objectives may also introduce distortions. The conditions for intervention and the choice of optimal policies are generally well defined for the different distortions, and service industries do not appear in themselves to raise new problems.[10] There is no reason to believe that the standard theoretical analysis particularly needs to be revised when distortions are brought into consideration.

Nonetheless, as Hindley and Smith (1984:377–81) point out, service industries are often prime targets of government intervention and regulation—to a much greater degree than goods-producing industries. The justifications given for government actions are the supposed dangers of destructive competition and the need to protect the interests of buyers who are imperfectly informed, especially when they are purchasing intangible services. The beneficial experiences many countries have had with deregulation suggest the dangers of destructive competition are exaggerated. When there are scarcity rents at stake, vested interests may have much to gain by maintaining government regulation, and imperfect information may constitute a

10. See Krugman (1986) for an analysis of the identification of strategic sectors when there are externalities that are country- or location-specific. He points out that, to the extent the products involved can be traded, it may not matter to a country where an industry is located. There is no necessary connection therefore between the availability of technology and the production of goods (and presumably also services) in a given country. Accordingly, it seems doubtful that governments have much to gain by seeking to identify and capture the returns associated with strategic sectors, whether these sectors produce goods or services.

genuine problem, but it is not unique to services. Even if it were, it is not clear that the nationality of providers should be the basis of government policy.

International trade and factor movements of services are subject to numerous impediments, as previously mentioned. These impediments may be due to conscious government policies, but natural barriers can also make certain kinds of international transactions relatively costly. For example, the market for some services may be limited geographically because of the need for direct contact between provider and consumer. However, with technical change, transactions costs may fall significantly, so that the service can be supplied at long distance in a separated form rather than by direct contact between provider and demander. The development of computers and satellites is a case in point. By using new technology, it might be possible in certain situations to circumvent government-imposed barriers that require the physical presence of providers.

To reiterate, the presence or absence of government-imposed and natural barriers will have an effect on decisions involving trade and factor movements, especially decisions about the location and mode of production of the service. This can be illustrated by the various options that may exist for providing architectural design services. An architect could transmit his drawings abroad by electronic means (case 1); have a draftsman do the drawings abroad based on instructions transmitted electronically (case 2 with separated factors); go to the importer's country of residence and do the drawings there (case 2 with physical factor mobility); have the buyer come to the architect's country of residence to obtain the drawings (case 3); or meet with the buyer in a third country (case 4). The first two options would probably be the most efficient way of providing this service, but existing government restrictions may necessitate choosing one of the other options. Many other examples could be constructed to illustrate this point. If existing barriers were relaxed or removed, the provision and consumption of the service would presumably correspond to the most efficient of the available alternatives.

Changes in Technology and Comparative Advantage

With the advent of computers and satellites, it has become possible to provide a variety of information, financial, and other services in a separated form rather than by the physical presence of the provider in the country of consumption. Technological change will thus affect the relative costs and prices of services (and goods) and the resulting pattern of production and trade. Trade flows and factor movements should still conform to the principle of comparative advantage, although there may be differences after the technological change takes place.

Because technological change is an ongoing process, what is important are the dynamics of comparative advantage rather than comparative statics, which is the basis for much of the analysis of trade theory. This distinction between statics and dynamics is well known, and is not unique when applied to services. The difficulty lies in modeling endogenous technological change in a comprehensive and general manner. This should not be taken to mean, however, that the principle of comparative advantage ceases to be valid.

Imperfect Competition

There has been a rapidly growing interest in recent years in the effects on a nation's trade and trade policies when there are imperfectly competitive firms either at home or abroad or both. Most of the analysis to date has dealt with production and trade in goods, but in principle the issues should carry over to services. Grossman and Shapiro (1985) have analyzed trade in technology services, and they stress the critical nature of market structure, especially when there is DFI and when the multinational enterprises involved seek to maintain exclusive control over the production and dissemination of their knowledge and expertise. The implication of imperfect competition for trade policy is that government intervention may enable a country to capture benefits that would otherwise accrue to other countries.

The assumptions and conclusions of trade models postulating imperfect competition have been criticized by Deardorff and Stern (1986) and Krugman (1986), among others, on a variety of grounds, and more work needs to be done to determine how these models withstand changes in their theoretical structure as well as the degree to which they apply empirically for given industries and countries.[11] As McCulloch (1985) has argued in her comment on Grossman and Shapiro, governments do not necessarily recognize and design appropriate policies to capture the benefits of intervention when there

11. The most critical assumptions of these models are whether (1) firms compete in terms of price rather than quantity; (2) factors of production are in inelastic supply; (3) there is a significant degree of competition among domestic firms and substantial exports; and (4) entry barriers are potentially or actually low. Further, the possible gains from government intervention may be limited because the excess profits of firms may not translate into large gains for a nation.

is imperfect competition. Furthermore, governments must consider the issue of foreign retaliation when contemplating intervention.

Effects of Liberalization of Trade and Factor Movements Involving Services

The preceding discussion dealt with the applicability of the principle of comparative advantage to trade and factor movements involving services. The analysis suggests that countries may realize significant gains from the removal of impediments to trade and factor movements related to services. Gains from liberalization arise from improvements in the efficient allocation of resources within and between countries, the lowering of prices, and the expansion of choices afforded to consumers and firms. The magnitude of gains from liberalization will depend on whether barriers are to be lowered only on trade in separated services—keeping existing restrictions on factor movements intact—or whether trade in separated services and factor movements will both be liberalized. This latter point is important because the complete liberalization of both trade and factor movements is unlikely to occur in the forthcoming GATT negotiations. (For more on this subject see the section, "Implications for Research.")

Empirical Considerations

The discussion to this point has been theoretical in nature, and it seems appropriate to ask what the facts show. In undertaking empirical studies of services the existing models of comparative advantage serve as a useful point of departure. These models suggest that in a given nation the composition of trade in services and factor movements both depend on relative factor endowments, technology, realization ot economies of scale, product differentiation, and government policies.

Some noteworthy work on services has been done by Sapir (1981) and Sapir and Lutz (1980) based on the empirical framework used to analyze trade in goods. An effort was made in these studies to analyze the determinants of international ocean freight, passenger services, insurance, and other services as classified in the International Monetary Fund (IMF) balance of payments statistics, which are based on a cross section of national data for as many as 52 industrialized and developing countries. The services trade data were for 1977, and the proxy measures for factor endowments and technology were calculated for reasonably adjacent years. The empirical results indicated the importance of physical capital abundance in explaining trade in ocean freight and passenger services and human capital abundance in explaining trade in insurance and other services. Scale and locational factors were significant in a few instances. With the usual caveats about the empirical implications of the underlying theory and the crudeness of the data, the results nonetheless lend support to the usefulness of the framework of comparative advantage as applied to trade in services.

Work by Saxonhouse (1985) is also pertinent. He sought to investigate in a comparative context whether the large size of Japan's distribution system and the small amount of Japanese exports in technology services were unusual by international standards. For this purpose, he used cross-sectional data for 11 countries for gross domestic product (GDP) in 23 sectors and for technology trade in 25 sectors for the years 1965, 1973, 1975, 1977, and 1979. His explanatory variables included national measures of capital stock, labor, educational attainment, distance, petroleum resources, iron ore, and arable land. Country-specific dummy variables were included in the pooled, cross-sectional regression estimates to allow for characteristics not included in the endowment and other variables. The results showed that few of the Japanese country dummies were statistically significant. Saxonhouse therefore concluded that the size of Japan's distribution system and its trade in technology services were not unusual by international standards when compared to other major countries. This example further illustrates the role that factor endowments and related variables may play in determining the structure of production and trade in services.[12]

Sapir and Schumacher (1984) calculated the direct employment effects of changes in the composition of trade in commodities and services for the United States, Japan, and six of the major European countries for individual years between 1970 and 1981. They primarily used a 16-sector breakdown of manufacturing industries, measures of sectoral labor/gross-output ratios for 1977, and trade in constant prices for the individual years. Traded services were represented by only three sectors—transport, travel, and other private services—based on the classifications in the IMF balance of payments statistics. The labor/output ratios were calculated from domestic data. The difficulty with this was that the labor/output ratios for services were based on

12. The determinants of Japanese technology trade have been analyzed in a factor-endowment context in Vestal (1985).

the domestic production data for essentially nontraded services. As Sapir and Schumacher (1984) themselves note, the resulting ratios may thus overstate the labor content of trade in services, and in the final analysis these ratios for services were larger than for goods. Calculations were made of the employment effects of changes in the value of trade in both goods and services for each of the eight countries globally as well as for the developing countries. In the latter case an equal expansion of the export of services and the import of manufactures was shown to be detrimental to employment in the industrialized countries.[13]

None of the aforementioned studies dealt explicitly with the determinants of DFI involving services. On the basis of work by Baldwin (1979), however, there is reason to believe that, at least for the United States, the same types of factor endowment and related variables that serve to explain the composition of trade in goods can be applied to DFI. This finding should carry over to investment in services, although whether it actually does remains to be seen. We are not aware of any empirical studies that have explicitly addressed the determinants of the international movement of labor used in providing services. To the extent such movement occurs in response to market forces, differences in national labor endowments, which in turn would reflect wage differences, seem to be important.

If it can be granted that international trade and factor movements involving services are governed by the conventional economic and policy-related variables determining comparative advantage, this will establish the basis for empirically analyzing the effects on economic welfare of the existing structure of trade and factor mobility in services and possible changes in this structure. Considerable attention has been given, especially in the United States, to documenting the foreign restrictions faced by U.S. firms engaged in trade and investment in services. It would be valuable to review the restrictions on services around the world in light of the models of the political economy of protection and lobbying that have been developed in recent years, in order to determine if the same considerations apply to services as to goods. We would not expect any important differences to emerge in such an analysis.[14]

13. See Stern (1985:152–53, 158) for some critical comments on the methodology used by Sapir and Schumacher.

14. See Kravis (1985) for a classification of service industries involved in current U.S. trade-liberalization efforts, categorized according to the motivations for foreign restrictions. These motivations include the preservation of cultural identity, financial stability, and national sovereignty or security, as well as the protection of the public from

Further, restrictions on trade and factor movements involving services can be analyzed using the same type of cost-benefit analysis used for goods. That is, it should be possible to determine what effects existing restrictions have on consumers, producers, and the return to factors and how these might change if restrictions were reduced or removed altogether. Data requirements may be an important limiting consideration, but this should not controvert the applicability of the cost-benefit analysis for determining how economic welfare may be affected in given empirical circumstances.

Implications for Research

Several questions relating to the international aspects of services deserve further study from both the theoretical and policy perspectives.

We noted earlier there may be an effort in the forthcoming GATT negotiations to remove from consideration services issues involving DFI and the international movement of labor. If the negotiations deal only with the liberalization of traded services they will be beneficial, but if existing restrictions on factor movements related to services remain intact, the benefits will be limited. Moreover, in cases in which countries have important interests in protecting against a foreign presence in services, the incentives to participate in international negotiations will be reduced. Thus, it will be important to determine the empirical magnitude of the various types of services and the stakes individual countries have in particular sectors, including the maintenance of barriers to trade and services-related factor movements.

Differences in factor endowments and technology have a major influence on the relative prices of services and returns to factors in the advanced industrialized and developing countries. It has been observed that many services are relatively more expensive in rich than in poor countries and that the real price of services relative to goods tends to rise with higher levels of per capita income. This suggests developing countries have a substantial advantage, especially in the provision of labor-intensive services. If so, it is important to identify the sectors involved and to determine the factors, including the removal of obstacles, that may be crucial in the efficient expansion of these sectors through time. The fortunes of some developing countries may thus lie in service industries as well as in goods. The mix between

---

monopoly power, fraud, or other undesirable practices not easily discerned by consumers.

a country's actual and potential comparative advantage in goods and services is important in charting future development and identifying the interplay between types of trade barriers and the possible benefits and costs of different patterns of liberalization.

The relationship between goods and services in international trade bears examination. We have noted that certain services may be complementary to goods, in which case liberalization of services-related transactions may lead to increased trade in goods. This contrasts with the case in which factor mobility substitutes for trade in goods. Djacic and Kierzkowski (1986) have shown that in some circumstances the liberalization of factor mobility in services might actually bring about a reversal in the pattern of trade in goods. In their model they assume exporters of goods also export servicing contracts (maintenance), which will require a physical presence in the consuming country. Restrictions on servicing contracts would therefore have an adverse effect on trade in goods. Djacic and Kierzkowski show that the pattern of trade may be reversed upon the removal of the restrictions. In cases in which services substitute for trade in goods (e.g., when a firm decides to franchise, lease, or rent abroad), it should be noted that removal of impediments to services actually reduces the volume of trade in goods.

Related to this is the impact of technical change on the volume and pattern of trade in goods and services. Thus, as noted earlier, technical change might result in services' changing categories, as in the case of separated services (case 1), which do not require physical proximity. Technical change may also result in increased trade in new goods that are splintered off from services and vice versa as Bhagwati's analysis (1984a) suggests. Bhagwati (1985) has also noted that organizational innovations may result in a change to the separated services category, in which a foreign presence is no longer required. Multinational enterprises may play a leading role in these developments, and for this reason it would be worthwhile to analyze the important features in corporate decision-making that shape the pattern of intrafirm specialization and the geographic location of foreign subsidiaries providing services. The factors affecting barriers to the entry of competitors and the ability of firms to sustain their competitive edge are also worthy of investigation.

Implications for Policy

This discussion of conceptual and empirical issues relating to the internationalization of the service sector is directly relevant to the ongoing effort to bring services into the GATT. Several pertinent questions have not been addressed, including (1) the choice of negotiating strategies; (2) the feasibility of extending existing GATT rules and nontariff barriers (NTB) codes to cover services; (3) the applicability of such concepts as fair and unfair trade in relation to services; and (4) the treatment of regulatory frameworks and government monopolies in services. Although it would take us too far afield to discuss policy issues in a comprehensive manner, certain issues deserve brief comment.

A crucial issue in the context of services concerns the definition of trade as opposed to investment. The GATT has traditionally avoided investment-related issues involving goods, and many countries believe this exclusion should extend to services. But, as our earlier discussion has made clear, investment is often a precondition for provision of services. It thus seems virtually impossible to avoid investment issues in future GATT discussions on services. The question of the right of establishment is of central importance in this context. If a country's regulatory system requires a physical presence as a condition for doing business, even though it is not economically necessary, the right of establishment could be interpreted as a trade issue in the case of services. As noted by Aronson (1986:32), this is essentially the U.S. position.[15]

Developing countries such as India that oppose bringing investment-related issues into the GATT have argued that services requiring labor mobility should be subject to discussion. Bhagwati (1985) forcefully articulates this view and, as we have noted, it may be that certain developing countries have a comparative advantage in labor-intensive services. The issue of labor mobility is a sensitive one for all countries concerned because of the universally stringent restrictions on the movement of nonimmigrant labor. Nonetheless, the failure to deal with this issue in some form could lessen the incentives for certain developing countries to participate in negotiations involving services.

Another important issue is that of linkages between goods and services. As noted in Stern (1985:154), it can be argued that the restrictions in the case of trade and investment in goods are far more important and damaging than in the case of services and that the GATT system, already fragile, is becoming increasingly unable to

15. It should be noted that the United States has already introduced investment issues into bilateral discussions and negotiation. Thus, for example, a recent Section 301 case directed against the Republic of Korea focused on the liberalization of access to the Korean insurance market. For more details, see Allgeier (1986).

cope with the situation. Perhaps by linking issues involving goods with those involving services that are of interest to both the advanced industrialized and developing countries, mutually beneficial agreements could be reached in a new round of negotiations.[16]

The exact form an agreement covering services might take remains to be determined. There are many issues that must be resolved in extending the GATT rules and the NTB codes to services and clarifying the various aspects of national treatment in the context of regulatory frameworks and government monopolies in services. The relevant issues can likely best be addressed by an umbrella code covering services, and details applicable to particular sectors can presumably then be worked out.

A final point worth mentioning is the inadequacy of existing data on services. As noted in Stern (1985:149), much greater attention has been given to the development of classifications and methods for reporting data relating to production and trade in goods.[17] As a consequence, it is difficult to determine the levels of and changes in particular types of services with anywhere near the accuracy with which they can be determined in the case of goods. This situation is being remedied to some extent, but there are still major gaps in the availability of information, especially on the effects of existing barriers to trade and investment in services.[18] Thus, before an attempt can be made to address some of the important research questions we have mentioned, more and better data will have to become available. Without knowledge of the levels and expected changes in particular types of services, evaluation of policy options involving services is fraught with uncertainty. In the context of the GATT negotiations on

---

16. Again, as in the investment case described in note 15, the United States has already linked goods and services issues in its bilateral negotiations with the newly industrializing countries (NICs). A case in point is the linking of the degree of U.S. preferences for eligible countries under the Generalized System of Preferences (GSP) with commitments to liberalize their market access in services. Brant Free of the U.S. Department of Commerce brought this example to our attention in his comment on Stern and Hoekman (1986). It should be noted that the developing countries were able to get the services negotiations on a separate track in the new GATT Round. However, this does not rule out the possibility that some linking of goods and services will occur in the course of negotiations.

17. This is perhaps due in large part to the intrinsic difficulty of monitoring trade in services because of its intangible nature as compared to trade in goods. Also, historically, services were for the most part not traded and thus not a potential source of tariff revenue, unlike goods.

18. Data needs for services in the Uruguay Round of multilateral trade negotiations are discussed in Stern and Hoekman (1986).

services, lack of information may hamper the attainment of an agreement or lead to a situation in which only a limited number of countries decide it is in their interest to participate in an agreement.

CHAPTER 2
Patterns of Trade and Investment in Services in the Asia-Pacific Region

Chung H. Lee and Seiji Naya

In recent years trade and investment in services have raised important international economic issues for the United States as its service industries have become increasingly internationalized.[1] Their foreign exchange earnings have become significant, and some economists have even argued that the comparative advantage of the United States has shifted from manufacturing to service industries (Shelp 1981). Among the developing countries of the Asia-Pacific region,[2] the Republic of Korea (South Korea) and Singapore are major exporters of services and have achieved surpluses in their services accounts in recent years. Nevertheless, little attention has been paid to trade and investment in services in the region, perhaps because they have been overshadowed by the highly publicized and important merchandise trade among the countries in the region.

Little is known about patterns of trade and investment in services and their determinants, yet much has been written in favor of liberalization of such trade and investment. To its advocates, gains from freer trade and investment in services are self-evident: they are seen to promote resource allocation in accordance with the principle of comparative advantage. Questions have been raised, however, about the applicability of this principle to trade and investment in services and even about the definition of trade in services. At the present state of knowledge, basic—even elementary—work at the empirical and conceptual level is urgently needed.

Empirical research on trade and investment in services is severely handicapped by the paucity of data. But even before empirical analysis

1. Internationalization is defined as the process of producing and distributing a good or a service for a foreign market, whether carried out at home or abroad.

2. In this paper the Asia-Pacific region consists of Hong Kong, Indonesia, Japan, the Republic of Korea, Malaysia, the Philippines, Singapore, Taiwan, Thailand, and the United States.

can begin, problems of basic concepts and definitions must be dealt with. There is confusion about whether trade in services refers to transborder transactions between residents and nonresidents or to sales of services by foreign affiliates as well (e.g., OECD 1983, 1984). These two types of transactions differ in determinants, effects on the trading countries, and the nature of impediments to transactions. A main point of this chapter is that trade in services should be defined in the narrower and more conventional sense, distinguishing it from direct foreign investment (DFI) in services and sales by service affiliates.

In analyzing trade in services, some authors include investment income from DFI and other internationally held private and government assets (Feldman and Proctor 1983). That is, trade in services is equated with the invisibles in the balance of payments; no distinction is made between factor services and nonfactor services. However, it is important to note that factor services are returns on the factors of production that have crossed national boundaries.

Another source of confusion lies in the joint sale of goods and services (Whichard 1984). For example, if in an international transaction the sale price of an airplane includes provisions for future services, part of the revenue is for services to be rendered in the future. The problem of separating the services component from the export revenue is similar to that of dividing the value added of a firm that has internalized service functions between the service sector and the industrial sector. If, for instance, the firm employs accountants instead of using the services of an accounting firm, should their value added be assigned to the service sector? In national income accounting it is assigned to the industrial sector, although internalized accounting services are not different in any essential way from those provided by an outside firm. Because it is impossible to get separate figures on services when they are sold jointly with goods, we have followed the convention of defining services as the output of service industries; however, this practice will lead to an underestimation of the magnitude of international transactions in services.

In this chapter trade in services refers to transborder transactions of service industries such as accounting, advertising, banking, building, construction, engineering, franchising, hotels and motels, insurance, leasing, legal services, motion pictures, telecommunications, data processing and information services, tourism, and transportation. Availability of data on transactions in these industries varies from country to country and from industry to industry. Consequently, data published by the International Monetary Fund (IMF) in its *Balance of Payments Statistics* are relied upon here. The data most closely corresponding to our definition of traded services are those on shipment, passenger services, travel, other transportation as well as private goods, services, and income.

The following section presents the reasons for treating trade in services, as we have them defined here, separately from investment in services and sales by foreign affiliates. Analysis of the patterns of trade and investment in services in the Asia-Pacific region then follows in a subsequent section.

Trade in Services versus Direct Foreign Investment in Services

Differences exist between trade in services on the one hand and DFI in services and sales by service affiliates on the other, although issues relating to the latter are often treated as trade issues. Determinants for trade in services differ from those for DFI in services, and the barriers to trade in services are not the same as those to investment. Liberalizing investment in services may thus have welfare implications for countries involved that are different from those arising out of liberalizing trade in services and may require a framework different from the General Agreement for Tariffs and Trade (GATT).

International transactions in services that are regarded here as trade in services may take place in one of the following ways: (1) Resident firms or individuals provide services to nonresident firms or individuals across national boundaries; (2) resident firms or individuals provide services to nonresident firms or individuals within national boundaries; and (3) some services—that is, the use of intangible properties—are transmitted across national boundaries through contractual arrangements. An example of the latter is an intangible property telematically transmitted across national boundaries and stored on magnetic tape upon receipt. This is a case of what Bhagwati (1984) calls the "disembodiment" of services from their providers or what Sampson and Snape (1985) call "separated" services. What is common to all three types of transactions is that they do not require the establishment of foreign affiliates and the long-term movement of the factors of production.

Are these transactions different in any fundamental sense from trade in merchandise? Hindley and Smith (1984) do not think so, and thus they argue there is no need for a separate theoretical framework for trade in services. As they see it, the wine and cloth in Ricardo's classic example could easily have been replaced by wine and insurance policies without changing his demonstration or altering the validity of the doctrine of comparative advantage.

Although Hindley and Smith are correct in saying the conventional trade models do not specify whether the commodity traded is a good or a service, it does not follow that there is no difference between the two in terms of tradeability. A key difference is that services—being intangible, nonstorable, and untransportable—cannot be traded (with the exception of disembodied services) without the providers or receivers moving physically at the same time. To quote Melvin (1985), "Not only must the consumer and the producer (of services) be at the same place at the same time, but the production and consumption activities are exactly the same process."[3] This inseparability of production and consumption activities accounts for the greater importance of transportation costs for services than for merchandise and for the preponderance of services in nontradeables. It also accounts for the importance of DFI as a means of selling services in foreign markets.

Besides the usual factors determining comparative costs—such as relative factor endowment—technological innovations that reduce transportation costs or render services disembodied affect the tradeability of services, transforming some nontraded services into traded services. In fact, recent increases in trade in services and the push for the liberalization of such trade may have had their origin in recent technological innovations in services such as communications and transportation.[4]

The same forces may account for the increase in DFI in services. There are transaction costs in carrying out DFI, and it follows that a reduction in these costs would lead to an increase in investment. But why are some services exported, whereas others are sold abroad by foreign affiliates? The answer lies in part in intrinsic differences among various services: tourism is exported, since travelers *must* go where

3. A further remark by Melvin is worth quoting for the explanation he offers of why standard economic theory seems incapable of handling services: "Standard economic analysis is almost entirely free from consideration of time and space dimensions.... Commodities are almost always assumed to be like apples, and the fact that consumption and production will generally occur at different points in space is seldom taken into account. We use the word 'services' to describe commodities that have characteristics distinguishing them from the usual commodities of economic analysis—they are associated with the time and space dimensions of economic activity. Perhaps one of the reasons that services seem to present problems in economic theory is that most economists are not accustomed to including these dimensions in their analysis."

4. In recent years there has been an increase in demand for services as the production of goods has become more automated and as the growth of multinational enterprises has increased the demand for business services. This increase in demand would also increase trade in services independently of the factors mentioned here (Feketekuty and Krause 1986).

services are provided, whereas services such as banking *can* be provided by foreign affiliates.

A modern theory of the multinational enterprise explains DFI as an alternative to exporting and thus as a process of internalizing market transactions. A firm may profitably internalize market transactions when there are market imperfections. A market may be imperfect because of its structural characteristics, such as economies of scale and differential advantage in knowledge, or it may be "naturally" imperfect because of costs inherent in market transactions. Thus, internalization through DFI is socially efficient when market imperfections are natural, but it may not be when they are structural (Dunning and Rugman 1985).

Establishing a service affiliate in a foreign country, which is the purpose of DFI, is a way of reducing the transaction cost of exporting services. They can then be provided by the affiliate to firms and individuals residing in the foreign country, and the international movement of providers or receivers of services need not take place for every transaction. The initial transaction cost of establishing the affiliate can be amortized over its life, and consequently services can be provided at a lower cost than if they were exported by the parent firm.[5]

The provision of services by a foreign affiliate can also be a more efficient alternative than exporting because a service establishment runs into diseconomies of scale at a relatively small scale of operation (Stanbeck 1979). Therefore, a service firm does not reap a cost advantage by centralizing production at one establishment and exporting its output. The firm is not subject to the same diseconomies of scale as a service establishment, however, so what is often found in service industries is a firm with multiple establishments. A foreign affiliate is simply an establishment located in a foreign country.

By treating trade in services separately from DFI in services a distinction can be made between the competitiveness of a country in service industries and the competitiveness of its firms in the same industries in the world market. The country's comparative advantage in service industries is location-specific, whereas firms' competitiveness in the world market is firm-specific and not bound to a particular location. As Lipsey and Kravis (1985) have pointed out, the country's comparative advantage and the competitiveness of its firms are not the same,

5. Carlson (1977) found in his study of Swedish multinational enterprises that products with an important software content, which had to be adapted to the needs of individual users, tended to be sold by foreign affiliates instead of being exported from Sweden. This can be explained in terms of economizing the transaction cost for providing software. Services are the extreme version of software-intensive products.

because firms in certain industries may be highly competitive in foreign countries even though their native country does not have comparative advantage in these industries. This distinction between comparative advantage and firm-specific advantage is central to explaining the empirical results herein. It also helps explain the fact that prices of services are higher relative to those of goods in rich countries than in poor ones (Kravis, Heston, and Summers 1983), yet the rich countries tend to make DFI in services. This distinction should also be kept in mind when interpreting the results of studies such as that by Sapir and Lutz (1981), which shows that the factors determining comparative advantage in trade in services (freight transport, passenger transport, and insurance) are physical and human capital. The same factors may not determine DFI in services.

Trade in Services in the Asia-Pacific Region

Traded services reported in this section consist of shipping; passenger services; other transportation; travel; and other goods, services, and income. The latter category includes communications, nonmerchandise insurance, and technical services of construction and related industries. This definition of traded services is narrower in scope than that proposed by the U.S. Department of Commerce, which includes the output of petroleum services; construction; transportation, communications, and public utilities; wholesale and retail trade; banking; finance (excluding banking), insurance, and real estate; agricultural services; hotels and other lodging places; and a variety of business, technical, professional, and personal services. Relying on the data reported by the IMF is likely to lead to underestimates of the magnitude of trade in services compared with those estimates using data based on the U.S. Department of Commerce definition. For the moment, however, a multicountry study like this must make do with the IMF data because of their intercountry comparability.

The relative importance of the service sector in the economies of the region is shown in table 2.1. The sector's share of employment ranged in 1981 from 66 percent for the United States to 15 percent for Thailand, and its share of gross domestic product (GDP) ranged in 1983 from 66 percent for the United States to 35 percent for Indonesia. With the exception of Singapore, the general pattern is that the more developed an economy, the larger its service sector as measured in terms of the share of employment or GDP.

The figures in the last two columns of table 2.1 show the share of services exported and the share of merchandise exported for the coun-

Table 2.1 Services' Share of Employment and GDP; The Share of Services and Merchandise Exported (percentage)

Country	Services' share employment[a] 1981	Services' share of GDP 1983	Share of services exported[b] 1983	Share of merchandise exported 1983
Indonesia	30	35	2	37
Japan	49	55[c]	4	29
Korea	37	47	17	57
Malaysia	34	44	14	86
Philippines	30	42	10	24
Singapore	59	62	87	216
Taiwan	39	43	12	86
Thailand	15	50	8	38
United States	66	66	2	18

Notes: a. Services are all branches of economic activities excluding the agricultural sector (agriculture, forestry, hunting, and fishing) and the industrial sector (mining; manufacturing; construction; and electricity, water and gas).

b. Services exported include shipment; passenger services; other transportation; travel; and other private goods, services, and income.

c. 1982.

Sources: IMF, 1984; World Bank 1985, Data for Taiwan are from ROC, 1985.

tries in the region. They may be taken as measures of the openness of the respective sectors. The figures indicate the service sector is less open than the other sectors, but the large variation in the share of services exported suggests diversity in services and varying degrees of tradeability of services.

Although the two most developed countries in the region—the United States and Japan—have a small share of services exported, they are nevertheless the region's two largest exporters of services. As can be seen in table 2.2, the sum of services exported from all the other countries during the 1976–1983 period does not match the sum of exports from these two giants. The same can also be said for merchandise exports.

The next largest exporters of services are three of the newly industrializing countries (NICs) of the region—Singapore, Korea, and Taiwan (no data are available on Hong Kong's services exports). It is well known these countries have achieved rapid economic development by heavily exporting labor-intensive manufactured goods. What is perhaps less well known is that these countries are also relatively large exporters of services. Why the countries that are relatively large exporters of merchandise are also relatively large exporters of services is

Table 2.2 Exports of Merchandise and Services of Asia-Pacific Countries, 1976–1983 (billions of SDRs)[a]

Rank	Merchandise		Services[b]	
1	United States	1,210.80 (100)	United States	171.61 (100)
2	Japan	765.09 (63)	Japan	106.83 (62)
3	Taiwan	114.39 (9)	Singapore	39.91 (23)
4	Indonesia	109.14 (9)	Korea	28.50 (17)
5	Korea	108.34 (9)	Taiwan	13.27 (8)
6	Malaysia	67.84 (6)	Thailand	7.51 (4)
7	Singapore	58.27 (5)	Philippines	7.00 (4)
8	Thailand	35.69 (3)	Malaysia	6.93 (4)
9	Philippines	29.63 (2)	Indonesia	2.25 (1)

Notes: a. Figures in parentheses are percentages and use figures for the United States as the base.

b. Services are shipment; passenger services, other transportation; travel; and other goods, services, and income. The last item, which varies from country to country, may consist of agents' fees, communications, construction services, management fees, nonmerchandise insurance.

Source: See table 2.1.

a question yet to be answered fully, although a complementary relationship has been suggested by Balassa (1983) and Praet (1985) for certain industries such as shipping (with trade) and software (with computer hardware).

Table 2.3 shows the same relationship between merchandise imports and services imports: the countries that are relatively large importers of merchandise are also relatively large importers of services.

Table 2.4 presents data on trade in services for the individual years 1976 through 1983 and cumulatively for the entire 1976–1983 period. All the countries experienced a high rate of growth both in exports and imports of services. The rate of growth in exports ranged from 31 percent for Indonesia to 10 percent for the United States, whereas the rate of growth in imports ranged from 26 percent for Malaysia to 11 percent for the United States. It is interesting to note that the developing countries in the region all had a higher rate of growth in both exports and imports of services than did the United States and Japan.

Table 2.3 Imports of Merchandise and Services of Asia-Pacific Countries, 1976–1983 (billions of SDRs)[a]

Rank	Merchandise		Services[b]	
1	United States	1,428.25 (100)	United States	180.29 (100)
2	Japan	654.97 (46)	Japan	176.12 (98)
3	Korea	124.46 (9)	Korea	21.71 (12)
4	Taiwan	99.57 (7)	Taiwan	18.20 (10)
5	Singapore	97.61 (7)	Indonesia	17.81 (10)
6	Indonesia	82.65 (6)	Singapore	16.18 (9)
7	Malaysia	59.84 (4)	Malaysia	15.17 (8)
8	Thailand	44.94 (3)	Thailand	8.84 (5)
9	Philippines	41.66 (3)	Philippines[c]	7.60 (4)

Notes: a. Figures in parentheses are percentages and use figures for the United States as the base.
b. See note on table 2.2.
c. 1977–1983.
Source: See table 2.1.

During the 1976–1983 period all but Korea and Singapore had deficits on the services account. Singapore's surpluses may be explained by the fact that it is an entrepôt economy. The case of Korea is different, however. Its surpluses were largely due to its export of construction services; during this period Korea had a surplus of 9,068 million Special Drawing Rights (SDRs) in the construction service account. Without this surplus Korea would have had deficits on the services

Table 2.4 Trade in Services, 1976–1983 (millions of SDRs)

Country/group	1976	1977	1978	1979	1980	1981	1982	1983	1976–1983	Average annual growth rate (%)
Indonesia										
credit	96	98	186	244	251	382	558	539	2,254	31
debit	-1,414	-1,426	-1,839	-2,172	-2,588	-4,134	-4,282	-4,021	-17,806	18
(net)	(-1,318)	(-1,328)	(-1,653)	(-1,928)	(-2,337)	(-3,752)	(-3,724)	(-3,482)	(-15,552)	
Japan										
credit ($\times 10^3$)	8.70	9.71	9.40	11.11	14.15	18.16	17.81	17.79	106.83	11
debit ($\times 10^3$)	-13.64	-14.92	-16.06	-20.00	-23.64	-29.37	-28.94	-29.55	-176.12	12
(net) ($\times 10^3$)	(-4.94)	(-5.21)	(-6.66)	(-8.89)	(-9.49)	(-11.21)	(-11.13)	(-11.76)	(-69.29)	
Korea										
credit	1,138	2,162	2,989	3,063	3,375	4,568	5,630	5,572	28,497	28
debit	-978	-1,666	-2,473	-2,616	-3,002	-3,556	-3,603	-3,813	-21,707	23
(net)	(160)	(496)	(516)	(447)	(373)	(1,012)	(2,027)	(1,759)	(6,790)	
Malaysia										
credit	335	413	497	609	876	1,119	1,412	1,667	6,928	26
debit	-707	-879	-1,061	-1,064	-2,255	-2,366	-2,799	-3,494	-15,165	26
(net)	(-372)	(-466)	(-564)	(-995)	(-1,379)	(-1,247)	(-1,387)	(-1,827)	(-8,237)	
Philippines										
credit	467	465	600	622	852	1,198	1,379	1,417	7,000	19
debit	-579	-674	-701	-856	-1,112	-1,285	-1,535	-1,436	-8,178	15
(net)	(-112)	(-209)	(-101)	(-234)	(-260)	(-87)	(-156)	(-19)	(-1,178)	

Table continues on the following page.

Table 2.4 Continued

Country/group	1976	1977	1978	1979	1980	1981	1982	1983	1976–1983	Average annual growth rate (%)
Singapore										
credit	2,391	2,615	2,890	3,401	4,563	7,141	8,612	8,408	39,911	21
debit	-907	-1,086	-1,230	-1,577	-2,157	-2,653	-3,144	-3,425	-16,179	21
(net)	(1,484)	(1,529)	(1,660)	(1,824)	(2,406)	(4,488)	(5,468)	(4,983)	(23,732)	
Taiwan										
credit	869	992	1,450	1,443	1,639	2,158	2,286	2,431	13,268	17
debit	-1,083	-1,050	-1,464	-2,142	-2,276	-2,941	-3,392	-3,854	-18,202	21
(net)	(-214)	(-58)	(-14)	(-699)	(-637)	(-783)	(-1,106)	(-1,423)	(-4,934)	
Thailand										
credit	352	408	600	735	1,051	1,278	1,461	1,623	7,508	25
debit	-618	-691	-765	-1,007	-1,212	-1,451	-1,406	-1,687	-8,837	16
(net)	(-266)	(-283)	(-165)	(-272)	(-161)	(-173)	(55)	(-64)	(-1,329)	
United States										
credit ($\times 10^3$)	14.96	14.89	16.01	18.27	21.64	27.45	29.17	29.22	171.61	10
debit ($\times 10^3$)	-15.84	-17.09	-18.02	-19.99	-21.64	-26.28	-28.82	-32.61	-180.29	11
(net) ($\times 10^3$)	(-0.88)	(-2.20)	(-2.01)	(-1.72)	(0)	(1.17)	(0.35)	(-3.39)	(-8.68)	

Note : Includes shipment; passenger services; travel; other transportation; and other private goods, services, and income.
Source: See table 2.1.

Table 2.5 Ratio of Services Trade to Merchandise Trade

Country/group	1976	1983	Average for 1976–1983	Standard deviation
Indonesia				
Exports	0.01	0.03	0.02	0.01
Imports	0.24	0.24	0.26	0.03
Japan				
Exports	0.15	0.13	0.14	0.01
Imports	0.28	0.28	0.27	0.01
Korea				
Exports	0.17	0.26	0.26	0.04
Imports	0.13	0.16	0.17	0.02
Malaysia				
Exports	0.07	0.13	0.10	0.02
Imports	0.22	0.28	0.25	0.02
Philippines				
Exports	0.21	0.30	0.23	0.05
Imports	0.18	0.20	0.19	0.01
Singapore				
Exports	0.44	0.44	0.40	0.05
Imports	0.12	0.14	0.13	0.01
Taiwan				
Exports	0.13	0.10	0.12	0.01
Imports	0.18	0.22	0.18	0.02
Thailand				
Exports	0.14	0.28	0.20	0.04
Imports	0.23	0.20	0.20	0.01
United States				
Exports	0.15	0.16	0.14	0.01
Imports	0.15	0.13	0.13	0.01

Sources: See table 2.1.

account during the period (table 2.4).[6]

To demonstrate whether the importance of services trade relative to merchandise trade has changed over time, the ratio of services trade to

6. Korea's case drives home a point recently made by Bhagwati (1985) regarding the liberalization of trade in services. He points out that the service industries for which the developed countries have pushed liberalization include banking, finance, "telematics," insurance, accounting, and other business services, but exclude others such as construction. The argument for liberalization is that since they have a comparative advantage

merchandise trade has been calculated. Table 2.5 shows values of this ratio for both exports and imports in 1976 and in 1983. There was some increase in the ratio of exports for Indonesia, Malaysia, the Philippines, and Thailand; there was a slight decrease for Taiwan. For Japan, Korea, Singapore, and the United States—the top four exporters of services in the region—there was no change, indicating that their exports of services and merchandise had increased at the same rate. In the ratio for imports there was a slight increase for Malaysia, but by and large there was no change in the ratio for the other countries.[7]

These findings seem inconsistent with the argument that U.S. comparative advantage has shifted in recent years to service industries. If it had, there would have been an increase in the ratio for exports and a decrease in the ratio for imports for the United States, and the converse would have been true for some of the other countries. However, this inconsistency may be due to the fact that there is a complementary relationship between services and goods transactions. As mentioned earlier, Balassa has argued that growth in services such as data processing, engineering design, and construction abroad are often linked with transactions in goods, with one or the other being the leading transaction or the two being jointly carried out. Given this relationship, even if there were a shift in comparative advantage from manufacturing to service industries, it would not be reflected in the pattern of trade.

To further shed light on this issue in the context of the Asia-Pacific region, we classified the countries in the region in terms of the balance of trade in merchandise and the balance of trade in services for the 1976–1983 period. Korea and Singapore had a surplus in the services account but a deficit in the merchandise account; Indonesia, Japan, Malaysia, and Taiwan had a deficit in the services account but a surplus in the merchandise account; and the Philippines, Thailand, and the United States had a deficit in both accounts. Given the numerous barriers to trade, the pattern of comparative advantage in the region can hardly be inferred from this pattern of trade balance. Nevertheless, it casts doubt on the contention that the United States now has a comparative advantage in services vis-à-vis other countries in the Asia-

---

in these industries, it would lead to welfare improvement for all trading partners. To limit liberalization to these industries and exclude construction seems unfair to countries like Korea, India, the Philippines, Egypt, and Pakistan, which appear to have a comparative advantage in the latter.

7. Stability in the ratio of services trade to merchandise trade was also found by Petit (1986) for the developed industrial countries.

Pacific region and the rest of the world.[8]

Direct Foreign Investment in Services and the Sales of Foreign Affiliates

As mentioned earlier, instead of exporting services, service firms may establish affiliates abroad to provide them locally. They do this because of their firm-specific advantages, even though their home country may not have a comparative advantage in services. An investigation of the magnitude of the sales of foreign service affiliates and comparison with a country's trade in services can shed light on the international competitiveness of its service firms and on its comparative advantage position in services. Such an investigation is also of practical importance—if a majority of international transactions in services are carried out by foreign affiliates, then the reduction of barriers to the entry or establishment of foreign affiliates and liberalization of the conditions under which they are allowed to operate will have a greater economic effect than liberalizing trade in services.

To discern patterns of DFI in services and in the sales of foreign affiliates in the Asia-Pacific region, data on the regional activities of multinational enterprises based in the countries of the region are needed. There are some multinational enterprises based in Hong Kong, Korea, the Philippines, Singapore, and Taiwan (Agmon and Kindleberger 1977; Kumar and McLeod 1981), but a majority of multinational enterprises in the region are based in the United States and Japan. Data on the activities of the former are not available; furthermore, there is a presumption that they are mostly in manufacturing and that those in construction have been operating in the Middle East. The focus here will therefore be on DFI in services in the region emanating from the United States and Japan.

U.S. Direct Foreign Investment in Services

Table 2.6 presents data on the U.S. DFI position (the net value of direct investors' equity and outstanding loans to foreign affiliates) by major sectors and service industries from 1977 through 1983. The total U.S. direct investment position in the rest of the world was approxi-

8. According to Kravis (1985), who has calculated revealed comparative advantage using the same definition of traded services and the same IMF data, the United States and Japan have a comparative disadvantage in services, whereas the non-oil-exporting developing countries as a group have a comparative advantage in services.

Table 2.6 U.S. Direct Investment Position[a] Abroad, Year-end (US$ millions)[b]

Industry/sector	1977	1978	1979	1980	1981	1982	1983
Mining and petroleum	$37,953	$40,780	$44,685	$54,350	$58,440	$62,934	$66,527
	(26)	(24)	(24)	(25)	(26)	(28)	(29)
Manufacturing	65,604	74,080	78,640	89,160	92,386	90,582	90,124
	(44)	(44)	(42)	(41)	(41)	(41)	(40)
Services	34,729	41,381	54,200	61,103	63,415	56,352	57,261
	(23)	(25)	(29)	(28)	(28)	(25)	(25)
Trade (wholesale and retail)	14,757	17,340	22,677	25,843	28,332	27,449	28,534
	(10)	(10)	(12)	(12)	(13)	(12)	(13)
Finance (including banking), insurance, and real estate	19,972	24,041	31,523	35,260	35,083	28,903	28,727
	(13)	(14)	(17)	(16)	(15)	(13)	(13)
All industries	148,782	167,804	186,760	215,578	226,359	221,512	226,117
	(100)	(100)	(100)	(100)	(100)	(100)	(100)

Notes: a. Investment position is the net value of direct investors' equity and outstanding loans to foreign affiliates. A change in investment position is due to net capital outflows, reinvested earnings, and revaluation adjustments.

b. Figures in parentheses are percentages.

Sources: United States, various issues.

mately US$149 billion in 1977, increasing to US$226 billion in 1983. Services—trade, finance (excluding banking), insurance, and real estate—accounted for 23 percent of the total DFI position in 1977 (US$35 billion) and 25 percent in 1983 (US$57 billion). These are lower than the figures for manufacturing, but compared to the low ratio of services exports to merchandise exports—14 percent for the 1976–1983 period—they are large, demonstrating the relative importance to service industries of DFI for providing services abroad. If figures for banking were included, the investment position in services would be even greater.

Since data on the U.S. direct investment position in services are not available for some individual countries in the region, it is impossible to find a direct measure of the importance of the region as a host for U.S. multinational service enterprises. However, if it is assumed that services' share of the U.S. direct investment position in the region is the same as that in the world, the importance of the region as a host can be inferred from the figures in table 2.7.

The figures in table 2.7 represent the U.S. direct investment position for all industries in the region as well as for individual countries during

Table 2.7 U.S. Direct Investment Position (All Industries) in Asia-Pacific Countries and Its Share in Total Investment Position, Year-end (US$ millions)[a]

Country/group	1979	1980	1981	1982	1983
Hong Kong	1,770	2,078	2,729	3,015	3,310
Indonesia	1,191	1,314	1,847	2,615	3,042
Japan	6,208	6,243	6,755	6,928	8,059
Korea	698	575	779	829	650
Malaysia	561	632	847	1,030	1,118
Philippines	1,254	1,259	1,320	1,297	1,102
Singapore	860	1,204	1,835	1,822	1,965
Taiwan	393	498	562	622	695
Thailand	200	361	551	585	729
Total Asia-Pacific countries	13,126	14,164	17,225	18,743	20,670
	(7)	(7)	(8)	(8)	(9)
World total	186,760	215,578	226,359	221,512	226,117
	(100)	(100)	(100)	(100)	(100)

Note: a. Figures in parentheses are percentages.
Source: See table 2.6.

1976–1983. Throughout these years Japan was the most important host country, followed by Hong Kong. The Philippines was more important than Indonesia and Singapore in the earlier years, but its relative position was later reversed as the U.S. direct investment position decreased absolutely in the Philippines but increased rapidly in Indonesia and Singapore. Korea, Taiwan, and Thailand were the least important countries in the region in terms of U.S. DFI.

The U.S. investment position in the Asia-Pacific region increased from US$13 billion in 1979 to about US$21 billion in 1983 (table 2.7), but it was only 7 percent of the total in 1979 and 9 percent in 1983. It is clear from these figures that although its share has increased over time, the U.S. investment position in the Asia-Pacific region remains only a small fraction of the total U.S. direct investment position. Given the assumption of services' share of DFI, U.S. direct investment position in services for the region can be estimated at about US$4 billion in 1979 and US$5 billion in 1983, or 2 percent and 2.3 percent respectively of the total U.S. direct investment position.

Tables 2.8 through 2.16 present data on the U.S. direct investment position by industry and by year-end for the individual countries in the region. Although data on services are not available for some countries, it can be seen that services' share of the position varied greatly from country to country. In 1983 services accounted for 60 percent of the U.S. investment position in Hong Kong, 2 percent in Indonesia, at least 20 percent in Japan, at least 37 percent in Korea, 12 percent in Malaysia, at least 21 percent in the Philippines, 31 percent in Singapore, 29 percent in Taiwan, and 18 percent in Thailand. It is interesting to note that Singapore, Korea, and Taiwan, which rank high among the developing countries in the region as services exporters, are also countries with a high percentage of U.S. direct investment position in services.

The data presented so far provide a rough picture of the importance of U.S. direct investment in services in the Asia-Pacific region; however, they say little about how important it is in comparison with services exports from the United States. For this, comparison of services exports with the sales of foreign affiliates in services is needed.

Table 2.17 shows sales made in 1982 by the majority-owned U.S. foreign affiliates located in the Asia-Pacific region and in all countries. These are for both goods and services and for sales made to markets outside as well as inside the United States. It is clear that the sales of foreign affiliates, whether in goods or in services, were primarily to markets outside the United States: for all affiliates combined, the share of sales going to these markets was 90 percent for goods and 89 percent

Table 2.8 U.S. Direct Investment Position in Hong Kong by Industry, Year-end (US$ millions)[a]

Industry	1979	1980	1981	1982	1983
Mining	0	0	0	0	0
Petroleum	159	219	271	317	294
	(9)	(11)	(10)	(11)	(9)
Manufacturing	297	373	467	506	540
	(17)	(18)	(17)	(17)	(16)
Services	1,057	1,154	1,480	1,698	1,975
	(60)	(56)	(54)	(56)	(60)
Trade	576	548	751	713	956
Banking	177	214	306	408	422
Finance (except banking, insurance, and real estate)	304	392	423	577	597
Other industries	257	333	512	494	502
	(15)	(16)	(19)	(16)	(15)
All industries	1,770	2,078	2,729	3,015	3,310
	(100)	(100)	(100)	(100)	(100)

Note: a. Figures in parentheses are percentages.
Source: See table 2.6.

for services, whereas for the affiliates located in the Asia-Pacific region, it was 83 percent and 96 percent respectively.

In 1982 the sales of services by the majority-owned U.S. foreign affiliates to the rest of the world amounted to 53 billion SDRs, whereas U.S. export of services was 29 billion SDRs (table 2.4). (Sales to the rest of the world by those located in the Asia-Pacific region were a little more than 3 billion SDRs.) These figures demonstrate that DFI, not trade, is the major vehicle for the internationalization of U.S. service industries.

Japanese Direct Foreign Investment in Services

Data of Japanese DFI in the Asia-Pacific region are presented by sectors and for all industries in table 2.18. By the end of March 1981 Japan had invested more than half its total DFI in this region, surpassing the United States as the region's largest foreign investor. The United States was by far the largest host for Japanese DFI, followed by

Table 2.9 U.S. Direct Investment Position in Indonesia by Industry, Year-end (US$ millions)[a]

Industry	1979	1980	1981	1982	1983
Mining	*	*	*	*	*
Petroleum	898	962	1,051	2,231	2,573
	(75)	(73)	(81)	(85)	(85)
Manufacturing	103	140	141	144	144
	(9)	(11)	(8)	(6)	(5)
Services	33	35	35	33	59
	(3)	(3)	(2)	(1)	(2)
Trade	16	20	20	19	41
Banking	11	9	9	6	11
Finance (except banking, insurance, and real estate)	6	6	6	8	7
Other industries	*	*	*	*	*
All industries	1,191	1,314	1,847	2,615	3,042
	(100)	(100)	(100)	(100)	(100)

Notes: a. Figures in parentheses are percentages.
* = Suppressed to avoid disclosure of data of individual firms.
Source: See table 2.6.

Table 2.10 U.S. Direct Investment Position in Japan by Industry, Year-end (US$ millions)[a]

Industry	1979	1980	1981	1982	1983
Mining	0	0	0	0	0
Petroleum	1,906	1,570	1,737	1,708	2,011
	(31)	(25)	(26)	(25)	(25)
Manufacturing	2,775	2,971	3,236	3,462	4,071
	(45)	(48)	(48)	(50)	(51)
Services	—	—	—	—	—
Trade	1,040	1,115	1,215	1,137	1,257
	(17)	(18)	(18)	(16)	(16)
Banking	*	*	*	*	*
Finance (except banking, insurance, and real estate)	160	186	221	254	347
	(3)	(3)	(3)	(4)	(4)
Other industries	*	*	*	*	*
All industries	6,208	6,243	6,755	6,928	8,059
	(100)	(100)	(100)	(100)	(100)

Notes: a. Figures in parentheses are percentages.
* = Suppressed to avoid disclosure of data of individual firms.
Source: See table 2.6.

Table 2.11 U.S. Direct Investment Position in South Korea by Industry, Year-end (US$ millions)[a]

Industry	1979	1980	1981	1982	1983
Mining	0	0	0	0	0
Petroleum	*	*	315 (40)	*	122 (19)
Manufacturing	218 (32)	179 (31)	161 (21)	163 (20)	150 (23)
Services	—	—	—	—	—
Trade	*	*	55 (7)	65 (8)	70 (11)
Banking	42 (6)	60 (10)	94 (12)	130 (16)	171 (26)
Finance (except banking, insurance, and real estate)	*	*	*	*	*
Other industries	20 (3)	8 (1)	*	*	*
All industries	689 (100)	575 (100)	779 (100)	829 (100)	650 (100)

Notes: a. Figures in parentheses are percentages.
* = Suppressed to avoid disclosure of data of individual firms.
Source: See table 2.6.

Table 2.12 U.S. Direct Investment Position in Malaysia by Industry, Year-end (US$ millions)[a]

Industry	1979	1980	1981	1982	1983
Mining	3 (1)	2 (0)	3 (0)	3 (0)	3 (0)
Petroleum	*	*	497 (59)	669 (65)	739 (66)
Manufacturing	109 (19)	179 (28)	242 (29)	246 (24)	241 (22)
Services	—	—	105 (12)	111 (11)	134 (12)
Trade	*	*	68	74	96
Banking	10	7	10	8	11
Finance (except banking, insurance, and real estate)	3	3	3	7	6
Other industries	29 (5)	27 (4)	24 (3)	22 (2)	21 (2)
All industries	561 (100)	632 (100)	847 (100)	1,030 (100)	1,118 (100)

Notes: a. Figures in parentheses are percentages.
* = Suppressed to avoid disclosure of data of individual firms.
Source: See table 2.6.

Table 2.13 U.S. Direct Investment Position in Philippines by Industry, Year-end (US$ millions)[a]

Industry	1979	1980	1981	1982	1983
Mining	**	**	**	**	**
Petroleum	378 (30)	335 (27)	263 (20)	297 (23)	*
Manufacturing	495 (39)	546 (43)	564 (43)	444 (34)	389 (35)
Services	261 (21)	231 (18)	—	—	—
Trade	95 (8)	86 (7)	93 (7)	80 (6)	58 (5)
Banking	138 (11)	116 (9)	141 (11)	166 (13)	181 (16)
Finance (except banking, insurance, and real estate)	28	29	*	*	*
Other industries	118 (9)	146 (12)	*	*	*
All industries	1,254 (100)	1,259 (100)	1,320 (100)	1,297 (100)	1,102 (100)

Notes: a. Figures in parentheses are percentages.
* = Suppressed to avoid disclosure of data of individual firms.
** = Less than 500,000 (±).
Source: See table 2.6.

Table 2.14 U.S. Direct Investment Position in Singapore by Industry, Year-end (US$ millions)[a]

Industry	1979	1980	1981	1982	1983
Mining	0	0	0	0	0
Petroleum	269 (31)	460 (38)	755 (41)	677 (37)	616 (31)
Manufacturing	294 (34)	392 (33)	587 (32)	574 (32)	655 (33)
Services	239 (28)	286 (24)	424 (23)	490 (27)	612 (31)
Trade	139	163	155	180	259
Banking	76	90	130	138	166
Finance (except banking, insurance, and real estate)	24	33	139	172	187
Other industries	58 (7)	67 (6)	70 (4)	81 (4)	82 (4)
All industries	860 (100)	1,204 (100)	1,835 (100)	1,822 (100)	1,965 (100)

Note: a. Figures in parentheses are percentages.
Source: See table 2.6.

Table 2.15 U.S. Direct Investment Position in Taiwan by Industry, Year-end (US$ millions)[a]

Industry	1979	1980	1981	1982	1983
Mining	0	0	0	0	0
Petroleum	35	38	37	63	93
	(9)	(8)	(7)	(10)	(13)
Manufacturing	252	321	341	363	382
	(64)	(64)	(61)	(58)	(55)
Services	100	132	173	183	204
	(25)	(27)	(31)	(29)	(29)
Trade	37	45	66	79	92
Banking	59	83	103	101	108
Finance (except banking, insurance, and real estate)	4	4	4	3	4
Other industries	5	7	9	13	16
	(1)	(1)	(2)	(2)	(2)
All industries	393	498	562	622	695
	(100)	(100)	(100)	(100)	(100)

Note: a. Figures in parentheses are percentages.
Source: See table 2.6.

Table 2.16 U.S. Direct Investment Position in Thailand by Industry, Year-end (US$ millions)[a]

Industry	1979	1980	1981	1982	1983
Mining	8	10	10	10	10
	(4)	(3)	(2)	(2)	(1)
Petroleum	*	*	406	426	564
			(74)	(73)	(77)
Manufacturing	65	87	26	30	33
	(33)	(24)	(5)	(5)	(5)
Services	—	—	113	124	128
			(21)	(21)	(18)
Trade	*	*	72	78	74
Banking	31	39	41	46	54
Finance (except banking, insurance, and real estate)	1	1	**	**	**
Other industries	10	5	−4	−6	−6
	(5)	(1)			
All industries	200	361	551	585	729
	(100)	(100)	(100)	(100)	(100)

Notes: a. Figures in parentheses are percentages.
* = Suppressed to avoid disclosure of data of individual firms.
** = Less than $500,000 (±).
Source: See table 2.6.

Table 2.17 Sales of Majority-Owned U.S. Foreign Affiliates, Country of Affiliate by Destination, 1982 (millions of SDRs)[b]

Geographical distribution of affiliates	Goods			Services[b]		
	Total	Sales to the United States	Sales to the rest of world	Total	Sales to the United States	Sales to the rest of world
Asia-Pacific countries[c]	63,563 (100)	10,614 (17)	52,949 (83)	3,533 (100)	149 (4)	3,384 (96)
World	601,375 (100)	62,800 (10)	538,575 (90)	60,070 (100)	6,747 (11)	53,322 (89)

Notes: a. Figures in parentheses are percentages.

b. Services include sales in the following industries: oil and gas field services; petroleum tanker operations, petroleum and natural gas pipelines, and petroleum storage for hire; finance (except banking) insurance, and real estate; services (as narrowly defined in the SIC); agricultural services; metal mining services; and transportation, communication, and public utilities. For a more detailed discussion of services included see Whichard and Shea, 1985.

c. Hong Kong, Indonesia, Japan, Malaysia, Philippines, Singapore, Korea, Taiwan, Thailand, and "Other" (excluding Australia and New Zealand).

Source: Whichard and Shea, 1985.

Table 2.18 Cumulative Sum of Japanese Direct Foreign Investment, End of March 1981 (US$ millions)[a]

Country	Services[b]	Manufacturing	Mining	All industries
Hong Kong	421	185	5	1,095
	(38)	(17)	(0)	(100)
Indonesia	101	1,527	2,522	4,424
	(2)	(35)	(57)	(100)
Korea	19	780	2	1,137
	(2)	(69)	(0)	(100)
Malaysia	26	456	120	650
	(4)	(70)	(18)	(100)
Philippines	33	236	277	615
	(5)	(38)	(45)	(100)
Singapore	90	688	—	936
	(10)	(74)	(0)	(100)
Taiwan	8	344	2	370
	(2)	(93)	(0)	(100)
Thailand	64	292	5	396
	(16)	(74)	(1)	(100)
United States	4,856	2,056	334	8,878
	(55)	(23)	(4)	(100)
Total for region	5,618	6,564	3,267	18,501
	(30)	(35)	(18)	(100)
Total for world	9,193	12,573	7,071	36,497
	(25)	(34)	(19)	(100)

Notes: a. Figures in parentheses are percentages.
b. Services include construction, trade ("commerce"), finance and insurance, and real estate.

Source: Japan, Ministry of Finance, 1981.

Indonesia, Korea, Hong Kong, and Singapore.

Almost a third of Japan's total direct investment in the region was in services, a proportion larger than that estimated for the United States. This relatively large share in services was due to the highly services-oriented investment in the United States and Hong Kong—55 percent and 38 percent respectively. Services' share of Japanese DFI in the rest of the region ranged from 16 percent for Thailand to a meager 2 percent each for Indonesia, Korea, and Taiwan. In fact, with the exception of Indonesia, the share of Japanese DFI in services in the developing countries in the region was smaller than U.S. DFI in the same countries.

The message from these findings seems to be that a developed service economy is a better host for multinational enterprises in services than a developing industrializing country. If this is true, the short-term prospect for increasing international activities of U.S. service industries in the region is poor unless their activities in Japan increase rapidly. By the end of 1983, services' share of U.S. DFI in Japan was probably slightly more than 20 percent, in contrast with 55 percent for Japanese direct investment in the United States by March 1981. There is still room for expansion in Japan by U.S. multinational enterprises in services.

Prospects for Liberalization

Because of the paucity of data, it is impossible to draw a detailed, comprehensive picture of the patterns of trade and investment in services in the Asia-Pacific region, but this investigation has revealed the broad contours of these patterns.

Among the countries in the region the United States and Japan are the two largest exporters and importers of services, although both export only a small portion of their services output. Following behind these economic giants in terms of the value of services exports are the NICs—Singapore, Korea, and Taiwan (there are no data on Hong Kong). What they export is relatively small in value, but nevertheless represents a much larger portion of their output than do services exports for the United States and Japan.

The cross-sectional and time-series data on trade in merchandise and trade in services suggest a roughly complementary relationship between the two. Some hypotheses have been proposed for this relationship, but more research is needed—especially at a less aggregate level—to find out whether there is any economic reason for the statistical relationship.

The evidence, albeit tentative, does not support the contention that the United States has a comparative advantage in services. Rather, Singapore and Korea seem to have this advantage. This finding is consistent with that of Kravis, which shows that it is the non-oil-exporting developing countries, not the United States and Japan, that have a comparative advantage in services.

Although the United States and Japan may not have a comparative advantage in services, some of their service firms possess firm-specific advantages. These advantages make these firms competitive in the world market, enabling them to invest overseas. In fact, U.S. service industries account for a significant portion of the total U.S. direct investment position in the rest of the world, and the sales of their foreign affiliates exceed their exports. Japanese service industries also account for a significant portion of Japan's total DFI, but their investment is highly concentrated in the United States.

The distinction between comparative advantage and firm-specific advantage raises some interesting points regarding the recent move toward liberalizing what is commonly referred to as "trade in services." If liberalization is limited to trade in services in the sense defined here, and if services are defined to include construction, it is not obvious that the United States will benefit from the liberalization in terms of its share of the regional or world market. If liberalization is based instead on the conditions of entry and operation of foreign affiliates in services, it is likely that firms in technologically more advanced countries such as the United States and Japan will dominate. Thus, what a country perceives as advantageous in the liberalization of "trade in services" may depend on how it defines both trade and services. Differences in their definitions may have much to do with the divergent attitudes shown by governments toward the issue of liberalization and the lack of consensus on it.

CHAPTER 3
Direct and Embodied Trade in Services, or Where is the Service Trade Problem?

Herbert G. Grubel

Analysis of trade and investment in services in the Asia-Pacific region is part of a worldwide effort to come to terms with two phenomena: the increase in the service industries' share of total employment and the decline in the percentage of foreign trade represented by the service sector. Examining data from Canada will help explain these two phenomena.[1]

Figure 3.1 shows the widely known historic changes in employment opportunities offered in agriculture, other goods-producing industries, and services. At the time of the 1911 census, all three sectors employed nearly equal proportions of the Canadian labor force. Since then, the share of employment in agriculture has fallen continuously and appears to have reached its lower limit at the 5 percent level. Other goods-producing industries employed a slowly rising share of the labor force after 1911. This share reached a peak of about 40 percent in 1951 and has been declining slowly since. The remarkable story is the strong growth in the share of total employment seen in the service-producing industries. Though this growth was interrupted briefly during the Second World War, it reached nearly a 70 percent share of total employment in 1981.[2]

Figure 3.2, which deals with the second phenomenon responsible

1. Although I have drawn heavily on data from Canada, almost all longer-run and real economic developments of that country are highly correlated with those of the United States and, to a considerable degree, with those in the industrial countries of Western Europe. In the following analysis, special note will be taken of developments that are particular to Canada.

2. The data are from the decennial census (Statistics Canada 1983). The aggregation of the categories followed the classification scheme adopted by Statistics Canada for later years and is standard in the literature on services. Construction is the one industry treated differently by different researchers. Here it was included in the goods-producing industry category. The category "industry unspecified" was included in the service sector.

Figure 3.1 Historic Shares of Employment in Canada

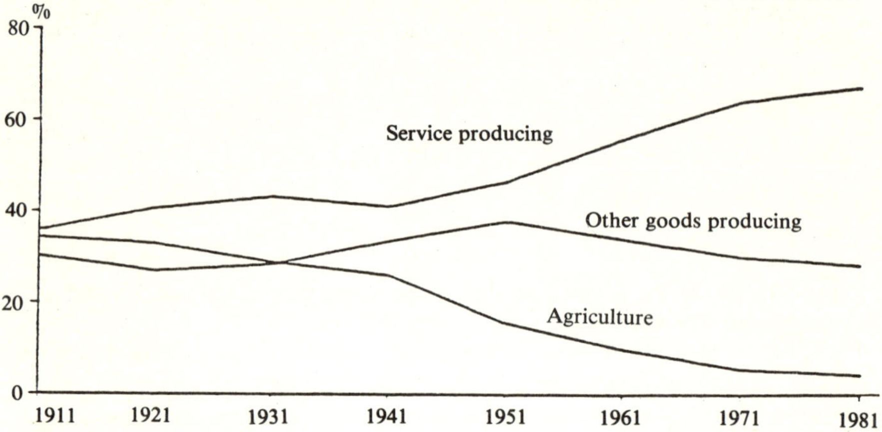

Source: Canada, 1983.

Figure 3.2 Service as a Percentage of Merchandise Trade in Canada in Current Canadian Dollars.

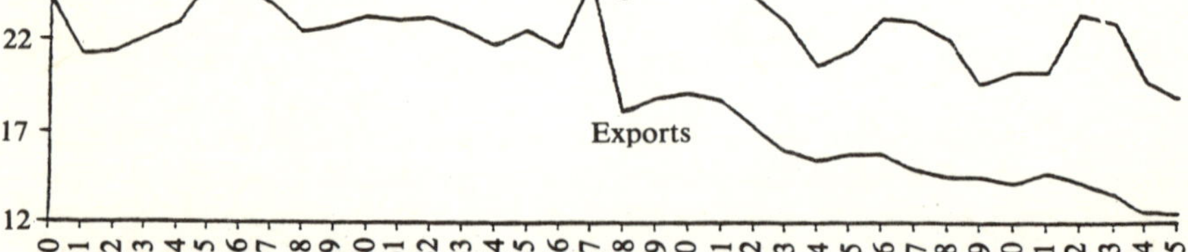

Note: Services are "other services" and consist of travel, freight and shipping, and other.
Source: Canada, 1986, Table J-2, Series D60501 and D60502 for merchandise trade and direct service trade.

for the current interest in trade in services, indicates Canada's nonfactor service imports constituted about 28 percent of the value of its merchandise imports in 1950.[3] Since then, this percentage has been declining; it reached about 21 percent in 1985. The pattern has been almost identical for exports during the same period, even though the figure has consistently been about four percentage points less than that for imports.[4]

Public concern over the implications of these two phenomena is summarized in a quote from the *Background Report of the Canadian Government Task Force on Trade in Services* (1982:19): ". . . Canada has become a service economy—at home. Despite the domestic importance of the service sector, however, Canada's trade orientation is concentrated on goods. . . ."

Similar developments have taken place in the United States and the industrial countries of Western Europe. These changes have attracted much attention because of their possible implications for the current account balances of the industrial countries in the future.[5] It is believed that as employment and output are shifted increasingly into the service sector, ever larger proportions of domestic demand for goods must be met through imports. And if nonfactor service exports perform in their historic pattern, they will fail to grow at a sufficiently rapid pace to pay for the goods imported.

These prospects have been responsible to a considerable degree for the efforts of the United States to convene a special round of General Agreement on Tariffs and Trade (GATT) negotiations.[6] The conventional wisdom is that U.S. service exports have been hampered by foreign trade restrictions. As a result, further evolution of the pattern of international specialization and global prosperity is threatened.

3. In this study I follow the suggestion made by Lee and Naya (1986) and consider only nonfactor service flows because less is known about them than about factor service flows. After all, the entire literature on international finance, DFI, migration, the brain drain—motives, balance of payments and welfare effects—is relevant to the latter.

In this context it is worth noting that the U.S. International Trade Commission (1982) has studied the gross sales of U.S. subsidiaries abroad and defined them to be U.S. service exports. This approach is unusual: it includes the sales of McDonald's hamburgers by its foreign subsidiaries in U.S. service exports. In this study, the sales of Canadian subsidiaries abroad are not considered service exports.

4. The spike in the ratio of service to merchandise exports in 1967 reflects the increased earnings of transportation accounts that accompanied the 1967 World's Fair in Montreal.

5. A convenient summary of current knowledge on several countries' service sectors is found in Gershuny and Miles (1983), Riddle (1986), and Petit (1986).

6. For an outline of the U.S. position and perception of the issues, see United States (1983). For a dissenting view on the merit of such negotiations, see Grey (1985).

Some questions arise about the interpretation of those trends in service employment and trade in services that have created these concerns. What is known about the nature of the domestic expansion of the service sector reveals that about half of the expansion has been in services that cannot be traded, such as education and medical and personal services.

The other half of the expanded service production represents increased capital deepening and specialization, which have resulted in greater factor productivity in the goods sector. Expanded service production has assured the persistence of comparative advantage in goods exports and led to substantial and growing export of services embodied in goods. This trend is likely to continue in the future, and if my analysis and data are correct, concerns about international trade in services are likely to be unfounded.

Domestic Service Industry Growth

Figure 3.3 illustrates the growth in employment enjoyed for the decade 1976–1985 by the 12 basic service industries for which Statistics Canada collects information. Recall from the preceding discussion that together these industries provided work for about 70 percent of the Canadian labor force in 1985.[7] The statistics reveal that the smallest employment gains were experienced by the following industries: transportation, communications, and utilities; education; and public administration. The highest growth rates were enjoyed by services to business management; personal services; miscellaneous services; and accommodation and food.

---

7. These data are reliable—they come from a monthly labor force survey with a good sample that has been consistently well administered since 1946. The survey's major shortcoming lies in the inadequacy of the industry definitions, which have not kept up with the profusion of new service sector activities. In addition, breakdowns of the major industry groupings are not published regularly, even though the data are available. However, with the recent interest in service industries, Statistics Canada is undertaking several projects to provide more detailed information on special sectors, such as services to business management.

Another source of information on employment service industries in Canada is the census. For 1981 a special compilation, "Labour Force by Occupation" (Population, 8-5200-623, 1984), provides data in extraordinary detail. However, because of differences in definitions and in the treatment of nonresponses, the census and the Labour Force Survey data are not fully consistent. In addition, different censuses cannot be compared.

Figure 3.3 Service Employment Growth Rates in Canada: 1976–1985

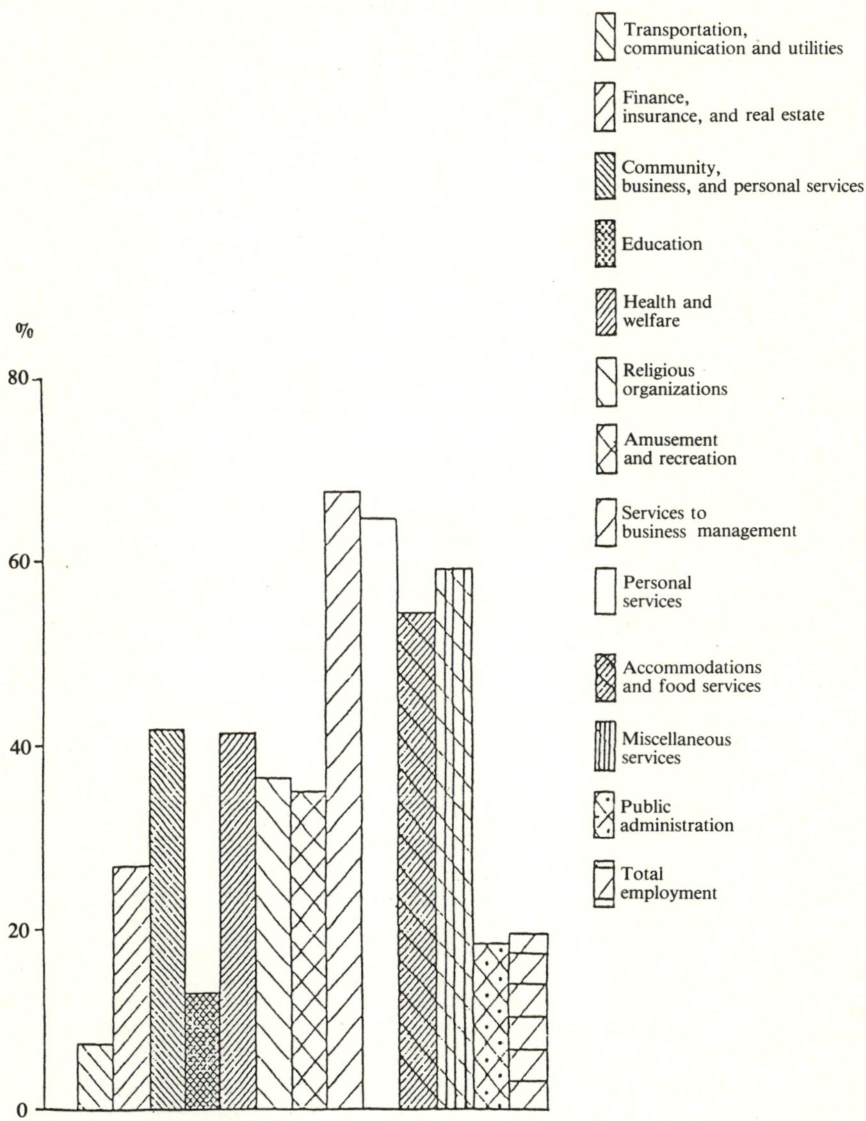

Source: Canada, 1985.

Figure 3.4 Growth Rates of Service Group Functions in Canada: 1976–1985

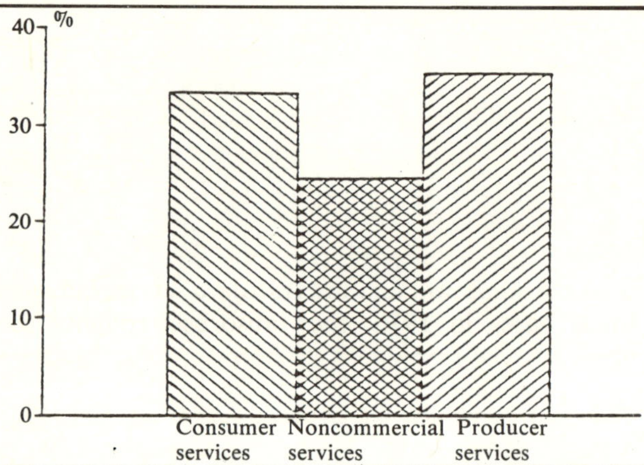

Note: In preparing the estimates shown in figures 3.4 and 3.5, the following scheme was used:

1. Consumer services consist of personal services; amusement and recreation; one-half each of accommodation and food services; community, business, and personal services; miscellaneous services; transportation, communication, and utilities; and two-thirds of wholesale and retail trade.
2. Noncommercial consumer services consist of education and related services; health and welfare services; religious organizations; and public administration.
3. Producers' services consist of services to business management; finance, insurance and real estate services; one-third of wholesale and retail trade; one-half each of transportation, communication, and utilities; miscellaneous services; community, business, and personal services; and accommodation and food services.

Source: Canada, 1985.

For analytical purposes, the aggregated data on the 12 industries were divided into three categories (figure 3.4).[8] The first category contains industries producing services for final consumption that are purchased in competitive markets. The second category includes final

8. I have not encountered studies that have classed Canadian industries in these three categories.

Changing the allocation of entire categories of services would affect the reported results substantially. However, since most of the service industries producing for both final consumers and for business were evenly divided, the results are not sensitive to the categories treated in this manner. It is clear, however, that changes in the proportions allocated to each category alter the outcome of my statistical representation and affect the main analytical conclusions.

For these reasons, this study must be considered indicative rather than definitive. An attempt will be made to use input-output tables to obtain a solid foundation for the assignment of individual industries to the three categories.

consumer services provided by the government; and the third comprises those services used as intermediate inputs into further production of goods and services.

During the period 1976–1985 employment grew most rapidly in the sector producing intermediate services (figure 3.4). Employment in marketed consumer services rose marginally less, whereas noncommercial consumer service employment increased but at a substantially smaller rate. However, growth rates in isolation may be misleading for certain types of analyses. For this reason, absolute employment levels in the three categories in 1976 and 1985 are given in figure 3.5. Because the final consumption and intermediate service categories had just about equal bases in 1976, they absorbed roughly the same absolute numbers of new employees. In contrast, the noncommercial service sector created only a relatively small number of new jobs.

For later analytical purposes, the information in figures 3.4 and 3.5 can be summarized as follows: The service industries in total generated 2,823,000 new jobs in the period 1976–1985, representing about 70 percent of all jobs created in the economy. Of those new service jobs, 40 percent were in marketed consumer services, 18 percent in non-

Figure 3.5 Service Employment, Absolute Levels in Canada (millions)

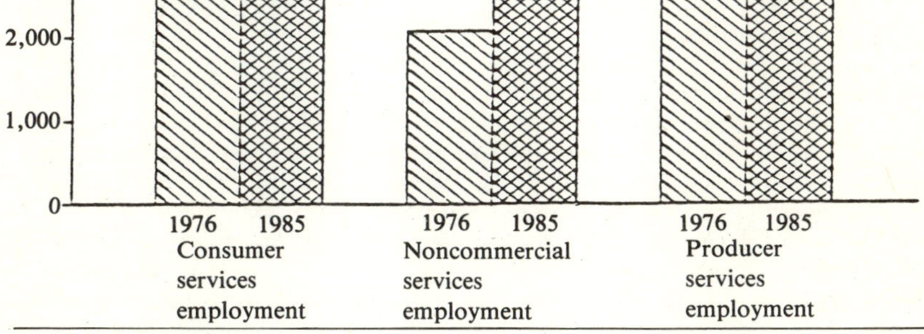

Note: See note to figure 3.4.
Source: Canada, 1985.

commercial consumer services, and 42 percent in intermediate input services.

The Three Types of Services and Their Importance in Trade

These facts about the growth of service employment are important because the two types of consumer services, by and large, are not tradeable, face no foreign restrictions, and are not an issue in international negotiations. The noncommercial services for final consumption in particular have these properties. Education, welfare, and general public services, which make up the bulk of the services in this class, are provided by the Canadian government for its citizens.[9]

The marketed consumer services consist of the textbook prototypes of nontradeables, such as personal care, amusement, recreation, accommodation, and food services. Consumption of these services requires that producers and consumers be in direct contact with each other. They are not involved in trade, primarily because transportation costs would typically constitute a multiple of the value of the services if they were exchanged internationally. International tourists and business travelers do consume these services, but the amounts traded in this manner make up a small proportion of the total, and they are neither a theoretical nor a policy issue in the debate over international trade in services.[10]

9. Noncommercial services also include religious organizations. Defense is included in public administration and in recent years represents about 2 percent of GNP (not employment) in Canada, as against about 5.5 percent of GNP in the United States.

Some education and medical services are tradeable through foreign student exchange and patients traveling to obtain specialized services in other countries. Also, one could interpret missionary work abroad as a form of international trade in religious services. However, all of this is likely to be a small amount of trade in noncommercial services. Nevertheless, special studies of the education and medical service industries should yield empirical information about this area. Grubel and Scott (1977) contains theoretical and empirical studies of international flows of human capital.

10. Again, the definition of nonfactor service trade in this chapter excludes from consideration the sale of services by a Canadian branch bank in the Caribbean. This type of activity generates earnings on the bank's investments and is reflected in the balance of payments as a dividend and therefore as factor service income. The same principle applies to the substantial international involvement of hotels, car rental agencies, and fast food service companies. Investment in these industries has given rise to many interesting and important theoretical, empirical, and policy issues, as the existing literature demonstrates. They have only a remote connection with the issues of trade in services. It is precisely because transportation costs for the final products are so high in these industries that internationalization involves DFI or licensing rather than conventional trade. Licensing fees and literary, film, and similar royalty incomes in this context are best considered as the return to knowledge and cultural capital and thus fall in the category of factor service flows.

Intermediate producers' services consist of the traditional services: finance, insurance, communications, transportation, wholesale trade, legal services, accounting, engineering, advertising, and management consulting. Intermediate producers' services also encompass the rapidly growing computer and information-processing services. It is believed that in these industries, the United States, Canada, and other highly industrialized countries have a comparative advantage that foreign restrictions prevent them from exploiting.

Direct Trade in Intermediate Services

There is some genuine, "direct" trade in intermediate services. In principle, it constitutes the numerator in the ratio of service-to-commodity trade shown in figure 3.2. Such trade occurs when firms in one country hire specialized engineering, management, accounting, transportation, and marketing experts in other countries. In the analytical framework adopted here, for the trade in these services to be relevant, the services should be effectively transferred abroad only through documents or electronic means, not through a permanent office. By the definition used here, services sold through such foreign offices require investment, and consequently net profits are reported as factor service income.

However, in practice, a large proportion of these services are transferred through persons working on sites abroad. Such travel also involves factor service flows in the form of labor and the human and knowledge capital attached to it. Such international migration will be defined as genuine trade in nonfactor services if an expert's stay abroad is determined by the need to service specific projects. Thus, a Canadian engineer employed by a pulp mill construction company who works for a year on a project in Malaysia is considered to produce a nonfactor service export equal to the bill paid by the Malaysian to the Canadian company. On the other hand, there is factor service trade if the Canadian engineer works abroad for a foreign subsidiary of the Canadian pulp mill construction company and moves from one job to another.[11]

11. To the best of my knowledge, statistical collection agencies do not make these distinctions between factor and nonfactor trade in intermediate services, though length of stay of foreigners is considered in determining whether its financial implications are recorded in the tourist accounts of countries or whether the individual is considered to be a permanent migrant. See White and Walker (1982) for a critical analysis of the travel account in balance of payments statistics of several countries. I present the discussion in the text as a preliminary attempt to sort out the conceptual issues surrounding the nature of international trade in services, which may result in practical propositions for improved data collection.

As in the case of final consumer services, intermediate services in general characteristically face a formidable barrier to international trade in the form of transportation costs. Therefore, it should not be surprising that direct trade in these services has been growing at a rate smaller than domestic production. This trend would probably exist without any government-imposed obstacles to trade in services.

One of my main conclusions follows from a second important characteristic of intermediate services. By their very nature, such services are an input into the production of traded goods. Therefore, to the extent the output and use of these intermediate input services has grown, they have been traded in growing quantities indirectly through embodiment in traded commodities. Before certain indicative and preliminary empirical estimates of Canada's trade in embodied services are presented, a discussion of theories on the causes of growth in domestic service production is necessary.

The Causes of Consumer Service Growth

The share of marketed consumer services in Canadian aggregate consumption expenditures rose in nominal terms from about 37 percent to 45 percent between 1947 and 1985 (figure 3.6). The two periods of falling values coincide with the introduction of government-financed hospital care (1961) and physicians' services (1971).

Figure 3.6 Market Service Consumption Expenditures in Canada (by percentage of total consumption expenditures)

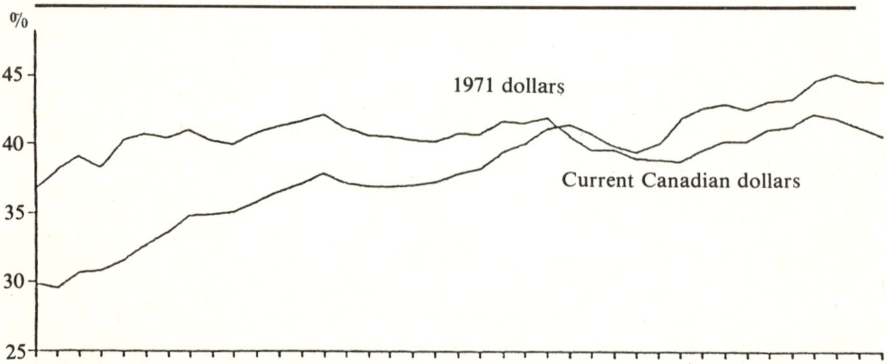

Source: Canada, Statistics Canada, *National Income and Expenditure Accounts*, Volume 1, Catalogue 13531, Table 6; Catalogue 13-01.

Also note in figure 3.6 that the real share of market services consumed has remained constant during the period under consideration.[12] In the literature on the demand for market services—for example, Gershuny and Miles (1983)—this fact is interpreted as being the result of the netting out of (1) an income effect greater than one that has operated on the growth in income and (2) a negative price effect that has operated on the increase in the relative price of services.

However, there is an alternative explanation for the constancy of the share of real services in the consumption basket. Grubel and Hammes (1986), using consumer expenditure surveys in Canada, estimate the elasticity of demand for market service goods, with respect to total spending on consumption, to be about 0.98. Since spending across income classes is free from relative price influences, this is a pure spending effect.[13] Estimates of the relative price elasticity of demand for market services made by others suggest a plausible value of −0.6.

An application of these income and price elasticity figures to the increases in total consumption expenditures of 392 percent and, in relative service prices, of 98 percent suggests that during the period the real demand for the services should have risen by only 325 percent. In fact, it rose 444 percent. It is postulated that the difference is due to the monetization of household production. This difference equals 27 percent, or US$8.1 billion out of a total of US$30.2 billion, of the total growth in consumption spending on services.

This monetization took place as the labor force participation rates of females increased and the purchase of food, laundry services, child care, and the like replaced previous home production of these services. Analogously, a growth in demand for effective leisure time

12. The deflation involves adjustment of the numerator for the increase in service prices and of the denominator for all the prices in the consumers' basket.

13. I should note that my colleague David Hammes estimated the service consumption values from the original survey data. He used the same definition of services as that found in the national income account data used in figure 3.6. The independent variable is total consumption expenditures, excluding personal income taxes paid. Both the service and total consumption values had to be adjusted for imputed rent on owner-occupied housing, since this item is contained in the national income data but not the consumer survey. This was done by multiplying real estate taxes paid by each income group by a factor of 10.

It is clear that the consumption elasticity computed in this manner is not the same as an income elasticity, though it should be similar. For this reason, it is necessary to treat with some caution the fact that Fuchs (1968) found an income elasticity of demand for services in general (i.e., not just market services of 1.05. Summers (1985) used international data and found the demand for most of the market services has an income elasticity of about or slightly less than one.)

has made many households give up domestic supply and begin to purchase home, garden, and automobile maintenance and similar services in the marketplace.

The demand for government-supplied consumer services in the form of education and medical care has been growing rapidly in Canada in the postwar years. This growth has been due partly to the rise in population, but mainly to the proliferation of the welfare state. However, the rate of increase in this service sector has slowed considerably in recent years. It is not clear whether this slowdown is due to a reduction in population and real income growth or to increasing resistance to the tax burdens generated by it.

The Causes of Intermediate Service Growth

There are two reasons for the growth of the intermediate service industries. First, firms have increasingly relied on the supply of intermediate input services from outside suppliers rather than internal sources. This process has been called "vertical disintegration" or "dehiving" by Momigliano and Siniscalco (1982). I have not seen any studies devoted to a theoretical or empirical investigation of the causes and magnitude of this phenomenon.[14]

---

14. The following are preliminary and speculative ideas on the causes of the vertical disintegration:

First, many business services have become more dynamic in recent decades as a result of a more rapid growth in knowledge due to (1) research and education (the MBA revolution), (2) database generation and manipulation opportunities due to the availability of greater computer and communications technology, and (3) increased complexity of tax codes and other such developments. The dynamism in these fields has resulted in a faster rate of obsolescence of knowledge and higher risks in acquiring it. Firms that use outside suppliers of these services effectively shift to them the risks associated with the acquisition and maintenance of this knowledge.

Second, the increasing internationalization and competitiveness of business due to the falling cost of transportation and communication has made it increasingly necessary for smaller business firms to hire intermediate business services. The scale of operation of these firms does not warrant the employment of full-time experts for this work. Use of outside suppliers in effect leads to the sharing of specialists among a number of buyers.

Third, the fixed costs of workers in Canada and most other industrial countries in recent years have been raised by costs of separation that stem from social welfare legislation and requirements of union contracts. These costs are manifested in more complicated procedures needed for the dismissal of employees and in required separation payments. By contracting out rather than supplying business services internally, firms are able to avoid these costs. Small-scale suppliers are typically not unionized and are often exempted from some of the social welfare legislation.

Fourth, other developments have also increased the supply of intermediate business services. The most important of these is the general growth of knowledge and the

Second, there has been an economy-wide increase in the endowment of physical, human, and knowledge capital per worker. This has resulted in greater "roundaboutness of production," to use a term of the Austrian School. Significantly, it has also produced greater specialization in all types of capital. From this perspective, the growth of the intermediate service input industries is simply the manifestation of growth of the capital stock, most especially human and knowledge capital, which is responsible for the secular rise in labor productivity and the development of comparative advantage in international trade.

An interesting challenge would be to empirically separate the relative importance of the two causes of the observed growth in intermediate service industry employment. However, this separation is not essential to the central argument here.

Embodied Service Trade

International trade in services continues to flourish as an input into the production of traded goods. This is as characteristic of trade in intermediate services as it is of trade in intermediate material goods. Both types of intermediate inputs are absolutely essential to the productive process and are often major sources of comparative advantage in manufacture for export.

The low cost of hydroelectric energy is an important source of Canada's comparative advantage in the production and export of aluminum, but so are the specialized engineering services used in the construction of the hydroelectric dams and transmission facilities. Similarly, engineering, use of computers, research and development, management control, advertising, shipping, and health-care services are continuously bought by aluminum producers to maintain and raise

---

specialization required to master it. In almost all fields of business services there has been an explosion in the stock of knowledge. As in all scientific and professional endeavors, specialization leads to increased productivity and lower cost per unit of effective service delivered. Legal, engineering, and marketing experts that have specialized in narrow fields are often expensive per unit of input but are in great demand because of low costs per unit of effective service delivered.

In general, the question of vertical disintegration seems amenable to treatment in the framework of the theory of the firms proposed by Coase (1937) and others. It is also worth noting that the magnitude of the disintegration phenomenon has important implications for the basic phenomenon and alleged problems of the decline of manufacturing and the growth of service employment. The greater the disintegration, the more the measured decline in the goods-producing industries is a statistical rather than a real phenomenon.

output and efficiency. Without these inputs the industry would begin to lose its comparative advantage and eventually fail as a domestic producer and exporter.

Intermediate service inputs are used by all industries, and their development is closely linked to the existence of comparative advantage based on other factors. For example, the Canadian forest industry, which is based on an abundance of forested lands, has led to the development of highly specialized engineering, management consulting, and other service industries. These service industries in turn have helped create an industry that exports machinery and processing plants used by forest industries around the world. Some of these services are exported directly; some firms have established consulting firms abroad and earn factor service income; but most of the services are embodied in equipment.

In addition to the forest and aluminum industries, there are other obvious examples, such as farm machinery and transportation equipment used in snow. However, service industries also exist to serve other service industries that are exported directly. Electricity services are a major export and require large quantities of specialized service inputs. In the case of the tourist industries also, the amount of intermediate service inputs per dollar of foreign tourist spending is relatively high.

International trade in embodied services does not alter existing trade theories, though there are important problems in operationally defining the concept of intermediate services. For example, are health-care services for workers intermediate or final consumer services? This issue has been brought to the fore by the allegation that the costs of health-care services embodied in an average automobile produced in the United States are greater than those for steel. If a similar statement can be made about steel and its material inputs such as coal and, in turn, the costs of health-care services embodied in coal production, it becomes clear how pervasive the phenomenon is. Should education be considered in this manner? More basic analysis is needed and probably will have to draw heavily on the concept of the creation and maintenance of human and knowledge capital.

These topics cannot be pursued further here. Instead, some thoughts concerning the measurement of embodied services trade will be considered. There are questions any student of international trade familiar with the Leontief paradox would want to ask: What is the value of service inputs per billion dollars of exports and imports? What has been the implicit balance of trade in embodied services, currently and historically? What is the ranking of Canadian export and import industries according to the proportion of service value added? Which service industries contribute the most to the embodied trade per billion dollars of exports and in relation to domestic production—engineering, scientific research, transportation, or accounting?

The theoretical and empirical research agendas appear promising and rich. Only a small contribution can be made here in the form of an exploratory, rather than an incisive, calculation.

Calculating the Value of Embodied Services

It is possible in principle, with the help of input-output tables and the techniques pioneered by Leontief, to estimate the direct and indirect amount of services embodied in a unit of a country's exports and imports. Since this approach has yet to be undertaken, the

Figure 3.7 Intermediate Service GDP (as a percentage of gross goods output)

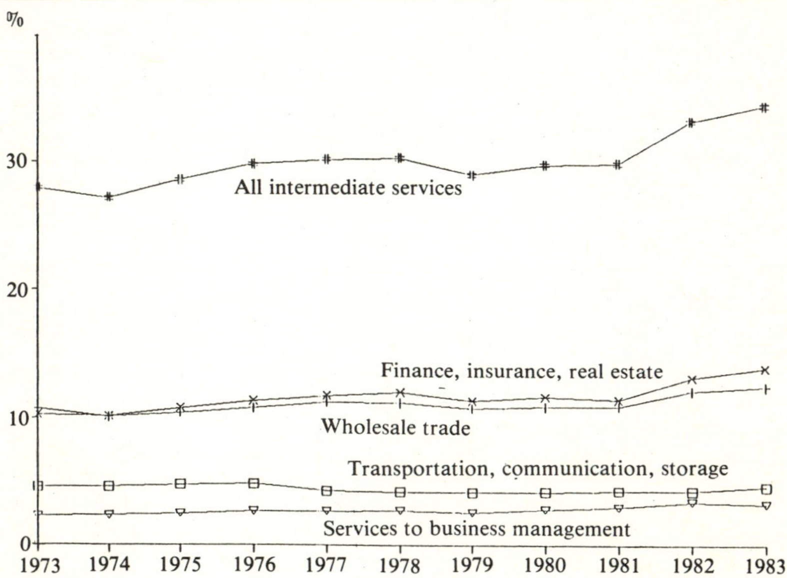

Source: Canada, Bureau Statistics, *Gross Domestic Product by Industry*, Catalogue 61-213.

Figure 3.8 Exports of Merchandise and Services in Canada (millions of current Canadian dollars)

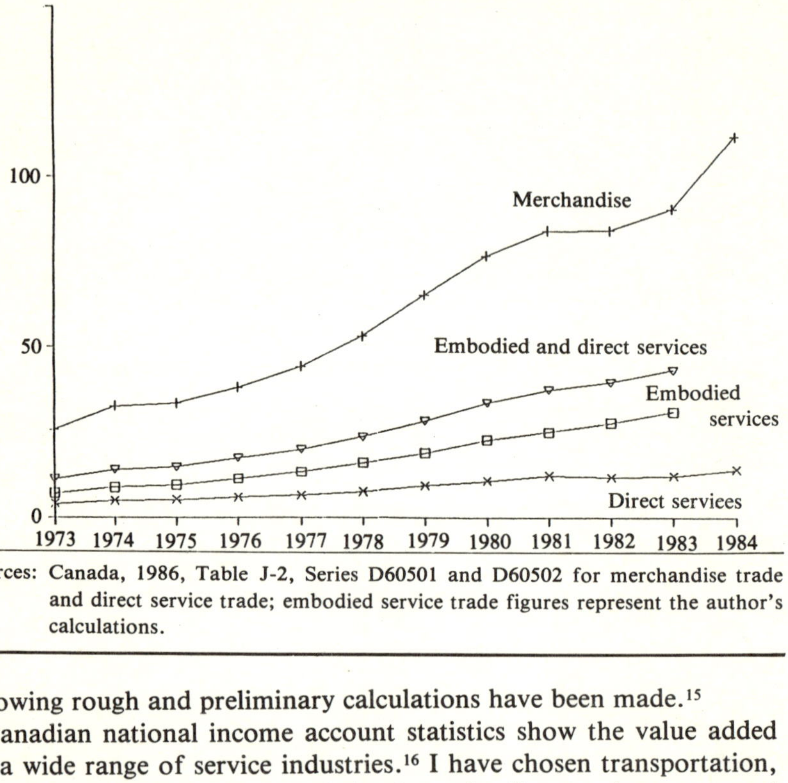

Sources: Canada, 1986, Table J-2, Series D60501 and D60502 for merchandise trade and direct service trade; embodied service trade figures represent the author's calculations.

following rough and preliminary calculations have been made.[15]

Canadian national income account statistics show the value added for a wide range of service industries.[16] I have chosen transportation, communication and storage; wholesale trade; finance, insurance and

15. Rick Harris of Queen's University will contribute a study of embodied service trade based on the use of Canadian input-output tables to the Fraser Institute. Campbell (1985) has measured embodied service trade for Australia and found that on average about 20 percent of the value of Australian exports consists of value added by service industries. This is remarkable, since these exports are mainly natural resources. Momigliano and Siniscalco (1982) have calculated the direct and indirect service input requirements of individual Italian industries from input-output tables, but have not explicity addressed international trade, though this could be readily done.

16. It should be noted that national income accountants generally do not put much faith in the quality of data on service industries, domestic production, and trade (Lederer et al. 1982). This fact further undermines the usefulness of the results presented here. However, the basic argument of this chapter is not affected by these data limitations, nor should the basic empirical results be.

real estate; and services to business management to represent intermediate services. The development of the value added of these industries as a percentage of gross goods produced in Canada in the years 1973–1983 is presented in figure 3.7. As can be seen, the level of these inputs has risen from about 28 to 33 percent.

The current dollar value of services embodied in goods exports was calculated under the assumption that Canadian exports of merchandise embodied the same proportion of service industry value added as all goods produced in Canada. These are referred to as embodied services and are compared with the dollar values of direct service and merchandise exports in figure 3.8. To bring out the relative growth rates of these analytical components of Canada's exports, the dollar values in 1973 were set at 100 and the cumulative indices were plotted over the following 10 years in figure 3.9.

Figure 3.9 Export Growth in Merchandise and Services in Canada (1973 = 100).

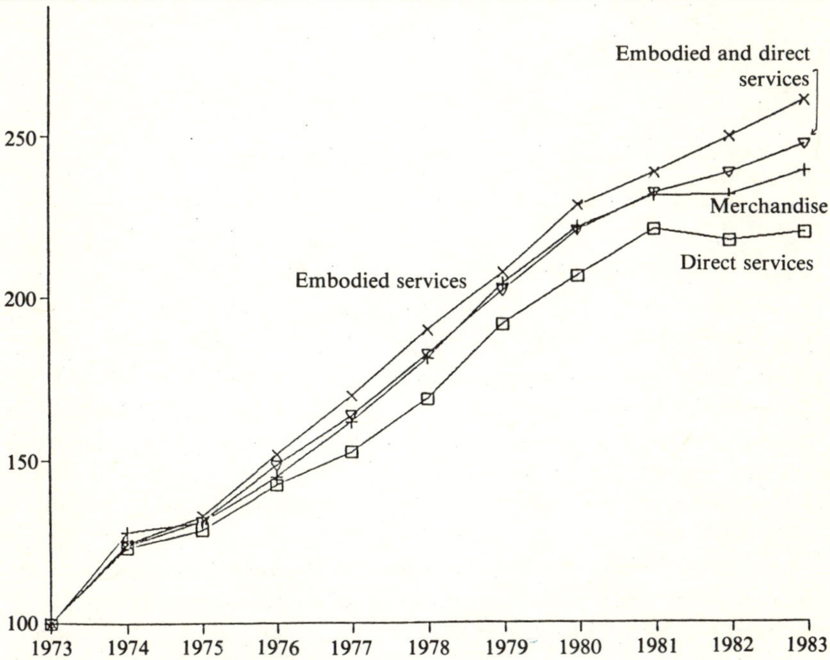

Sources: Same as figure 3.2 for merchandise and direct service trade; embodied service trade figures represent the author's calculations.

Figure 3.10 Import Growth in Merchandise and Services in Canada (1973 = 100).

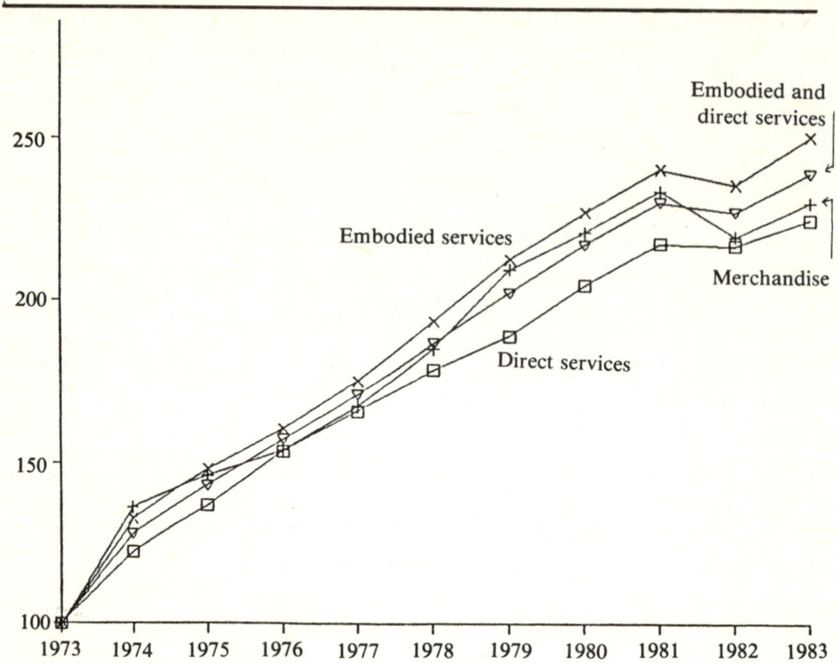

Sources: Same as figure 3.9.

According to these calculations, Canada's trade in embodied services has grown more rapidly than merchandise trade. The combined direct and embodied service trade grew at approximately the same rate as the merchandise trade.

The values of embodied and direct service trade implicit in Canadian imports were calculated and their growth rates charted in figure 3.10. The balance of trade in direct and embodied service trade is shown in figure 3.11 and is dominated by the extraordinary trade surplus in recent years, which has been as high as 4 percent of GNP.

The specific results of my calculations do not deserve detailed discussion, primarily because they are based on assumptions that are unlikely to be realistic. For more reliable results, a careful choice of intermediate service industries must be made, and above all, estimates of both the direct and indirect service inputs used by a billion dollars' worth of actual merchandise imports and exports must be computed.

However, my basic hypothesis is supported by the calculations of embodied service trade in imports and exports. The growth in direct

Figure 3.11 Service Trade Balances for Canada (millions of current Canadian dollars)

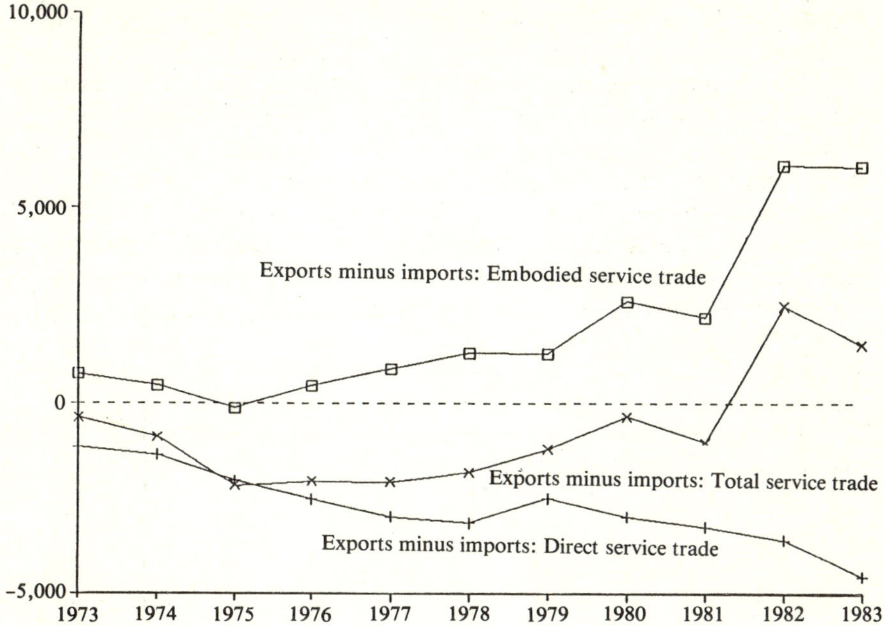

Sources: Same as figure 3.9.

service trade has lagged behind the growth in merchandise trade and domestic service industry output, but trade in services embodied in merchandise trade has expanded more rapidly than the merchandise trade. This result follows directly from the empirical fact that the value added by intermediate service inputs is becoming an ever larger proportion of the value of goods produced and traded. This process is likely to continue as long as there is further accumulation of human and knowledge capital per worker and an accompanying growth in specialization.

Some Final Observations

Because about half of the growth in service production is in the form of services used as inputs in the production of goods, the simultaneous growth in domestic service employment and decrease in service exports does not portend a crisis. Through trade in goods there is trade in embodied services. Often these services are an important source of comparative advantage in specific industries.

In spite of the preliminary nature of this study, the findings are sufficiently encouraging to permit a tentative conclusion regarding the problems of trade in services.

Neither Canada nor other industrial countries, such as the United States, need fear a reduction in international trade and the benefits derived from it as a result of the growth of the service industries in their economies. Trade in commodities will increasingly involve trade in embodied services. For this reason, the need for a GATT incentive on service trade is much less urgent than it has been made out to be. The highest priority in trade policies remains the lowering of tariff and nontariff barriers on goods. Yet there is still the issue of lowering barriers to foreign investment, and there are special issues regarding investment in service-producing industries. But these are a separate topic. The pursuit of resolutions to problems in this area is not aided by a fundamental confusion between trade in services and international investment in service industries.

PART II
SPECIFIC SERVICE INDUSTRIES

OVERVIEW

CHAPTER 4
Jussawalla, Snow, and Braunstein on Trade in Information Services

This chapter addresses major issues relating to international trade in information services. The rapid technological changes in recent years have greatly affected the content as well as the conduit of information services. New technologies have rendered inadequate the existing laws governing the ownership of intellectual property; and how to legally cope with the effects of rapidly changing technologies—by copyright law, patent law, or a special-purpose law—is an issue yet to be settled. New technologies such as satellites have also increased the difficulty of reconciling the status of property rights among different countries.

Transborder data flows (TBDF) have become an important part of international trade in information services, linking subsidiaries of transnational corporations to their headquarters and providing information to members of closed user networks and to subscribers to computer service bureaus. The growth of TBDF has led to the introduction of new financial services, such as electronic funds transfer, and has made major financial markets of the world more fully integrated than before.

Barriers in telecommunications impede the flow of information between nations; nevertheless, telecommunications is one of the most heavily regulated industries in many countries, whether developed or developing. Regulation of the industry is usually justified on the grounds of the economies of scale and thus economic efficiency of natural monopoly. Recent studies in industrial organization have made natural monopoly an issue of greater complexity and the case of maintaining the telecommunications industry as a regulated monopoly a more contentious one. The authors also examine other factors, such as "cooperation instead of competition" and military and strategic considerations, that work against deregulation of the industry.

The authors correctly point out that the charter of the GATT has no provision for dealing with services trade, agricultural goods, nontariff barriers, and direct foreign investment and that leading countries of the world have bypassed GATT in dealing with these issues. They argue that the future of the GATT will depend on its ability to structure internationally acceptable codes and provisions for dealing with these issues and that free flows of information are crucial to the growth of non-information trade.

CHAPTER 5
Miklius on Ocean Shipping

To analyze trade in ocean shipping in the Asia-Pacific region, Miklius first looks into the shipping industries of the countries in the region. He finds that Japan has by far the largest fleet for every category of commercial ship (oil tankers, ore and bulk carriers, and general-cargo carriers). He also reveals that the shipping industries universally suffer from heavy debt and a stagnant demand for their services and that the existing overcapacity they are experiencing is due to a worldwide overcapacity in the shipbuilding industry.

He notes that governments have actively intervened in liner shipping, leaving nonliner shipping relatively free of government intervention. Governments have used such practices as "cargo reservation," construction and operating subsidies, and preferential tax treatment for national flag carriers as market intervention devices. They have also intervened indirectly in the market by supporting the liner conference system.

Miklius finds it puzzling that governments have supported the liner conference system, which is a cartel arrangement, despite widely accepted economic arguments against it. He examines several arguments that rationalize such government decisions, but finds them all less than satisfactory.

Although there have been occasional signs of liberalization in a few shipping industries, Miklius finds the outlook rather bleak. He notes that resistance to liberalization has come from the governments of developing countries as well as those of certain developed countries and foresees the increasing use of flag reservation and unilateral or bilateral measures to protect national merchant marines. It seems that, unlike other service industries that have experienced growing domestic pressure for deregulation and liberalization, the shipping industries have been immune to such pressure.

CHAPTER 6
Mak and White on International Tourism

This chapter addresses the development of international tourism in Asia and the Pacific and issues relating to travel restrictions in the region.

Mass tourism in the region began in the late 1960s, but lagged behind that in Europe and North America. Recently, however, the region has become the fastest-growing area for mass tourism in the world. This rapid growth is due to an increasing number of Asia-Pacific residents visiting intraregional destinations, reflecting the general prosperity of the region's economies and the technological innovations in transportation that have reduced both the money and time cost of travel. Mak and White also point out two additional events affecting the rapid growth in mass tourism in the region: the opening of China to international tourism in 1978, and a series of measures taken by the Japanese government to ease restrictions on overseas travel by Japanese nationals.

Tourist trade in the region is dominated by the major countries in East and Southeast Asia plus Australia and New Zealand. Of all these countries, China has experienced the most spectacular growth in visitor arrivals with an annual growth rate exceeding 25 percent—4.2 million in 1979 and nearly 13 million in 1984. In terms of visitor departures, it is Japan that leads the group, generating 4.7 million departures in 1984 and expenditures valued at US$4.5 billion. By all accounts Japan has become the major tourist-generating country in the region.

An interesting and important byproduct of this "Japanese saga" in international tourism is the growth of Japanese direct foreign investment in tourism and tourism-related industries as evidenced by the growing number of hotels and golf courses in Hawaii acquired by Japanese nationals or corporations.

Mak and White note that although a growing number of Japanese now travel abroad, they still constitute a small portion of Japan's population, smaller in fact than that portion of the population in other countries in the region. They interpret this as an indication that Japan can raise its rate of overseas travel in the near future. They also anticipate expansion of leisure travel for the other countries in Asia and the Pacific, aided by the lifting of restrictions.

International tourism can be restricted by indirect as well as direct measures on the movement of tourists. Examples of indirect measures are restrictions on hotel acquisition and franchising by foreigners. Liberalizing international tourism thus requires comprehensive measures dealing with restrictions in a number of related industries as well as on the movement of tourists.

CHAPTER 4
Major Issues in Information Services Trade

Meheroo Jussawalla, Marcellus S. Snow, and Yale M. Braunstein

Information services, in a broad sense, consist of both the "content," including intellectual property such as patents, trade secrets, and copyrighted works, and the "conduit," such as telecommunications or broadcasting. According to one definition, information services comprise 10 sectors of the economy, ranging from telecommunications and broadcasting to financial, medical, and educational services (table 4.1). As a result, although transborder data flows (TBDF) are an important part of trade in information services, trade in information services encompasses more than trade in data services.

Although there are data for certain areas, such as advertising services and motion pictures, little from the content category is ever measured. However, detailed data for the various point-to-point, nonbroadcast conduits (e.g., telephone, telegraph, telex) are available.[1] It is useful to note that, despite the growth and size of the information sector in the industrialized nations, trade in information services is a relatively small proportion of the goods and services traded internationally. For example, U.S. exports of information services accounted for approximately 4 percent of total exports in 1978, and information services imports were only 1 percent of total imports that year. By comparison, the U.S. information services sector amounted to approximately 18 percent of domestic production in 1977.[2]

Although international trade in information services may be relatively small, there has been an increasing recognition of its importance. Because information about resources and markets is fundamental to the

1. For example, Rubin and Sapp (1981) present U.S.annual export and import data for 1965-1978.

2. Robinson (1986:196). There may be small inconsistencies in the definitions of information services used by Robinson and Rubin, but the relative magnitudes are nevertheless instructive.

Table 4.1 The Information Services Sectors of the Economy

Sector name	Sector number		
	Rubin	BEA	SIC
Telecommunications	14	66	48*
Radio and TV broadcasting	15	67	483
Information trade margin (wholesale and retail trade)	16	69*	—
Finance and insurance	17	70	61-4, 7
Real estate	18	71*	65-6*
Repair of information products	19	72.02	72*
Miscellaneous business services information (including advertising)	20	73*	73, 81, 9
Motion pictures	21	76*	78-9
Medical and educational services	22	77	80*
Postal services	23	78	4311

Note: * After additions or deletions.
Source: Rubin and Sapp, 1981.

efficient operation of the various organizations in an economy, debates are taking place about control of and access to information in both domestic and international forums.

Property Rights in Information

Nations have adopted a variety of laws to provide for ownership of intellectual property. Copyright, patent, and trade secrecy laws provide different degrees of protection for the ownership of information and impose correspondingly different requirements on the property-right holder. Developed long before the era of electronic communications, these laws have undergone major changes over time in many countries. As new technologies change the economics of information creation and dissemination, pressure is often exerted for change in this body of laws. Several countries have recently reviewed their laws regarding the appropriate form of protection for computer software, databases, and microchips. The economic and legal problem is to balance the incentives that increased protection of property rights give to the creator of new intellectual works with the desire for widespread dissemination of useful products, processes, and ideas.

Since 1980 at least eight countries have explicitly extended copyright

Table 4.2 Legal Protection for Computer Programs as of March 1986

Nation	Copyright	Trade secret unfair competition	Trademark	Patent
Australia	yes*	yes	yes	unclear
Austria	—	—	—	unclear
Belgium	unclear	yes	yes	no[c]
Brazil	maybe[b]	very limited	—	no
Canada	yes[b]	yes	yes	sometimes
China	—	—	yes	unclear
Denmark	maybe[b]	limited	—	unclear
Egypt	unclear	—	—	—
Finland	maybe[b]	yes	—	unclear
France	yes*	unclear	—	perhaps
Germany (Fed. Rep.)	yes*	yes	—	no[c]
Germany (Dem. Rep.)	—	—	—	no[c]
Hong Kong	unclear	—	—	—
Hungary	yes*	—	—	—
India	yes[a]	—	—	—
Indonesia	no	—	—	—
Italy	yes	yes	—	unlikely
Japan	yes*	limited	—	sometimes
Korea	unlikely	limited	yes	sometimes
Malaysia	no	maybe	—	unclear
Mexico	yes	very limited	yes	no
Netherlands	yes[b]	yes	yes	possibly
New Zealand	probably	probably	—	unlikely
Nigeria	maybe	—	—	—
Norway	maybe[b]	—	yes	unclear
Philippines	yes*	—	—	—
Poland	—	—	—	no
Singapore	unclear	probably	limited	see UK
South Africa	yes	yes	—	—
Spain	a	maybe	sometimes	—
Sweden	b	—	—	no[c]
Switzerland	unclear	maybe	yes	no
Taiwan	maybe*	—	pending	—
Thailand	maybe	—	—	—
United Kingdom	yes*	yes	yes	sometimes
United States	yes*	yes	yes	sometimes
Venezuela	no	limited	—	—
Yugoslavia	—	—	—	no

Notes: * Special legislation passed.
a. Legislation pending.
b. Special legislation proposed.
c. Perhaps, if included in process.
Source: Bigelow, 1986.

protection to computer software. Table 4.2 summarizes the state of legal protection of software in 37 countries. However, the situation is both complex and changing. The question of whether the best approach is to use copyright law, patent law, or a special-purpose law continues to be discussed in several countries.

There are many bilateral and multilateral agreements whereby countries have extended protection to intellectual property created by citizens of other nations. In the copyright area, the two major multilateral agreements are the Berne Convention and the Universal Copyright Convention (UCC).[3] The Berne Convention has been in force since 1886 and was most recently revised in 1971; the UCC was negotiated in 1952 and was revised, parallel to the Berne revision, in 1971. The fundamental provisions of the two conventions convey the same protection to works created by nationals of member states that exist for works created by citizens of the home country.[4]

In the broadcast area, new technologies such as satellites have highlighted the difficulty in reconciling the status of rights in different countries. The combination of noncompatible standards and technical constraints such as limits to signal range have enabled nations to develop television broadcasting policies virtually in isolation from their neighbors, but the growth of satellite and cable retransmissions has led to policy dilemmas in many countries (Canadian-U.S. Conference on Communications Policy 1984).

Currently in each country, broadcasting is controlled to varying degrees by domestic regulation, international copyright law, and international satellite agreements. Often domestic employment considerations and national culture and sovereignty arguments are raised in debates over existing and proposed laws. The emergence of new technologies such as direct broadcast satellites will create new challenges.

---

3. The World Intellectual Property Organization (WIPO) is Secretariat to the Berne Convention for the Protection of Literary and Artistic Property, and UNESCO is Secretariat to the Universal Copyright Convention. The United States is a member of the UCC, but not of the Berne Convention.

4. See, for example, Article II, Clause 1 of the UCC: "Published works of nationals of any Contracting State and works first published in that State shall enjoy in each other Contracting State the same protection as that other State accords to works of its nationals first published in its own territory."

Transborder Data Flows

In recent years telecommunication networks have become widely used to transmit and receive data within and outside a country. These data flows can be either information that is an input into any given economic activity or information that results from such economic activity. The exchange of these data electronically by computer across the boundaries of nation states is called transborder data flows. The signals and messages are not visible in physical form within the conduit, but take physical form on the printout or on the screen of the receiving computer.

Transborder data flows (TBDF) can be divided into marketable and nonmarketable flows. Even though marketable flows lack a palpable physical construct, they are essentially a market manifestation of the demand for information. This demand may come from firms in manufacturing, mining, agriculture, banking, or a variety of related services, since marketed data provide them with valuable knowledge unavailable internally.

Nonmarketable data flows are those that occur within a firm, such as communications between the headquarters and subsidiaries of a transnational corporation. It is estimated that 90 percent of the current volume of TBDF is of this intrafirm variety. These data flows are nonmarketable in the sense that they are protected by an exclusion mechanism and are not accessible to all individuals willing to pay. Thus, users of such TBDF consist of (1) subsidiaries of transnational corporations (TNCs); (2) members of a closed user network; or (3) paying subscribers of a computer service bureau.

Table 4.3 lists the countries linked with five major public network systems. In addition to the public networks appearing in table 4.3, there are also private networks, not accessible to public users, that are provided by service bureaus such as CYBERNET. As these networks expand, so do the termination points to which user equipment is attached. In Western Europe alone, according to LOGIGA, there are 1,620,000 network termination points. It is estimated that the number of data transactions on an average working day has grown from 136 million in 1979 to a projected 800 million in 1987. For example, the international public on-line database market had 1,100 databases with a sales volume of US$1.5 to US$2 billion (Sauvant 1983).

As telematics becomes more widespread, information processing becomes more profitable. Some argue that automated data processing (ADP) causes low-income countries to be dependent on those that are technologically advanced. This has led to a debate sponsored by the

Table 4.3 Regional and International Data Transmission Networks: Members 1982

Telenet	Tymnet	Uninet	Euronet	Nordic Network
Argentina	Argentina	Argentina	Austria	Denmark
Australia	Australia	Australia	Belgium	Finland
Austria	Austria	Austria	Denmark	Norway
Bahrain	Bahrain	Bahrain	Finland	Sweden
Belgium	Belgium	Belgium	France	
Bermuda	Bermuda	Bermuda	Germany, Fed. Republic of	
Canada	Canada	Canada	Greece	
Chile	Chile	Denmark	Ireland	
Denmark	Denmark	Finland	Italy	
Dominican Republic	Finland	France	Luxembourg	
Finland	France	Germany, Fed. Republic of	Netherlands	
France	Germany, Fed. Republic of	Hong Kong	Portugal	
Germany, Fed. Republic of	Hong Kong	Israel	Sweden	
Hong Kong	Israel	Italy	Switzerland	
Ireland	Italy	Japan	United Kingdom	
Israel	Japan	Kuwait		
Italy	Luxembourg	Netherlands		
Japan	Mexico	New Zealand		
Kuwait	Netherlands	Norway		
Luxembourg	New Zealand	Philippines		
Mexico	Norway	Portugal		
Netherlands	Philippines	Qatar		
New Zealand	Portugal	Saudi Arabia		
Norway	Singapore	Singapore		
Philippines	Spain	Spain		
Portugal	Sweden	Sweden		
Qatar	Switzerland	Switzerland		
Saudi Arabia	United Arab Emirates	United Arab Emirates		
Singapore	United Kingdom	United Kingdom		
Spain	United States	United States		
Sweden				
Switzerland				
United Arab Emirates				
United Kingdom				
United States				

Source: Computed by Meheroo Jussawalla.

Intergovernmental Bureau of Information (IBI), the Organization for Economic Cooperation and Development (OECD), and the Council of Europe. The technology has made it vital for the countries participating in data trade to become aware of its implications and to arrive at policy decisions on whether to protect data flows or to permit the free flow of information. Conceptually speaking, technological changes have made information increasingly vital as a resource and as a factor of production. But as Madec (1980) points out, there is economic ignorance and a legal void surrounding TBDF.

Dramatic technological changes have made many service industries increasingly information-based. This is especially true of banking and finance. In these services, not only is information concomitant with power, but prior information means wealth (Gallant 1985). Markets have become more volatile, financial instruments more numerous, and information about money as important as money itself. Digits stored in computers are transferred around the world's financial systems, replacing paper currencies and paper transactions (Jussawalla 1985). Technical networks for handling such information are vital, and electronic delivery of this information is a saleable product.

TBDF is composed of those economic services that represent different segments of the computer communications process, such as data collection, storage, retrieval, processing, dissemination to users, and provision of access. The first stage in the production process is the generation and collection of raw data comparable to extractive industries. The processing and analysis of data is similar to a postextractive economic activity. Therefore, economic theory would describe the production of TBDF as dependent on the supply of three resources: computer systems, telecommunication networks, and data.

These computer and communications systems can be further classified as either private or public systems. A private system is owned or leased in its entirety by the final user, whereas public systems are those in which users can only buy or rent some part of the system or its services. Given the present industrial organization under which TBDF takes place, a nesting of public systems is often found at two levels: (1) a public database provider (e.g, DIALOG) using (2) a public data network (e.g., TELENET), so that the public can have low-cost access to an available database.

Because access to telecommunication networks and computing power are both necessary inputs, suppliers that exploit the interdependence between different segments of the system may enjoy cost advantages. The trade-off is often between an integrated computer = cum = communications system and having several information services using a large communications network. In either case the scale of the operation may cause barriers to the entry of new firms.

Potential subscribers can often avail themselves of the same production techniques and market demands as the monopoly suppliers in the absence of legal restrictions on interconnection or market entry. European post, telegraph, and telecommunications (PTTs) feel threatened by this rampant penetration by private enterprise. In TBDF there may be potential for competition that is sufficient to ensure efficiency among incumbent suppliers and that many contend obviates the need for economic regulation.

What makes the international policy decisions on trade in information services so complicated is the fact that regulatory bodies and multilateral agreements, even if designed to address appropriate issues, may not be able to respond to the continually changing flows of vast streams of data moving across continents. New rules may need to be devised to govern international transactions in data flows as part of the services sector of the world economy. But the fact remains that governments have not been able to monitor service transactions, mainly because of revolutionary changes in the methods of delivering services. For TNCs, the value added of these computer-communicated information services is diffused geographically, even though the final fee may be booked to a particular location for tax reasons. Furthermore, the configuration of service industries is rapidly changing because of acquisitions and mergers that transcend separate types of services. These factors make the data available to governments often inaccurate and may understate the contribution of services to the gross national product.

Financial Information

As a consequence of dynamic innovations in telecommunications systems, two hitherto separate industries, banking and telecommunications, have become interlinked, bringing about powerful changes in the global velocity of the circulation of money as well as in foreign exchange rates, interest rates, and international capital flows. Nonbanking financial intermediaries are also providing new services that take advantage of telecommunications technology. Consequently, the electronic integration of financial markets has created greater competition in this part of the services sector.

Transnational industrial corporations have been the major beneficiaries of the banking industry's entry into the electronic age. International competition in banking, together with the economies of scale generated by electronic funds transfer (EFT), have challenged the principles by which banks tradionally priced their services.

In countries where the government PTT or a monopoly provider is the sole vendor of telecommunication services, the vendor pricing scheme has determined a large portion of the bank's telecommunications costs. In many countries this power of the monopoly telecommunications provider has been reduced by the entry of competing carriers, including the banks themselves. As communications costs have been reduced, banks have changed both their mix of products and their pricing policies. New electronically delivered banking services have been introduced, and as a result, the geographic segmentation of the market has broken down. This internationalization of markets, along with the entry of nonbanking and nonfinancial institutions into traditional markets hitherto dominated by banks, has led to greater competition. The result has been a trend toward more cost-based pricing and the provision of new services in banking itself. Often the incremental costs of these new services are low. One additional result may be that the combination of new services and increased information enables financial institutions to further reduce risk through diversification (Malmgren 1985).

Specialized financial information networks include the Society for Worldwide Interbank Financial Telecommunication (SWIFT), a specialized international financial transactions messaging system between member banks. Formed in May 1973, it is the only system that permits banks located throughout the world to obtain instant transfers

Table 4.4 Membership and Traffic of SWIFT, 1977–1988

				Traffic (1,000 messages)		
Year	Member banks	Member countries	Active countries	Actual volume	Cumulative volume	Peak day
1977[a]	518	21	15	3,187.0	3,187.0	—
1978	586	24	16	21,409.4	24,596.4	—
1979	683	29	16	34,351.3	58,947.7	—
1980	768	35	21	46,918.3	105,866.6	—
1981	900	39	26	62,575.6	168,441.6	318.6
1982	1,017	44	32	79,988.0	248,429.6	384.8
1983[b]	1,073	53	37	66,731.7	315,161.3	455.1

Notes: a. August-December only.
b. January-August only.

Source: SWIFT, Annual Reports, various years, computed by Sauvant in 1986.

of funds 24 hours a day, seven days a week. In 1985 its membership extended to 1,200 banks in 50 countries with a volume of 500,000 transactions per day (table 4.4). The system will attain greater efficiency with decentralization and when financial markets become more integrated under the SWIFT II network. This computerized network permits even developing-country banks to join and provides greater flexibility in services.

Due to advances in telematics, an international securities market has emerged with the establishment in 1971 of the National Association of Securities Dealers Automated Quotations system (NASDAQ). It is now the third largest market in the world in terms of equity trade, following the Tokyo and New York Stock Exchanges. The computerized system enables large numbers of securities dealers across continents to handle stocks and creates an international pool of capital to support these stocks. Over 300 non-U.S. companies are traded over the counter. However, nontariff barriers in terms of restrictions imposed by European PTTs and the high cost of international telecommunications stem the expansion of this type of global services trade. Sophisticated networks such as Reuters Financial Services and NASDAQ give an impetus to developing countries to improve and upgrade their domestic stock markets and to establish a conduit for foreign capital investment.

In addition to EFT, clearinghouse transactions are computerized and can effect same-day transfers to interbank accounts. In New York the system is called CHIPS (Clearinghouse for Interbank Payments System); in London it is called CHAPS (Clearinghouse for Automated Payments System); and to meet the vast increase in transfers of funds in the Asia-Pacific region, Hong Kong has CHATS (Clearinghouse Automated Transfer System). The SWIFT system has member banks in 60 countries and provides an even more cost-effective system for interbank transaction by eliminating the reliance on PTTs for the telecommunications part of its services since it has its own private computerized network.

Impediments to Trade in Telecommunications

There are a number of reasons why impediments to trade in telecommunications (and thereby in information) exist. Most of these are associated with tendencies toward monopolization of the international telecommunications sector by state-controlled enterprises.

Monopolization: Natural and Administrative

In theory a monopolist, if adequately regulated, can be obliged to provide a sufficient quantity of output at an equitable price and in a combination of quality and diversity sufficiently responsive to users' needs, but this ideal is seldom realized. Thus, an examination of types of and reasons for monopolization in the telecommunications sector is important in understanding the impediments to trade in information services.

Telecommunications is one of the most heavily monopolized sectors, whether in the industrialized or developing countries; and communication links are even more likely to be under state supervision internationally (i.e., when they enter information trade) than domestically. Why is this the case, and what exactly is meant by monopoly?

At the outset, it is convenient to distinguish between an administrative monopoly—an organizational form imposed on a given market or industry for whatever reason by the state—and a natural monopoly, which is a function of the production and cost relations in a given industry apart from any legal or administrative actions. The former type of monopoly can be usefully considered *de jure*; the latter is what can be called a *de facto* monopoly.

Of the two, the natural monopoly is of greater interest in the present context. A rich body of relatively recent publications in the literature of industrial organization has added to our understanding of the cost, production, and technological relationships that must obtain if monopoly is to be economically more efficient than competition.[5]

Classically, natural monopoly has resulted from economies of scale in production, which, as a result of declining unit costs, gave a single producer with a large output a cost advantage over two or more producers sharing that output. This led to a case for enshrining such a *de facto* cost relationship in a *de jure* administrative monopoly (whether public or private), as long as suitable regulatory oversight prevented the monopolist from maximizing profit by charging the highest possible price. This line of analysis, however, depends on the assumptions of a single output and the lack of close substitutes. By the mid-1970s it had become clear that the assumption of multiple outputs by a single producer—a particularly realistic point of departure in industries like

5. The definitive reference is Baumol, Panzar, and Willig (1982). Bailey and Friedlander (1982) provide a useful bibliographic essay on the literature. Sharkey's (1982) book is the most accessible general treatment. Brock (1983) and Spence (1986) each review the volume by Baumol, Panzar, and Willig. Shepherd (1983, 1984) and Snowberger (1978) offer critical perspectives.

telecommunications—rendered much of the previous theory useless. For example, neither economies of scale nor average unit are well defined in a multiproduct setting. The most important and perhaps counterintuitive result of the new natural monopoly literature, however, has to do with the sustainability of monopoly.

In the single-output setting, a monopolist sharing the same cost function and technology with rivals need not fear market entry, as long as potential entrants are constrained to cover their costs. This invulnerability to entry is assured by declining unit costs. In the multi-output mode, however, matters are not so simple. Even if a single firm can produce a given basket of outputs more cheaply than can any combination of two or more firms, it has been proved that financial incentives might exist for small-scale entry by rivals that, through competition, can take away part of the monopolist's business, perhaps through specialization in individual product lines. Thus, a solution other than that of least-cost production can arise (with its attendant inefficiencies and welfare costs) if entry is allowed against a monopolist. In such a case, the natural monopoly is said to be unsustainable. Conditions under which a natural monopoly is sustainable or unsustainable—and tariff structures under which sustainability can be assured—are as yet poorly understood.

To the limited extent that the sustainability-of-monopoly theory has found empirical application, most of the attention has been directed to telecommunications.[6] Indeed, as Snow (1985) has shown, the contention that the telecommunications industry is a natural but unsustainable monopoly constitutes the single most potent argument against deregulation of telecommunications in the advanced industrialized countries. Nonetheless, this line of argument has an uneven record of effectiveness. The natural monopoly argument, for example, formed the basis of AT&T's unsuccessful claim before the U.S. regulatory and judicial authorities that it should not be subjected to divestiture.

Natural monopoly arguments against telecommunications deregulation have encountered three major rejoinders. First, some of the assumptions have been challenged as being overly simplistic (Shepherd 1983, 1984; Snowberger 1978). For example, it is assumed that all producers have the same cost functions and that the monopolist does

6. The first major empirical study using natural monopoly theory was conducted by Baumol and Braunstein (1977), who estimated economies of scope in a scholarly journal publication. Evans and Heckman (1983, 1984) test for natural monopoly in the predivestiture Bell System in the United States and do not detect any. Snow (1987), in a preliminary study, uses a similar econometric methodology with INTELSAT data and finds evidence for the presence of natural monopoly in INTELSAT's cost function.

not react strategically to the entry attempts of a rival. Second, as noted, the empirical work needed to document the cost relations underlying natural monopoly is complex and difficult, even assuming the necessary data exist and are both available and accurate. Third, as von Weizsacker (1986) has argued, natural monopoly theory is essentially static and therefore does not fully capture the dynamic welfare benefits, such as product diversity and responsiveness to user needs, that experience has shown to flow from deregulation.

Cooperation versus Competition

There are three major variations on this theme, each of which provides a rationale for governments to avoid, circumvent, or eliminate the structures and mechanisms of the competitive marketplace. To the extent that such recourse to nonmarket solutions adversely affects the quality of information flow via international telecommunications, it can be considered an impediment to trade in information services.

Consider first the technical sense in which INTELSAT is a financial cooperative of owners and users.[7] The ownership share of each member country is periodically realigned to reflect its recent past usage of the system, thereby equating the incentives of members as users with their incentives as owners. It is argued this decreases the need for competition in international public commercial satellite communications, at least given the presence of natural monopolies.

Second, as Voge (1986) points out, the telecommunications organizations of the French government are based on the philosophy that cooperation in telecommunications is superior to competition and that decentralization—at least in the context of the historically over-centralized French state—is preferable to deregulation. Despite having recently installed a new government opposed to various forms of socialism, France still has the most centralized and monopolistic telecommunications administration in Western Europe. Cogent arguments have been advanced for this arrangement, however, and it cannot glibly be concluded that information trade is being impeded simply because monopolistic governmental structures exist. Nonetheless, the consensus of opinion among economists familiar with telecommunications is that the free flow of information is generally facilitated in an environment of competition and deregulation of telecommunications services.

Third, there is a non-Marxian variant of socialist thought known as social economy, derived from the insights of the English cooperatives

7. See Snow (1976) for a financial model of INTELSAT.

and German economic thinkers of the 19th century, that argues for continued state ownership and operation of vital sectors in the economy such as telecommunications, transportation, health, education, and energy. Thiemeyer (1983) makes the connection between telecommunications and *Gemeinwirtschaft*, the German variant of social economy, whereas Snow (1984) compares social economic theory with natural monopoly theory as alternative arguments against deregulation of the telecommunications sector. In the Federal Republic of Germany (Germany), where social economy still enjoys considerable influence, it is used by trade unions, the Social Democratic Party, and other groups to justify continued governmental provision of various vital services and to resist efforts at privatization and introduction of competition. Even proponents of social economy, however, have argued that it relies too heavily on value judgments and does not have the theoretical undergirding or methodology of neoclassical economic thought.

Taken together, these and other facets of the cooperation-versus-competition outlook contribute to impeding the flow of information services to the extent that protection of telecommunications from the effects of competition creates unnecessary barriers to the quantity, quality, and diversity of services available to users.

The Political Economy of Deregulation

Mancur Olson's (1982) seminal work examines the actions of interest groups in the political arena and the economic marketplace opposing economic policies they view as inimical to their welfare. Such groups can be particularly effective when the interests of the status quo are clearly identified and sharply focused, but the interests of those standing to benefit by departures from the status quo—typically those of consumers and the business community—are poorly understood and diffuse. Olson's fundamental question might be phrased as follows: Given a policy change that demonstrably increases overall social welfare, how is it possible for the legislative enactment or administrative implementation of such a policy to be frustrated by interest groups perceiving their own welfare to be threatened by the policy? Noll (1983, 1986), Noll and Owen (1983), and Noam (1986) add rich institutional detail to illustrate the influence of such groups in attempting to frustrate deregulation of the telecommunications sector in the United States and other industrialized countries.

Naturally, the efforts of interest groups to oppose changes that serve the overall interest of society are not always successful. The trucking, civil aviation, and telecommunications sectors of the United States have been extensively deregulated since the mid-1970s. In addition, both Great Britain and Japan have recently privatized their major state-owned domestic telecommunications carriers and subjected them to some measure of competition.[8] Derthick and Quirk (1985) have attributed deregulatory successes in the United States in large measure to the patient and politically astute efforts of the economics profession.

Other industrialized countries are in a state of political stalemate regarding deregulation of telecommunications. Germany, discussed by Neumann (1986) and Snow (1982, 1983), is an instructive example. In a consultants' report issued several years ago for the German Monopoly Commission, Knieps, Muller, and von Weizsacker (1981) pointed out many arguments for subjecting the Deutsche Bundespost to various forms of competition. Neumann, Schweizer, and von Weizsacker (1983), in an excellent applied study, showed that the Deutsche Bundespost could have increased overall national welfare by more than DM 1 billion in a single year by using a form of demand-based pricing instead of its current tariff structure, which is politically dictated and based on heavy cross-subsidies. Nonetheless, the Deutsche Bundespost argues that to maintain a political consensus favoring redistributive policies, "optimal" cost-based pricing of the type developed by modern neoclassical economic groups plays a significant role in posing obstacles to the introduction of competition and privatization in the industry. On balance, such efforts indirectly impede trade in information services.

Inertia, Conservatism, and Organizational Obsolescence

Lamberton (1986) has documented and offered a conceptual framework revealing bureaucratic conservatism, inertia, and obsolescence in the Australian telecommunications administration, a phenomenon by no means limited to that country. In addition, he has noted a preference on the part of telecommunications users for prices that are predictable but on average higher when compared to an unpredictable but declining tariff structure. In a similar vein, Noam (1986) cites institutional incentives for preservation of the status quo in the PTTs of Western European countries. He also outlines the political and economic dynamics by which entrenched civil servants find allies among other interest groups—such as intellectuals, trade unions, the poor, farmers, and political parties—in opposing the liberalization of domestic and international telecommunications regimes.

8. Baughcum (1986) discusses such developments in the United States, whereas Jonscher (1986) considers Great Britain and Ito (1986) examines Japan.

Strategic, Military, and National Security Issues

Concerns for national security, military prowess, and prestige are seldom discussed in the context of information and telecommunications. Yet it is clear that the resolute pursuit of those goals has impeded economic efficiency, marketplace competition, and the flow of information within and among countries.

Whereas industrialized countries, for example, enjoy the luxury of separate public, administrative, and military telecommunications systems, developing nations strapped for foreign exchange must often combine all of these functions into a single network. Indonesia's acquisition of its PALAPA system in the 1970s, for example, made ample allowance for military requirements and might not have been justified in terms of civilian needs alone. In the United States, the Department of Defense has historically insisted on a degree of redundancy in international telecommunications, often including obsolescent cable links that violate criteria of either economic or engineering optimality. A number of regional systems, arguably including EUTELSAT and ARABSAT, owe their genesis in large part to regional political pressures to bypass INTELSAT, which many European and Third World members have long held is too strongly influenced by the United States. Domestic pilot and operational satellite systems in a number of countries, notably Canada, have been built well ahead of demand, but other countries, such as the United States, Japan, and Australia, have adopted domestic satellite systems only to the extent that demand and commercial considerations justified them.

Finally, the rapid spread of communications of all kinds is not viewed as an unmitigated blessing in many developing countries. On the contrary, some authoritarian regimes view such information flow as a threat to their stability and legitimacy. The Western ideal of "free flow of information" is far from an accepted notion in some countries of the Third World.

International trade in information services can be impeded to the extent that domestic and international telecommunications links and systems respond to national needs for prestige, military power, and national security. Naturally, such needs are legitimate considerations in every country, and there is an implicit trade-off between the realization of these goals and the benefits of international trade that could have been made possible by greater emphasis on civilian, market-based telecommunications facilities and services.

GATT and Its Role in Reducing Impediments in Information Trade

Launching and sustaining multilateral trade talks has become increasingly difficult, and yet, as Aronson and Aho (1986) point out, the trade ministers from 92 countries meeting at Punta del Este had to choose between trade talks and trade wars. In the Tokyo Round of GATT negotiations, tariff reduction on manufactured goods was easier to agree upon, since goods are tangible and characteristically have quantifiable content and prices. Nontariff barriers raise conceptually difficult issues, especially when trade in services is the matter being negotiated. Countries cannot even agree on how to define and measure trade in services, be they telecommunications, banking, insurance, or managerial services. This difficulty is compounded by the fact that today trade, investment, and monetary developments are closely linked. Economic policies of industrialized countries are interdependent partly because of the expansion of information technology. As integration advances, national autonomy has to be gradually sacrificed. Currently there are no international institutions that have jurisdiction over these matters. GATT finds itself challenged because its charter does not extend to agricultural goods, services trade, or nontariff barriers. Leading countries are bypassing GATT and entering into bilateral agreements like the one negotiated between the United States and Japan to share the market for semiconductors.

GATT has adapted its rules to accommodate high-technology products, services, direct foreign investment (DFI), subsidies, nontariff barriers, and government procurement. In July 1985 negotiations in GATT were challenged by the developing countries at a meeting held in Stockholm at which they spelled out conditions for opening trade talks on services. Their stand is that trade in services should be dealt with separately from trade in merchandise, yet parallel to it. At the outset, India and Brazil wanted trade in services to be negotiated under the auspices of the United Nations Conference on Trade and Development (UNCTAD), but they later withdrew this demand. The United States has accepted this twin-track compromise.

Bilateral agreements between the leading trading nations have been termed "black protection" because they are symptomatic of managed trade rather than free trade. An example of such managed trade is the agreement between the United States and Japan on market sharing and supervision of the cost and price of semiconductors. It is called "black protection" because the agreements are outside the official rules contained in 38 articles of the GATT, which are binding on its 92 member countries. Whether GATT is being eroded to the point of collapse is an issue that was raised at the Uruguay meeting. Although government officials deny this, there is widespread agreement that political commitment to the system is crumbling (Tyler 1986b). The developing countries have come to regard GATT as a rich man's club that allows discrimination against LDC exports, despite the privileges developing countries enjoy under the generalized system of preferences (GSP).

It is difficult to measure the impact of nontariff barriers on information trade, but the World Bank calculates that for 1985, 27 percent of imports from 16 industrial countries are subject to invisible control. Such control becomes all the more difficult to perceive when nations erect invisible barriers to invisible trade such as data flows. Black protection is applied in many ingenious ways, such as local content requirements, pollution and safety tests, and standards compliances. The World Bank has counted an increase of 2,500 nontariff barriers in two years. Consequently, this eighth round of trade talks of GATT members will attempt to halt the proliferation of barriers to trade in services, from banking to air travel to consultancies. The link between goods, services, and overseas investment has to be recognized for GATT talks to achieve any measure of success. But even the planning of this meeting did not cover such vital issues as transborder data flows, protection of patents and trademarks, and trade-related investments.

The future of GATT will depend on its ability to structure a services code and to supplement this with specific provisions for information services. It will have to examine how such a code can deal with most-favored-nation (MFN) treatment. The most difficult problem facing the new GATT round is that of linkages, that is, whether countries can exchange concessions in the goods sector for concessions in the services sector (Mizoguchi 1986). Also at issue is whether special treatment for developing countries will be conceded by the technologically advanced nations. The issue of "graduating out" the Asian NICs from GSP schemes may be possible in the new round of trade talks.

Whereas the Pacific nations have different interests in various sectors of the negotiations, the Association of Southeast Asian Nations (ASEAN) is interested in revitalizing GATT and the international trading system. Five years ago this group had the fastest growth rate in the world, but now they are plagued by slow growth and protectionism abroad. This forces them to have greater economic cooperation among themselves. These countries are interested in services trade because their services sectors are expanding. In 1985 Singapore had a services sector that accounted for 69 percent of its GDP, followed by Thailand (48 percent), Malaysia (43 percent), and the Philippines (40 percent). They are at an advantage in the services sector because they can diversify and differentiate their exports, whereas in the goods sector they export similar products, mainly basic food grains and raw materials.

Implications of Trade in Information Services for Trade and Investment in Goods and Other Services

The growth of the world economy depends on trade. Since goods and services related to information are among the most dynamic sectors of industrial economies, restrictions on trade in this area affect growth opportunities. Barriers to international information flows would impede the availability of data on market opportunities, on the credit worthiness of foreign enterprises, and on financial assets. They could thus disrupt future trade and investment in goods and services. Restrictions on telematics trade and investment opportunities could sidetrack efforts to stimulate world growth and could disrupt world trade (Brock 1982).

Flows of data accompanying trade are also important because they deal with information about markets, commercial information, product description, technical data, and information about the general framework of trade and monetary policies. There are specialized firms that make such information available. There are also information needs for transactions such as after-sales services, maintenance, and updating of information. These flows accompanying trade are similar in nature to intrafirm flows. Efficiency of such flows is essential for the development of noninformation trade. International access to such information accompanying trade encounters difficulties because of the heterogeneous legal environments encountered and because of the telematics barriers. International access to markets is a condition of competition, which makes access to information a counterpart of access to markets.

CHAPTER 5
Issues in Ocean Shipping and the Asia-Pacific Region

Walter Miklius

The Asia-Pacific region contains many important maritime nations, among them Japan, which has the world's largest fleet of commercial ships. Although gross revenue from the two general types of shipping services, liner and nonliner, have increased monotonically in all countries in the region except Japan, there are serious problems in the industry. Bankruptcies and enormous debts plague practically all countries in the region to some degree; and government intervention in many forms is pervasive throughout the industry. The effects of such intervention, the justifications for government-approved cartels, the potential benefits from liberalization, and the possibility of liberalization occurring are important issues. However, the current state of economic knowledge and the unsettled state of the ocean shipping industries in a number of countries make predictions regarding liberalization difficult.

Merchant Marine Fleets

The distribution of ships and deadweight tonnage (DWT) of vessels by country of registry for selected countries in the Asia-Pacific region is shown in table 5.1. The statistics are hardly surprising. Japan has by far the largest fleet in the region and accounts for 13.5 percent of the world's total fleet and for 9.4 percent of all the world's DWT. The fleets of eight other Asian countries account for 8.7 percent of the world's total fleet and for about 7.2 percent of the world's DWT.

Marine transportation can be classified in various ways, for example, by the type of vessel used. The major categories are oil tankers, ore and bulk carriers, and general-cargo carriers. The distri-

I wish to thank David Bess, Reuben Kyle, Chung Lee, and Robert Nevel for their helpful comments on an earlier draft of this paper.

Table 5.1 Distribution of All Ships and Deadweight Tonnage by Country of Registry, Selected Asia-Pacific Countries, 1985

Country of registry	Number of ships	Percent of world's fleet	DWT	Percent of worlds's DWT
PRC[a]	1,991	2.6	22,615,443	3.4
Hong Kong	396	0.5	11,322,555	1.7
Indonesia	1,653	2.2	2,673,698	0.4
Japan	10,288	13.5	63,451,188	9.4
Korea [b]	1,847	2.4	11,772,926	1.7
Malaysia	467	0.6	2,582,744	0.4
Philippines	1,000	1.3	7,571,141	1.1
Singapore	758	1.0	11,187,280	1.7
Thailand	244	0.3	863,424	0.1
World total	76,395		673,691,787	

Notes: a. People's Republic of China.
b. Republic of Korea.

Source: *Lloyd's Register of Shipping*, 1985. Statistical Tables.

Table 5.2 Distribution of Ships and Gross Tonnage by Country of Registry and Type of Ship, Selected Asia-Pacific Countries, 1985

	Oil tankers		Ore and bulk carriers		General cargo [a] carriers	
Country of registry	Number of ships	Gross tonnage	Number of ships	Gross tonnage	Number of ships	Gross tonnage
PRC[b]	140	1,461,781	178	3,518,441	744	4,525,386
Hong Kong	27	384,020	135	4,326,385	53	476,652
Indonesia	183	481,268	11	128,255	730	891,455
Japan	1,267	13,837,455	331	12,045,583	2,605	3,790,333
Korea [c]	100	990,893	157	3,547,098	368	952,220
Malaysia	68	224,068	19	386,685	199	438,189
Philippines	63	556,396	122	2,468,800	362	915,589
Singapore	124	2,004,263	78	2,048,346	215	1,298,715
Taiwan	18	628,199	50	1,481,746	118	406,960
Thailand	63	143,710	1	12,649	105	347,523
World total	6,156	134,860,580	5,007	110,257,281	21,135	75,091,683

Notes: a. Single and multideck.
b. People's Republic of China.
c. Republic of Korea.

Source: *Lloyd's Register of Shipping*, 1985. Statistical Tables.

bution of ships by type as well as by country of registry is shown in table 5.2. Japan again has the largest fleet of each type, accounting for 20.6 percent of all the world's tankers, 6.6 percent of all ore and bulk carriers, and 12.4 percent of all general-cargo carriers. Similarly, it accounts for 10.3 percent of the world's gross oil-tanker tonnage, 10.9 percent of the total ore and bulk-carrier tonnage, and about 5 percent of the general-cargo-carrier tonnage. The fleets of nine other Asian countries account for 11.2 percent of the world's oil tankers, 11.5 percent of ore and bulk carriers, and 10.5 percent of general-cargo carriers. In terms of gross tonnage these fleets account for 4, 13, and 8 percent, respectively.

These statistics include fleets servicing domestic as well as international trade; nevertheless, some adjustments are possible. As shown in figure 5.1, the distribution of the world's fleet by size of vessel is bimodal, indicating comingling of two separate populations. The distribution of fleets by vessel size in different countries shows the same pattern. Thus it appears that vessels smaller than 8,000 DWT are used predominantly in the domestic trade and those larger than this in the international trade.

Figure 5.1 Distribution of World's Fleet in 1985 (by size of vessels)

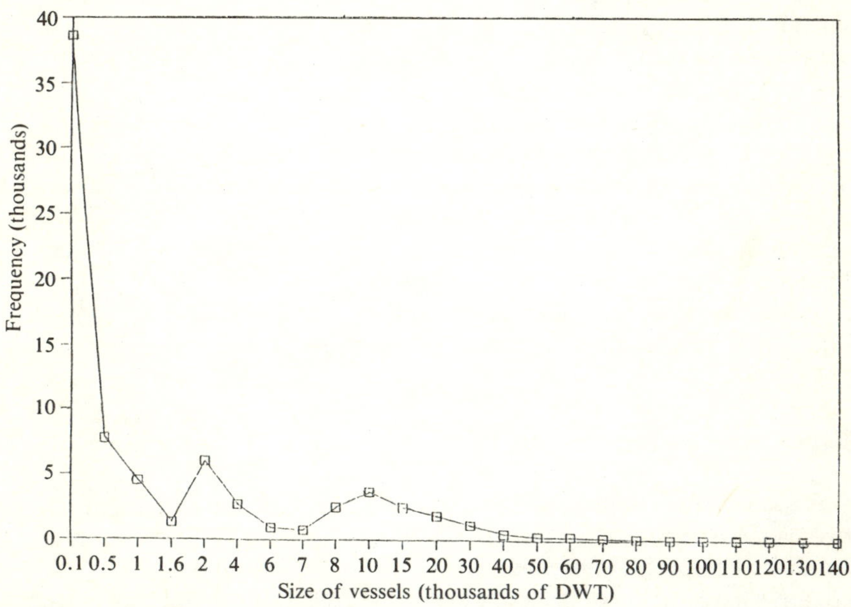

Source: *Lloyd's Register of Shipping*, 1985, Statistical Table.

Table 5.3 Distribution of Ships of 8,000 DWT and Larger by Size, Median Size, Age, and Country of Registry, Selected Asia-Pacific Countries, 1985

Country of registry	Number of ships	Gross tonnage	Median size (gross tonnage)	Median age (years)
PRC[a]	582	8,298,043	11,408	14.60
Hong Kong	211	6,684,863	25,818	7.00
Indonesia	50	625,267	10,166	8.75
Japan	812	32,368,708	27,631	7.20
Korea[b]	230	5,814,235	16,420	12.50
Malaysia	43	1,223,831	19,999	9.09
Philippines	173	3,663,503	16,956	9.00
Singapore	246	5,677,257	17,034	9.96
Taiwan	121	3,925,760	30,750	8.40
World total	13,575	343,743,057	16,550	11.07

Notes: a. People's Republic of China.
b. Republic of Korea.

Source: *Lloyd's Register of Shipping*, 1985. Statistical Tables.

The distribution of ships of 8,000 DWT and larger by size and country of registry is shown in table 5.3. The effect of excluding smaller ships is not significant. In terms of the number of ships, Japan's share in the world's total fleet drops from 13.5 percent to 9.4 percent, but the share of total tonnage remains the same. The share of the world's fleet for the six other Asian countries (Hong Kong, Indonesia, the Republic of Korea, Malaysia, the Philippines, and Singapore) for which data are available also decreases from 8 percent to 7 percent, but the tonnage share remains the same. Table 5.3 also reports the median size and age of the vessels in each country's fleet. In general, according to these measures, the fleets of developing countries are neither older nor do they consist of predominantly small-sized vessels when compared to the fleets of other countries.

Types of Shipping Services Provided

An alternative classification of marine transportation is by the two general types of service provided: nonliner and liner shipping. Nonliner shipping is unscheduled, tends to deal in shipload lots, will go anywhere, and its prices are set by free competition. Nonliner

Table 5.4 Vessels Operating in U.S-East Asia Liner Trade, May 1981 Breakdown by Operator Nationality and Flag of Registry

Operator nationality	Under flag of operator's nationality[b]	Under flags of convenience[b]	Under other flags[b]	Total
U.S.	50	—	—	50
Japan	26	3	—	29
Korea	15	8	6 (European)	29
Taiwan	15	19	11 (European)	45
Hong Kong	—	4	—	4
Philippines	12	—	—	12
Thailand	—	—	—	—
Malaysia	—	—	—	—
Singapore	4	—	—	4
Indonesia	10	—	—	10
East Asian total	63	26	11 (European)	110
Third parties	65	3	12 (Other European)	79
European	49	3	12 (Other European)	64
India	8	—	—	8
USSR	7	—	—	7

Notes: a. Number of vessels is approximate.
b. Regional totals do not equal sum of country totals because vessels used in joint service are counted under both countries.

Source: E.G. Frankel, Inc. 1981b, Table 11-3.3-10.

shipping can be subdivided into the carriage of liquid bulk (crude oil, oil products, chemicals, and other liquid bulk), dry bulk (grains, metal ores, coal), or combination dry- and liquid-bulk carriers that can shift between the liquid and dry trades.[1] Vessels engaged in dry-bulk shipping are known in the trade as "tramps." In contrast, liner trade tends to transport less-than-shipload lots, usually sails on rigid schedules and defined routes, and is ordinarily organized into liner conferences, which are organizations resembling classical cartels.

The statistical information on liner and nonliner shipping is not readily available except for the U.S.-East Asian trade.[2] In this trade in

1. In addition, a large fleet is engaged in transporting proprietors cargoes. For example, roughly one-third of all tankers are owned by major oil companies.

2. E.G. Frankel, Inc. (1981a, 1981b, 1981c).

1979, liner traffic accounted for 52 percent of the total value and 16 percent of the tonnage of U.S. imports from the Far East and Southeast Asia. On the export side, the liner sector represented 37 percent of the value and 10 percent of the tonnage. Inclusion of neobulk carriage increased tonnage more than value and imports more than exports. As expected, the share of nonliner shipping varied among commodities and was particularly significant for some export commodities, such as wood, coal, grain, and fertilizer.

In 1981 there were 28 conferences and rate agreements operating in U.S.-East Asia trade. On the average there were 7 member lines per conference or rate agreement, and the range was 3 to 21. Shipping lines belonging to these conferences operated 239 vessels. The distribution of these vessels by the nationality of the operator and the flag of registry is shown in table 5.4.

Trade in Shipping Services

Statistics on trade in ocean transport services are reported in table 5.5. With the exception of Japan and the Republic of Korea (Korea) all remaining countries in the Asia-Pacific region are net debtors on the shipping account. In 1984 the gross revenues earned from ocean shipping varied from an amount equal to 5.9 percent of the FOB value of all merchandise exports for Japan to about 2.5 percent for Malaysia and the Philippines.

It is difficult to reconcile these statistics with information supplied by other sources. According to the Japanese Ministry of Transport (1985c), in the "mariner transport sector" Japan's international balance of payments in 1984 registered a deficit, with US$10.8 billion received and US$12.8 billion paid, but the deficit decreased on a year-to-year basis for the first time in three years. The report attributes the smaller deficit to cross-trade growth, generating the first increase of freight revenues in three years; increased port charge revenues, reflecting more frequent calls by foreign vessels at Japanese ports; and a decrease in chartering foreign tonnage, resulting from a drop in cargo-ship charter rates. Apparently these statistics pertain to a more broadly defined marine transport sector.

The demand for shipping services is sensitive to business cycles. The reported 1985 earnings from shipping were affected by the economic recovery in a number of countries. This led to some recovery in freight rates from the depressed levels of the late 1970s. However, this recovery appears to have been short-lived and did not

Table 5.5 Earnings and Payments for Ocean Transportation Services, Selected Countries in the Asia-Pacific Region: 1984 (millions of SDRs)

Country	Shipment[a] credit	Shipment[a] debit	Shipment net	Merchandise exports, FOB	Merchandise imports, FOB	Ratio of shipment credit to merchandise exports
Japan	7.20[c]	− 3.72[c]	+ 3.48[c]	164.31[c]	-121.00[c]	4.38
Korea	1,518[b]	-497[b]	1,021[b]	25,735	-26,716	5.90
Malaysia	396	-1,273	-877	15,967	-13,295	2.48
Philippines	132[b]	-343	-211	5,264	-5,926	2.51
Singapore	703	-1,468	-765	21,799	-26,081	3.22
Thailand	280	-1,051	-771[b]	7,163	-9,042	3.91

Notes: a. Ocean freight and insurance.
b. Ocean freight only.
c. In billions of SDRs.

Source: IMF, 1985.

Figure 5.2 Value of Merchandise Exports, Fleet Gross Tonnage, and Gross Revenue Earned from Shipping, Japan: 1969–1984

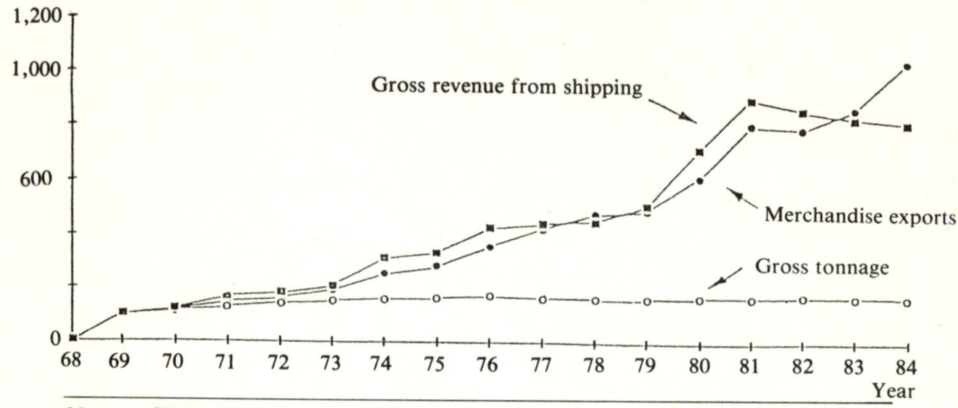

Note: a. SDR = Special Drawing Rights, t = tons.
Source: IMF, 1985.

Figure 5.3 Value of Merchandise Exports, Fleet Gross Tonnage, and Gross Revenue Earned from Shipping, Korea: 1969–1984.

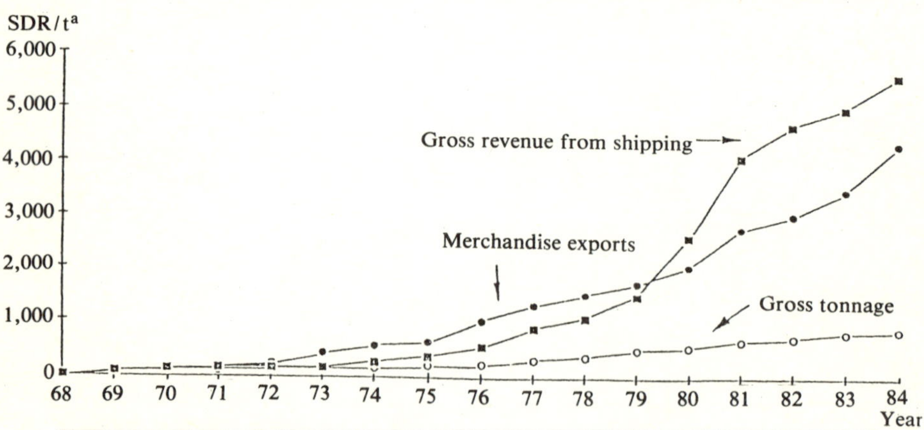

Note: a. SDR = Special Drawing Rights, t = tons.
Source: IMF, 1985.

Figure 5.4 Value of Merchandise Exports, Fleet Gross Tonnage, and Gross Revenue Earned from Shipping, Philippines: 1969–1984.

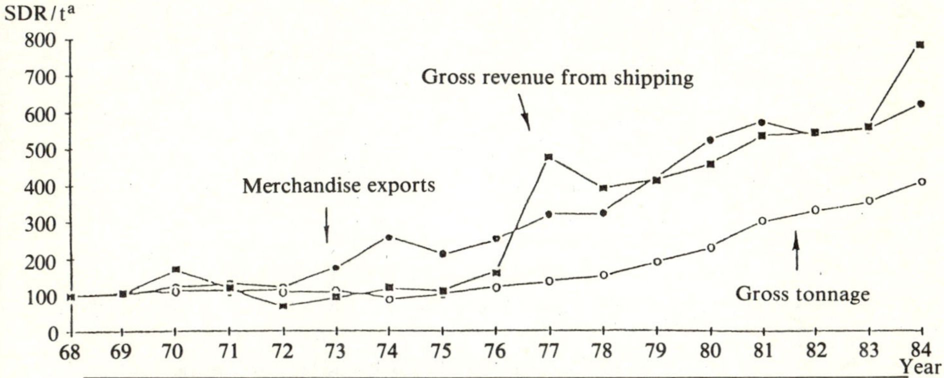

Note: a. SDR = Special Drawing Rights, t = tons.
Source: IMF, 1985.

Figure 5.5 Value of Merchandise Exports, Fleet Gross Tonnage, and Gross Revenue Earned from Shipping, Singapore: 1969-1984.

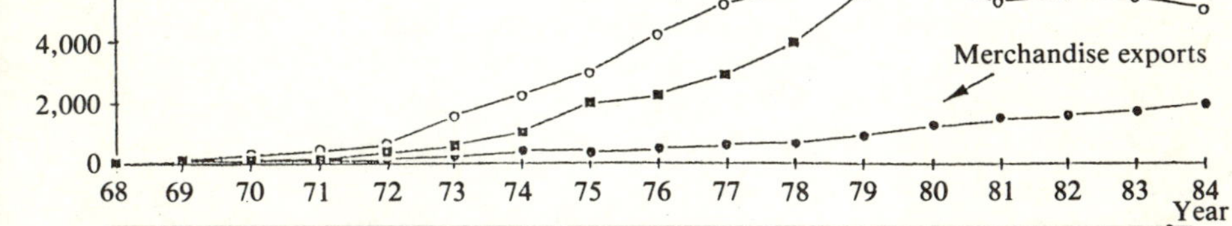

Note: a. SDR = Special Drawing Rights, t = tons.
Source: IMF, 1985.

affect all routes. Because of this sensitivity of shipping trade to short-term fluctuations, it may be instructive to examine longer-term trends.

Figures 5.2 through 5.5 show the trends for four countries (Japan, Korea, the Philippines, and Singapore) in gross revenue earnings from shipping services, fleet size (measured by gross tonnage), and the total value of merchandise exports for the period 1968–1984. During this period, with the single exception of Japan since 1981, gross revenues from shipping have increased monotonically in all countries. In fact, in all four countries the trend in gross revenues from shipping either exceeded that of the value of merchandise exports or closely followed it. The sizes of Korea's and the Philippines' fleets continued to increase during this period while Japan's fleet size remained relatively stable. However, Singapore's fleet began decreasing in 1979.

Current Problems and Future Prospects

The fleet and earnings statistics fail to convey the seriousness of the financial problems in the shipping industries in virtually all of the countries considered here.[3] During the past three years a number of shipping companies have been forced into bankruptcy. In the summer of 1984, Eddie Steamship Company, Taiwan's largest bulk-carrier operator, collapsed under an avalanche of debt. In August 1985, Sanko Steamship Company, Japan's largest bulk-carrier operator, went into bankruptcy with debts of US$2.6 billion and additional sums owed to trade creditors and ship owners. In September 1985, Hong Kong's largest ship owner, the Tung Group, declared insolvency with current liabilities and indebtedness totaling at least US$2.8 billion.

There were other, less publicized bankruptcies, and governments were forced to take drastic measures to salvage their shipping companies. Korea's shipping industry, for example, had a net operating loss of US$193 million in 1984 and had accumulated an aggregate debt of US$3.2 billion. To prevent wholesale bankruptcy, it has gone through a radical restructuring over the past two years under the government's two-phase consolidation program. Under the first phase, enforced early in 1985, a total of 63 large and small shipping companies were merged into 6 integrated companies and 11 holding companies. The recently implemented second phase involved a further merger of the 11 into 9 new units.

Yet restructuring of the industry is not likely to resolve the long-run financial problems, since it does not tackle the fundamental problem of the enormous collective debt. In most cases the surviving companies simply took over the debts of companies they absorbed. However, some restructuring of loan repayments, provided by the program, will offer short-term relief.

3. Each year in February, the *Far Eastern Economic Review* devotes the better part of one issue to a survey of ocean shipping in the region. Unless otherwise indicated, this section is based on information supplied in these surveys. For the latest, see "Shipping '86," *Far Eastern Economic Review*, Vol. 131, No. 7, February 13, 1986.

The causes of the shipping industry's financial difficulties are numerous and interrelated. In part they are due to the stagnant demand for shipping services as a result of the worldwide recession and the relatively long lag between the placement of orders for ships and their delivery. The optimistic expectations that prevailed prior to the recession would by themselves have produced some excess capacity. But the main source of overcapacity in the shipping industry is probably the worldwide overcapacity in the shipbuilding industry. This overcapacity has resulted in falling prices of new ships. For example, the China Ship Building Corporation, owned by the government of Taiwan, is selling a 150,000-DWT bulk carrier for US$22 million; only three years ago it was able to sell a 130,000-DWT bulk carrier with a significantly less advanced control system for US$42 million.

Overcapacity has also resulted in attractive purchase terms being offered by governments, private lenders (spurred by their governments), and shipyard owners in an effort to keep work-starved shipyards busy. Even in late 1982 Sanko Steamship Company was able to order 123 new handy-size bulk carriers on terms that amounted to a 10-year hire-purchase plan with nothing but the interest payable for the first three years. In 1984 Singapore's Neptune Orient Lines (NOL) bought two large 3,000-TEU (20-foot equivalent unit) new containerships from Korea's Hyundai Industries for only US$54 million, of which US$12.4 million was paid in new NOL shares and the remainder financed by long-term credit from the Korean Eximbank. Those shares later had to be sold at a 20 percent loss by Hyundai because of deterioration in the line's financial performance.

The shipowners' willingness to add capacity is traceable to the events of the early 1970s when anyone with available ships realized high profits. The apparent expectation is that this will happen again when the long-awaited recovery finally arrives, and no shipowner wants to be caught short of capacity.

The overcapacity problem has been further aggravated by technological change—the shift to containerization. This technology is characterized by substantial economies of ship size, which have yet to be exhausted. Consequently, the new container ships belonging to the fleet have reached a 4,500-TEU total. Total capacity is increasing as older, smaller ships are being replaced by much larger vessels.

The Organization for Economic Cooperation and Development reports the following:

> At the end of February, 1985, the capacity of the world container and

> ro/ro fleet (ships with an individual capacity of more than 400 TEUs) was estimated by Drewry's to be 1.2 million TEUs. However, the current order book amounted to 0.28 million TEUs, an increase of 23 percent, with the great majority scheduled for delivery before the end of 1986. A number of further orders are expected to be placed for the largest sizes of container ships as other lines and groups of lines seek to defend themselves against Evergreen and United States Lines by acquiring similar vessels. Because of the relative youth of fully containerized ships, 90 percent of whose tonnage is less than fifteen years old, there is little prospect of the surplus capacity being reduced by scrapping and the surplus vessels will move down into the trades which have, to date, not been fully containerized, with a knock-on effect upon the other types of shipping which have previously serviced these routes. . . . OECD 1985: 61-62.

The report concludes that on the major trade routes at the beginning of 1986, container-ship capacity will most likely exceed demand by about 40 percent. Similarly, on the East Asia-West Coast route the container capacity between 1984 and 1987 is expected to increase by 46 percent and the overcapacity to reach between 20 and 40 percent in the best-case scenario. Although the exact estimate is not available, as a result of current overcapacity the 1985 freight rate level was believed to be even lower than the depressed 1984 rate level.

Because none of the causes of the current problems have been remedied, the future promises more of the same. Although Japanese shipyards are expected to reduce their shipbuilding capacity, the Korean government, in order to shore up its struggling shipbuilding industry, has resorted to the short-run solution of improving the export financing terms for the purchase of new ships. In addition, China, which entered the world's export-shipbuilding market at the beginning of the 1960s, is expected not only to contribute to the overcapacity, but also, because of its high volume and ultra-low-cost competition, to cause continuous problems to the shipbuilding industries of Korea and Japan in the future.

The adoption of new technologies is likely to continue, and this will be unfavorable to the shipping industries of developing countries. Although providing transport services by general-cargo ship is highly labor intensive and therefore favors developing countries, the containerized ship is relatively capital intensive. However, the shift to containerization has produced a by-product—a trend toward intermodal transportation—which in turn has a significant impact on cost structure. Table 5.6 offers a comparison between the profiles of costs for a typical U.S.-registered conventional liner operation (employing a C-4-type general-cargo vessel) and a full-scale intermodal operation

Table 5.6 Comparative Cost Profiles: U.S. = Flag Conventional versus Intermodal Liner Operation

Operation	Conventional, mariner class (%)	Container 1,700 TEU (%)
Marine operations	59	19
Terminal/cargo-handling	24	24
Land operations	0	19
Equipment (containers, etc.)	2	9
Sales	5	6
Administration	5	6
Capital	5	17
Total	100	100

Source: Temple, Barker & Sloane, Inc., 1984. *Strategic Options for U.S. Liner Operations.*

Table 5.7 Comparison of Estimated Marine Expenses: U.S. = and Asian = Flag Operators, U.S. Dollars per Day (1984)

Cost component	Type of recently built diesel-powered ship			
	850 TEU		1,700 TEU	
	U.S.[a]	Asian	U.S.[a]	Asian
Crew	$ 6,400	$ 1,800	$ 6,700	$ 2,000
M&R, stores	2,500	2,500	3,600	3,600
Fuel	6,600	6,600	9,000	9,000
Insurance, other	1,700	1,500	2,400	2,100
Total vessel	$17,200	$12,400	$21,700	$16,700
Port[b]	3,600	3,600	5,000	3,000
Total marine	$20,800	$16,000	$26,700	$21,700
Marine cost per slot	$24.47	$18.82	$15.71	$12.76
U.S./Asian cost ratio	1.30		1.23	

Notes: a. Nonsubsidized.
b. Based on 42-day round-voyage.
Source: Temple, Barker & Sloane, Inc., 1984.

(employing state-of-the-art 1,700-TEU vessels). Whereas well over half of the conventional operator's expenses are for marine operations, with cargo handling a distant second, the container operator's combined landside costs of terminal and inland operations significantly outweigh marine costs.

Table 5.7 presents the estimated differential in marine costs between nonsubsidized U.S. carriers and Asian (non-Japanese) carriers operating in the trans-Pacific trade with an 850-TEU or 1,700-TEU vessel. The cost differential resides primarily in the area of crew wages and insurance. Given that U.S. crew costs are about 25 percent of total marine expenses (and marine costs are 19 percent of total costs), and that Asian crew costs are around 30 percent of the U.S. costs on a 1,700-TEU vessel, a U.S. operator's cost disadvantage, compared to an Asian competitor, is only 4 percent. The cost disadvantage would have been even smaller if the range were expanded to cover 4,400-TEU vessels.

The trend toward larger container vessels is expected to continue, subject only to the constraints imposed by port and canal restrictions and service requirements such as frequency and transit time. This trend is likely to further erode the comparative advantage of developing countries in supplying ocean transport services.

In general there appears to be some consensus that (1) the worldwide slump in shipping will continue for another three to four years; (2) during this time governments, banks, shipyards, and shipowners will lose substantially more than they have to date; and (3) only a few firms currently in business will remain so to benefit from the long-expected recovery.

Government Intervention in the Trade in Shipping Services

Nonliner shipping has been relatively free from government intervention. As was pointed out in the discussion of types of shipping services, the freight rates for nonliner services are established in the competitive market and fluctuate in response to supply and demand. The opposite is true in liner shipping, in which intervention by governments has been ubiquitous.

Although this intervention has taken a variety of forms, it can be divided roughly into direct and indirect intervention. The most popular tool of direct intervention is cargo reservation, a government's policy of reserving certain cargo, a specified share of total cargo, or certain services in a particular geographic area to its own flag carriers.

Direct intervention also includes construction or operating subsidies or both, as well as preferential tax treatment for liner shipping companies. Indirect intervention pertains to government's long-standing support of the conference system. Although these issues are not really independent, it is convenient to discuss them separately.

Direct Intervention

Cargo reservation has been used by nations to support their merchant marines since the mercantilist era. In the United States, for example, cargo reservation began in 1798 when Congress established discriminatory tonnage taxes on foreign-flag vessels.[4] In 1817 the tonnage tax was replaced by legislation that strictly prohibited foreign-flag vessels from operating in the domestic trade.

As it has for other transport modes, the federal government initially provided financial assistance to the merchant marine through mail contracts, the first of which was awarded in 1845. And although this practice continued, the Military Transport Act of 1904 required that all military cargo transported overseas to defense installations be carried by U.S.-flag vessels. This law marked the beginning of cargo reservation as a major tool to subsidize the merchant marine. Thirty years later Congress expanded the scope of cargo preference in Public Resolution 17, which requires that only U.S.-flag vessels be used to transport agricultural commodities purchased abroad with loans made by the U.S. government or its agencies. This resolution established the precedent of allocating a fixed percentage of all cargo purchased or financed by government loans to the merchant marine. As a general rule, to comply with this resolution and subsequent legislation, today 50 percent of government-generated cargo must be transported by U.S.-flag operators.

Flag discrimination continues to be a favorite policy of developing countries eager to improve and augment their merchant fleets. This flag discrimination policy began to be adopted in the second half of the 1960s, mainly by nations in Latin America. It later spread to developing nations in other regions, including Southeast Asia.

Brooks (1985) describes the maritime policies of the ASEAN countries, stating that, with the single exception of Singapore, all ASEAN countries have adopted a policy of cabotage—reserving domestic shipping for national-flag ships. Again with the single exception of Singapore, all ASEAN countries reserve government cargo for national-

4. The history of U.S. cargo reservation policy is from Kyle and Phillips (1983).

flag ships. However, in some countries the term "government cargo" is defined so broadly as to include almost all cargo.

The most popular new policy instrument, however, is the cargo-sharing agreement, which is either the result of bilateral negotiations between trading countries or is declared unilaterally. Although in use much earlier, flag discrimination through cargo-sharing agreements was legitimized by the adoption in 1974 of the Convention on a Code of Conduct of Liner Conferences.

Prior to 1974, the liner conferences, like any other cartel, were eager to prevent entry in order to maximize their joint profits. They were therefore closed when possible. The developing countries were dissatisfied, since in some cases their shipping companies could not take part in conferences, even those serving transport routes to the countries themselves. Developing countries therefore vehemently demanded that, in order to promote their merchant marines, their shipping lines be allowed to join liner conferences. As a result of these demands, the Convention on a Code of Conduct for Liner Conferences was adopted in 1974.

The code has two primary mandates: (1) requirements for partici-
routes served by the conferences; and (2) there is a provision for cargo sharing within liner conferences through pooling agreements in which the two national shipping lines of the countries at both ends of a route each be given 40 percent of the cargo and third-country shipping lines 20 percent of the cargo.

Many developing countries and East European nations became contracting parties to the convention, but the ratio requirement for the signatory nations' combined merchant tonnage was not fulfilled until the Federal Republic of Germany and the Netherlands became the first developed countries to ratify or accede to the convention on 6 April 1983. When the ratio requirement had been satisfied, the convention came into force on 6 October of that year.

According to Brooks (1985), all ASEAN countries have negotiated cargo-sharing agreements or have adopted them unilaterally. Thailand signed an agreement with Korea in late 1983 and adopted the 40-40-20 cargo allocation rule in Thailand-Korea trade. Malaysia has signed agreements with Bangladesh, Turkey, and Indonesia and plans to negotiate similar pacts with Korea, Pakistan, India, and Japan. Indonesia has negotiated bilateral agreements with Japan, Taiwan, and Korea for carriage of logs and with Taiwan for carriage of general cargo. Even Singapore has signed a 50-50 cargo-sharing agreement with Indonesia for Indonesia-Singapore trade.

In 1982, to support its failing fleet, the government of the Philippines adopted cargo sharing on a 40-40-20 basis for all liner cargo, an action taken unilaterally by executive order. This led to a confrontation with the United States. Faced with action by the Federal Maritime Commission (FMC), which would have effectively barred Philippine-flag vessels from United States ports, the government of the Philippines was forced to withdraw the executive order.

It is not clear how much effect cargo-sharing agreements will have. Some shipping company executives believe that only trade routes between developing countries will be affected and that, because of the opposition of developed countries as well as the opposition of shippers, the agreements are not likely to affect shipping on main trade routes.

In addition to cargo sharing, ASEAN countries, like many others, have adopted a variety of financial assistance schemes. These include such measures as lowering income and other taxes, tax holidays, lower interest rates on loans to finance ship purchases, and lower (or no) import duties. Other schemes include equity participation and government ownership and operation of shipping companies.

Yet current problems in the shipping industries of some countries are directly traceable to these financial aids. For example, when world shipping rates jumped in the 1970s following the first oil shock, Korea—without a significant fleet or much experience in the shipping business—suffered badly from prices imposed by foreign carriers. At that time Korea decided to expand its fleet. However, because the worldwide shipping boom was forcing up secondhand prices, the timing was unfortunate.

In the midst of the boom, the Korea Maritime and Port Administration (KMPA) declared that effective subsidies in the form of guaranteed employment would go to the designated major shipping companies. That started a veritable stampede in the world market by Korean buyers purchasing secondhand vessels. This demand led brokers to charge a "Korean rate" for aging ships. The outcome should have been expected: the Korean shipping industry ended up with a huge aggregate debt and a fleet in which 32 percent of the ships are more than 15 years old and at least 50 percent are more than 10 years old.

Some countries have also used licensing and regulation as tools of flag discrimination. The most extreme case is Indonesia, where all nonpetroleum exports must be shipped from one of four ports; that is, ships unloading imports at any of 48 other ports open to foreign vessels cannot pick up exports, but must ballast to one of the four designated ports. There are also regulations restricting the use of transshipment ports, and the multiple permit system is widely known to be a bureaucratic nightmare.

Indirect Intervention

Governments have also interfered with free trade in shipping services through their support of liner conferences. As previously mentioned, liner shipping conferences are shipping cartels that—in addition to jointly determining prices—control entry, operate revenue and cargo pools, and set the frequency of sailings and ports of call in order to prevent nonprice competition. In effect, liner conferences are indistinguishable from industrial cartels.

It is therefore not too surprising that concern over the effects of conferences has a long history. The Royal Commission on Shipping Rings conducted an inquiry into the conference system in 1907, and in the United States the Alexander Commission held hearings in 1913–14. Since then conferences have been the subject of numerous other hearings. These hearings notwithstanding, the conference system has survived primarily because of the support it has received from various governments. Even in the United States, where similar activities among competitors in other industries would be judged per se violations of the antitrust laws, liner conferences enjoy immunity from those laws.

The support of the conference system by developing countries is even more surprising, because one of the stated reasons for developing their national fleets was dissatisfaction with the conduct of conferences—the Far Eastern Freight Conference (FEFC) in particular.

Two questions may be asked: (1) Why are governments willing to support liner conferences? and (2) Does the liner shipping industry have unique characteristics that require cartelization for it to survive? To answer these questions, Kyle (1984) scrutinizes both the arguments made by the proponents of the conference system and the counter-arguments offered by opponents. He examines the following arguments in favor of liner conferences: (1) Liner conferences are natural monopolies; (2) liner conferences are subject to ruinous competition; (3) the liner industry has a common carrier obligation or public utility status; (4) ocean shipping is an international industry; and (5) the liner industry is essential to national defense. He also investigates the extent to which liner conferences inhibit competition and the potential benefits of rationalization of liner services.

Because the first three arguments are a rehash of those used to debate regulation versus deregulation in other transportation modes, they have been discarded. Gomez-Ibanez and Morgan (1984) find no validity in the fourth argument, that the special status of liner shipping is due to the international nature of the industry and cannot be subjected to unilateral regulation by one participant. Citing the example of the airline industry, they argue that the strongly pro-competitive U.S. airline policy forced liberalization of international aviation policy, resulting in welfare gains for not only U.S. but also other travelers. They expect a pro-competitive shipping policy would have a similar effect, but in this area the U.S. stance is not pro-competition.

In general, the arguments offered by the proponents are not persuasive; that is, they do not support the contention that unique economic characteristics of the industry or the environment in which it operates require cartelization. The counterarguments of the opponents (economists for the most part) are based on widely accepted arguments against cartels and the welfare loss resulting from their profit-maximizing behavior.[5] However, the opponents do not explain why governments support liner conferences.

Several testable hypotheses could be suggested to explain the support of shipping cartels by governments and the need for cartelization in the liner industry. Kyle and Phillips (1983) have estimated that the annual welfare loss that would result from reserving 40 percent of dry bulk cargo for U.S.-flag vessels would be between US$13.5 and US$136 million. The transfer of income from shippers to the maritime sector, however, would be between US$645 million and US$1.08 billion annually. In other words, the welfare loss is much smaller than the transfer of income. If the preceding ratio of welfare loss to income transfer is accurate and is sufficiently general, it may be rational for a government to support liner conferences, since the share of the income transfer captured by the nationally owned flag line exceeds the welfare loss to the country's economy. It should be possible to estimate the welfare loss and the income transfer in other situations and to derive necessary and sufficient conditions to explain support of conferences as a rational government policy.

Taplin (1983) offers a different explanation for the existence of liner conferences. He starts with the Turvey-Mohring findings that service frequency effects can result in marginal social cost being less than average costs in an industry experiencing constant production costs.[6] He then argues this phenomenon is also applicable to shipping conferences. He states, "The fact that conferences tend to form in the absence of government prohibition may be evidence that liner

5. For a concise statement of the case against liner conferences with which most economists would agree, see Shneerson (1986).

6. Mohring (1972), Turvey and Mohring (1975), and Jansson (1979).

shipping is a multi-product natural monopoly. By banding together, the operators are able to offer frequent services and, at the same time, achieve substantial economies of ship size. As before, more patronage means more frequency, which confers benefits on all shippers. The conference increases patronage by discriminatory pricing and is an evident case of a multi-product monopoly defending itself against the threat of entry by Ramsey-optimal pricing, in the manner indicated by Baumol, Bailey and Willig (1977). . ." (Taplin 1983:36).

Taplin does not test this hypothesis, but merely argues that, even if this is the case, conferences should not be protected in any way. On the contrary, he holds that conferences should be continually exposed to actual or threatened competition in order to determine their sustainability. His hypothesis could be tested, since methods for estimating the value of sailing frequency to shippers are now available.[7]

The third hypothesis pertains to the claimed benefits of conferences by allowing the rationalization of liner services. Although proponents of this argument have failed to supply a clear definition of rationalization, it appears to refer to the reduction in costs due to restriction of nonprice competition, subject to the constraint that all available cargo is transported. This, however, is not an appropriate objective criterion to be minimized from the social point of view, unless the value of the quality of services to shippers is equal to zero. For example, taken to its logical conclusion, rationalization would imply that ships would never sail until fully loaded. This in turn would be optimal only if the value of the frequency of sailing and transit time to shippers is equal to zero.

The rationalization argument implies that if nonprice competition is not restricted, too many sailings would be produced if each competing shipping firm made independent decisions. This would result in a low utilization factor and high costs. However, although this is true in a cartel, in which rates are set above the competitive level, it is not clear this would occur in the absence of liner conferences.

This hypothesis can be tested by two methods. First, it is possible to use simulation to determine the outcome of two alternatives: (1) free competition among liner firms, and (2) a conference with rationalization that would include a positive value for the frequency of sailings and the value of time to shippers. Second, a synthetic experi-

7. For application of one such method, see Garrod and Miklius (1983).

ment could be designed to replicate the market functioning with and without a conference system-*cum*-rationalization. Both methods should be able to answer the question of whether conferences with rationalization would produce net benefits to society under more normal assumptions (i.e., both the value of the frequency of services and the value of time to shippers are greater than zero).

The national defense issue is even more complex and has not been resolved. The value of the merchant marine to national defense in conventional wars has been amply demonstrated. The latest example is the Falklands campaign, for which 54 ships were chartered and requisitioned from 33 civilian companies. In his assessment of this war's logistics Tustin (1984:296) concludes that without these ships "... and their resolute volunteer crews, the task would have been impossible. . . ." Furthermore, the conversion from civilian to military use was swift: the Canberra was at sea with 2,500 troops and a helicopter deck less than 60 hours after fare-paying passengers had disembarked.

Still, the use of conventional ships presented some problems. Tustin notes problems in off-loading merchant ships without roll-on-roll-off ramps. Also difficult was the considerable restowing and cross-decking of men and materials made necessary by the particular design of commercial ships.

Nevertheless, commercial ships have performed well in Falklands-type conventional wars. But there is no assurance that future wars will be of this type. Therefore, an assessment of defense needs should start with the development of various war scenarios and an assignment of probability to each. The required size and mix of ships for each scenario could then be estimated. This information in turn would allow estimation of the optimum fleet at an acceptable level of risk. Next, the cost of alternative ways of constructing and maintaining this fleet should be estimated. At one extreme, a specialized fleet could be built and maintained for defense purposes only. At the other, a commercial fleet devoted to international trade but available for defense purposes could be relied upon. There are other options, as well as mixed strategies. Research for this paper indicates that no such assessment has been made, although one has been commissioned by the Department of Transport in association with the Ministry of Defence in the United Kingdom to determine which ships are needed for national defense.

In the United States, the Commission on the Merchant Marine and Defense has been established. The purpose of this commission, as defined in Public Law 98-525, is to study problems relating to the transportation of cargo and personnel needed to meet national security requirements in time of war or national emergency, the capability of the U.S. Merchant Marine to meet the need for such transportation, and the adequacy of the U.S. shipbuilding mobilization base to meet the needs of naval and merchant ship construction.

The Outlook for Liberalization of Trade in Shipping Services

A recent OECD (1985:16) report notes, "... there are some signs that some developing countries are beginning to rethink their shipping policies and to perceive the damage that protectionist measures do to their own national interests...." It cites as evidence two liberalizing measures introduced in Brazil during 1984. The first cancelled three earlier resolutions reserving conference cargo to Brazilian-flag vessels in Brazil's northbound trade. The second authorized the Brazilian Merchant Marine Supervisory Body (Sunaman) for a limited time to grant permission for foreign ships to be chartered by Brazilian shipping companies to operate in coastal services. (Recall also that in 1984 the Philippines withdrew the executive order that had reserved 40 percent of U.S.–Philippine liner trade, but this was done under duress.)

In spite of these encouraging signs, outlook for liberalization of trade in shipping services appears bleak. In fact, governments of developing countries, encouraged by adoption of the UN Code of Liner Conferences, have made concerted efforts to have similar cargo reservation schemes adopted in the bulk trade on the pretense that merchant fleets of developing countries have been excluded from transportation of this cargo. The pretense is groundless, however, since this trade is competitively organized, and there are no barriers to entry.

So far these efforts have failed because of the opposition of developed countries. If they succeed, they will have an unfortunate side-effect. In 1985 the Baltic International Freight Futures Exchange commenced trading in freight futures. This provided an opportunity for participants in the shipping industry, both operators and shippers, to hedge against future-freight rate fluctuations. However, the futures market can function only in the absence of gross interference from governments.

The governments of developing countries have also made efforts to eliminate competition from the flag-of-convenience vessels under a variety of pretenses. Thus far these efforts have failed, but they are likely to continue.

The conference system itself faces multiple challenges, and its future is by no means certain. It is being threatened not only by overcapacity, but also by competition from independent, particularly government-controlled, East European lines. For example, OECD (1985) report that in the Far East trade the Soviet-controlled Balt Orient Line (BOL) charges rates 30 percent lower than those of FEFC. To defend itself against this competition, the FEFC started negotiations to admit BOL to the conference, but negotiations have failed because BOL demanded an annual entitlement to carry 36,000 TEUs eastbound and 42,000 TEUs westbound. This would have represented more than 25 percent of the FEFC's total westbound liftings from the Far East liftings from the Far East area served by BOL and some 16 percent of eastbound liftings. Although BOL later reduced its demand to 35,000 TEUs westbound and 32,000 eastbound, this still significantly exceeded the FEFC's offer of approximately 25,000 TEUs eastbound and 22,500 TEUs westbound. It has been estimated that by the end of 1985, BOL capacity in the trade was about 125 percent above the level offered in early 1982.

As the experience in the Europe-Central America/Caribbean trade indicates, a successful agreement admitting these lines to the conference may not produce the stability hoped for. In 1983 an agreement was concluded admitting two Soviet-controlled lines, Baltic Shipping Company and Scan Pacific Line to the WITASS Conference. Almost as soon as the agreement entered into force, its stabilizing effects and benefits were undermined by the appearance of the German Democratic Republic's shipping line, Deutsche Seereederei (DSR), as a nonconference operator, quoting rates 17 to 70 percent below those of the conference. By aggressive rate-cutting DSR was able to increase its monthly sailing from about 700 weight-tons in 1983 to 1,100 weight-tons in 1984. Because of its practice of price discrimination, the conference was vulnerable to "cream skimming." Thus it was badly hurt, because the cargoes shifted to DSR were high-value cargoes and most tariffs were already fixed at low levels to meet commercial outside competition.

The future promises more of the same as conferences encounter competition from the China-owned and -controlled fleet, which now stands at about 620 ships totaling 13 million DWT. About one-third of this fleet is comprised of general-cargo carriers, including 55 container-carrying vessels with a total slot capacity of some 37,000 TEUs.

The volume of sailings by Chinese shipping has increased by an average of 25 percent a year since 1976. However, even if a lower projected growth rate of 10 percent is assumed, China's general-cargo trade will be at the same level as Japan's by the end of the decade.

Even in bulk trade China is expected to catch Japan within the next 10 years, provided Chinese port and infrastructure construction problems are successfully resolved.

Marcus (1986) believes the immediate future will bring a continuation of vessel overcapacity, rate-cutting, and bankruptcies. Once the shakeout is complete, the remaining carriers will be ready to cooperate with each other, and cooperation will be easier because their number will be smaller. But the remaining firms will be larger because of the economies of scale and will be engaged in intermodal transportation. These changes will create substantial barriers to entry. In short, Marcus visualizes strong conferences, relatively stable rates, and emphasis on services competition.

His scenario, however, assumes passive governments. It is more reasonable to assume that, in order to protect their merchant marines, governments will increasingly resort to flag protectionism and to unilateral or bilateral interference in the trade in shipping services. Neither scenario even remotely resembles free trade in shipping services.

CHAPTER 6
Tourism in Asia and the Pacific

James Mak and Kenneth White

In the broadest sense, tourism encompasses all expenditures for goods and services by travelers. It includes purchases for transportation, lodging, meals, entertainment, travel agency and sightseeing tour services, and various other personal services. Hence, tourism encompasses the output of many industries.

Before we can talk about international tourism, we must first define an international tourist. According to the World Tourism Organization (WTO), an international tourist is someone who makes a trip of at least 24 hours' duration outside his or her country of residence for purposes other than emigration. The definition therefore includes travel for many different purposes: pleasure, business, employment, religious pilgrimage, and education.

International tourism is a large source of income for many countries in the world. Even after excluding international transportation, tourism accounts for one-quarter of the world trade in services and more than 5 percent of the total value of world exports. It is the largest of the individual service industries. International tourism is proportionately more important for developing countries than for developed countries, accounting for about one-third of their service trade. Typically, industrialized countries have deficits in their travel accounts, whereas developing countries have surpluses.

In 1985 international tourist arrivals totaled 325 million, accounting for over US$105 billion in gross travel receipts, excluding transportation payments (table 6.1). Since 1965 international arrivals have grown at an average annual rate of 5.5 percent and gross tourism receipts have grown at 12.0 percent per annum. However, tourism receipts have not kept up with the value of world trade. The ratio of tourism receipts to the total value of world exports has fallen from 6.3 percent in 1965–1970 to 5.3 percent in 1980–1984, although this ratio has recovered from the low years between 1974 and 1977, when it fell to

Table 6.1 International Tourism Development and Exports, 1965–1985

Year	International tourist arrivals (millions)	Index	International receipts (US$ billions)	Index	Total value of world exports (US$ billions)	Index	Ratio of tourism receipts to world exports
1965	112.7	100.0	11.6	100.0	184.1	100.0	.063
1966	119.8	106.3	13.3	114.7	203.4	110.5	.065
1967	129.5	114.9	14.5	125.0	214.5	116.5	.068
1968	130.9	116.1	15.0	129.3	239.5	130.1	.063
1969	141.1	125.2	16.8	144.8	273.0	148.3	.062
1970	159.7	141.7	17.9	154.3	312.0	169.5	.057
1971	172.2	152.8	20.9	180.2	349.4	189.8	.060
1972	181.9	161.4	24.6	212.1	414.7	225.3	.059
1973	190.6	169.1	31.1	268.1	574.0	311.7	.054
1974	197.1	174.9	33.8	291.4	836.0	454.1	.040
1975	214.4	190.2	40.7	350.9	873.0	474.1	.047
1976	220.7	195.8	44.4	382.8	991.0	538.2	.045
1977	239.1	212.2	55.6	479.3	1,125.0	611.1	.049
1978	257.4	228.4	68.9	594.0	1,303.0	707.8	.053
1979	274.0	243.1	83.3	718.1	1,635.0	888.1	.051
1980	284.1	252.1	101.4	874.1	1,985.0	1,078.2	.051
1981	287.3	254.9	103.0	887.9	1,970.0	1,070.1	.052
1982	286.0	253.8	97.4	839.7	1,842.0	1,000.5	.053
1983	292.3	259.4	97.5	840.5	1,807.0	981.5	.054
1984	312.3	277.1	100.8	869.0	1,915.0	1,042.2	.053
1985	325.0	288.4	105.0	905.2	—	—	—

Source: WTO, 1985a.

less than 5.0 percent.

This chapter describes and explains the development of international tourism in Asia and the Pacific and addresses the issue of travel restrictions on international tourism development in the Asia-Pacific region.[1]

1. The WTO definition of East Asia and the Pacific has been used. The countries included in this region are Australia, Brunei, China, the Cook Islands, Kampuchea, Fiji, French Polynesia, Hong Kong, Indonesia, Japan, Laos, Macau, Malaysia, the Marianas, New Caledonia, New Zealand, Papua New Guinea, the Philippines, Republic of Korea (Korea), Samoa, Singapore, Thailand, Tonga, and Vanuatu.

Table 6.2 International Tourist Arrivals by Region, 1950–1985 (in thousands)

Year	Africa	North America	Latin America and the Caribbean	East Asia and the Pacific	Europe	Middle East	South Asia	World
1960	750	14,000	2,705	680	50,351	630	180	69,296
1965	1,423	19,355	3,868	1,600	83,732	2,351	400	112,729
1970	2,407	27,400	9,248	4,859	113,000	1,864	912	159,690
1975	4,654	29,360	13,603	7,804	153,859	3,520	1,557	214,357
1980	6,413	35,376	18,270	19,981	195,966	5,821	2,280	284,107
1985	8,000	33,491	20,009	34,000	220,000	7,000	2,500	325,000

Source: WTO, 1985a.

Table 6.3 International Tourism Receipts by Region, 1960–1985 (in current US$ millions)

Year	Africa	North America	Latin America and the Caribbean	East Asia and the Pacific	Europe	Middle East	South Asia	World
1960	178	1,388	1,064	195	3,918	89	35	6,867
1965	220	2,071	1,289	411	7,270	270	73	11,604
1970	400	3,519	1,281	1,100	11,200	300	100	17,900
1975	1,127	6,410	3,809	2,164	26,363	500	329	40,702
1980	1,992	12,342	13,180	7,465	61,654	3,228	1,549	101,410
1985	2,150	14,710	11,890	11,650	59,000	4,000	1,600	105,000

Source: WTO, 1985a.

Tourism in Asia and the Pacific

In comparing international tourist arrivals and receipts by region, Europe has historically dominated both arrivals (table 6.2) and gross receipts (table 6.3), accounting for more than two-thirds of all international tourist arrivals and nearly 60 percent of gross receipts. In 1960 the developed countries in North America and Europe accounted for 93 percent of world tourist arrivals and 77 percent of the gross tourism receipts.

The development of mass tourism in the Asia-Pacific region began in the late 1960s. Since then it has become the fastest-growing region in terms of tourism in the world, followed by South Asia, the Middle East, and Africa. Its share of total world tourist arrivals grew from 1 percent in 1960 to 10.5 percent in 1985 (table 6.4). In terms of the more important measure—that is, tourism receipts—the Asia-Pacific region's share has nearly quadrupled, rising from 2.8 percent to 11.1 percent over the same period. By contrast, the shares in gross receipts for the Middle East and South Asia have both tripled, while those for Africa, North and South America, and Europe have declined during this period.

Table 6.4 Regional Shares in Tourism

	Arrivals		Receipts	
Region	1960	1985	1960	1985
Africa	.001	.025	.026	.020
North America	.202	.103	.202	.140
South America and Caribbean	.039	.062	.155	.113
East Asia and Pacific	.010	.105	.028	.111
Europe	.726	.677	.571	.562
Middle East	.009	.022	.013	.038
South Asia	.003	.008	.005	.015

Source: WTO, 1985a.

World tourism is primarily intraregional travel. Data on tourist arrivals indicate that more than 80 percent of world travel is within the same region. However, this was not true of Asia and the Pacific in the 1960s. In 1967, 56 percent of all international tourist arrivals in Asian and Pacific destinations were composed of interregional travel and 44

Table 6.5 Distribution of Regional versus Interregional Arrivals

	1967 (%)	1976 (%)
World		
Regional	84.4	82.9
Interregional	15.6	17.1
East Asia and Pacific		
Regional	44.0	57.9
Interregional	56.0	42.4

Source: WTO, 1980.

percent of intraregional travel. By the mid-1970s the percentages had reversed (table 6.5). In 1984 intraregional travel in Asia and the Pacific accounted for slightly more than two-thirds of international travel, excluding overseas Chinese visiting their country (WTO 1986a). The rapid growth of tourism in the region during the past 20 years can therefore be traced to the increasingly larger number of Asia-Pacific residents visiting other Asia-Pacific destinations. Furthermore, whereas business travel was previously the predominant purpose of travel, most tourists arriving at Asian and Pacific destinations today are traveling for pleasure.

The Asia-Pacific region also generates tourism to other regions. Unfortunately, comprehensive visitor departure data are unavailable. Receipts and expenditure data compiled by the WTO indicate that until 1982, Asia-Pacific countries collectively spent more on travel than they received (table 6.6); but with receipts rising faster (19.6 percent per year) than expenditures (16.3 percent per year from 1973 through 1984), the Asia-Pacific countries now enjoy a positive balance in their aggregate travel account. In 1984 travel expenditures among the Asia-Pacific countries totaled approximately US$10 billion and receipts were approximately US$10.5 billion. Collectively, they held roughly the same share (10.7 percent) of aggregate world tourism expenditures as they did of receipts.

It is more useful to examine the data for the individual countries, since they reveal substantial differences in the performance of each country in the tourist trade. Aggregate data are also less reliable. The aggregate data reported by the WTO are flawed because the WTO makes no effort to adjust for missing data for individual countries in

Table 6.6 Tourism Receipts and Expenditures for East Asia and Pacific Countries, 1973–1984

Year	Receipts (US$ millions)	Expenditures (US$ millions)	Balance (US$ millions)
1973	1,544	2,117	-563
1974	1,722	2,440	-718
1975	2,164	2,817	-653
1976	2,576	3,230	-654
1977	3,577	3,790	-213
1978	4,675	5,963	-1288
1979	6,027	8,547	-250
1980	7,465	8,778	-1313
1981	8,859	9,370	-511
1982	9,398	9,126	272
1983	9,821	9,295	529
1984	10,602	9,949	653

Source: WTO, 1985a.

compiling its aggregate travel statistics. This has probably resulted in serious underestimation, particularly in the aggregate tourism expenditure data and aggregate travel statistics in earlier years, when reliable national tourism statistics were difficult to obtain.

It is well known that tourism expenditure estimates are among the most unreliable data in the balance of payments accounts. As detailed by White and Walker (1982), it is rare for one country's estimates of receipts to match the other country's estimates of expenditures. Discrepancies of more than 100 percent in these figures can be found. However, for a given country, a consistent methodology is usually applied from year to year, so time-series estimates of expenditures can normally be considered reliable indicators of changes in trends, even if the precise dollar figures are unreliable.

Among the Asia-Pacific countries, the major countries in East and Southeast Asia as well as Australia and New Zealand clearly dominate the Asia-Pacific tourist trade. Relative to their larger neighbors, the island countries of the South Pacific still remain unimportant in international tourism. Fiji—which in 1984 received only 235,000 visitors, who spent a total of US$160 million—is the largest.[2] The rest—French Polynesia, New Caledonia, the Marianas, Tonga, Samoa, Vanuatu, the

2. By contrast, total departures other than for emigration numbered 38,379 for 1984. Resident travel expenditures abroad were valued at US$18 million for 1983.

Table 6.7 Country Tourism Data, 1984

Country	Visitor arrivals (in thousands)	Departures (in thousands)	Receipts (US$ millions)	Expenditures (US$ millions)
Singapore	2,991	480	2,076	587
Hong Kong	2,427	1,140	1,371	—
Australia	1,015	1,400	1,211	2,109
Taiwan	1,457	750	1,066	2,011
Thailand	2,347	508	1,156	298
Japan	2,036	4,660	970	4,500
Korea	1,297	470	673	563
Malaysia	2,874	—	546	1,065
Philippines	804	703	358	190
Indonesia	701	297	442	498
New Zealand	388	380	309	446
China	12,852	—	1,130	—

Source: WTO, 1985a. *Far Eastern Economic Review,* various issues; official tourist publications from the individual countries.

Cook Islands, and Papua New Guinea—had combined annual receipts of less than US$250 million from nearly a half million visitors.

Table 6.7 displays individual-country tourism data for 1984 for the major tourist countries in the Asia-Pacific region. In terms of arrivals, China leads with nearly 13 million arrivals in 1984, more than 90 percent of whom were residents of Hong Kong. The 13 million arrivals constituted about 40 percent of all visitor arrivals in the region. If these and other overseas Chinese are excluded, total arrivals still numbered nearly 1.2 million. This is a remarkable achievement considering that China only officially opened its doors to international tourism in 1978. Since liberalization, tourist arrivals have increased at an annual growth rate exceeding 25 percent (1979–1984), rising from 4.2 million in 1979 to nearly 13 million in 1984.

Singapore, which has vigorously promoted its tourist industry, is the leader in revenue received from tourism, with receipts in excess of US$2 billion annually. All others trail far behind.

Japan is clearly the leading tourist generator among Asia-Pacific countries with nearly 4.7 million Japanese overseas departures in 1984. Total spending on international tourism, excluding international transportation, was valued at US$4.5 billion. This is a significant change from 1964, when the monetary liberalization of overseas travel began and only 128,000 Japanese traveled overseas. Between 1964 and 1979, annual overseas travel increased at an average rate of 34.7 percent; since then it has averaged 7.3 percent per annum, although expenditures grew at 15 percent per annum. In 1984 Japan accounted for 46 percent of all international tourist expenditures by Asia-Pacific countries; its share in 1973 was even more impressive at 59 percent. Indeed, the major story in world tourism after 1970 is the emergence of Japan as a major tourist-generating country.

Travel flows can be a critical element in a country's balance of payments. For many countries, revenues from tourism are an important source of funds that help offset deficits in other sectors. However, increased travel has also resulted in substantial travel account deficits for a few countries, notably Japan, whose deficit is among the highest in the world. Countries that fear a travel account deficit could be damaging to their balance of payments accounts have often imposed various types of travel restrictions on their own residents. For example, all the major Southeast Asian countries, with the exception of Singapore, impose hefty exit taxes on residents traveling abroad.[3] Their intention is not to prevent their nationals from traveling, but to make it more costly to do so. The extreme case is the Republic of Korea (Korea), which until 1983 had forbidden its nationals to travel abroad for pleasure.

When the figures for travel account balances for selected Asia-Pacific countries are examined (figures 6.1 through 6.10), the countries showing a surplus on their travel accounts are the Philippines, Singapore, and Thailand. China and Hong Kong probably also have substantial surpluses in their travel accounts, although no data are available on travel expenditures for them. Korea's travel balance remains positive despite several recent years of deficits.

Historically, Indonesia, Malaysia, Australia, New Zealand, and Japan have run deficits in their travel accounts. In 1984 the three high-income countries—Australia, New Zealand, and Japan—accounted for more than 70 percent of all travel expenditures by the Asia-Pacific countries, but only 23 percent of the gross receipts.

Travel account deficits for high-income countries are to be expected, since their residents allocate high proportions of their incomes to leisure travel. Because of the substantial surplus in its trade account, this situation is hardly a matter for concern in Japan. However, in the case of Australia and New Zealand, deficits have been a problem, and at times both countries have imposed unpopular exchange controls on residents wishing to travel abroad. Recently these countries have vigorously

3. Taiwan also imposes an exit tax of US$100 to discourage overseas travel by its nationals.

Figure 6.1 International Account for Tourism for Singapore: 1967–1986

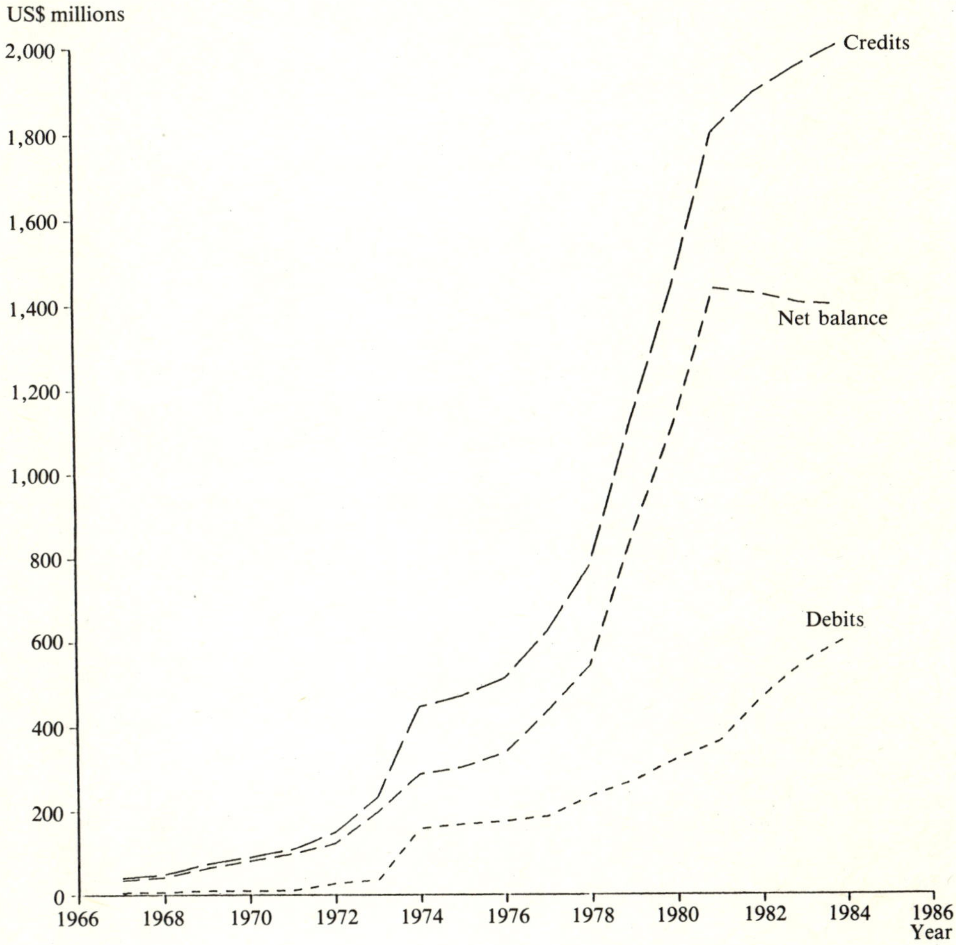

Figure 6.2 International Account for Tourism for Japan: 1967–1986

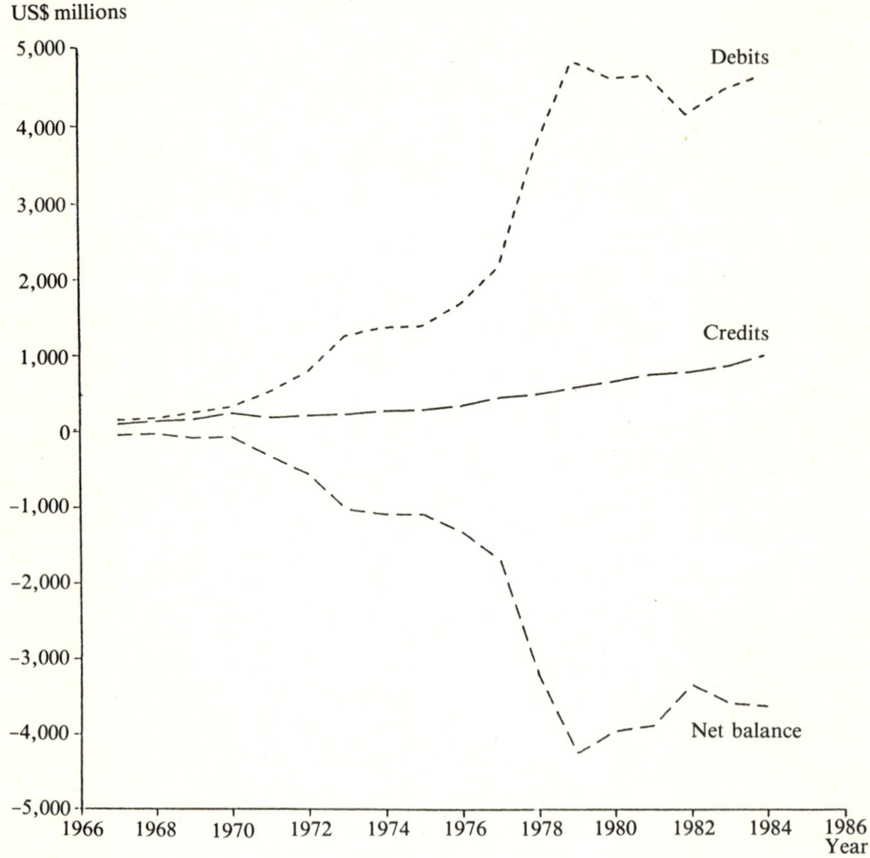

Figure 6.3 International Account for Tourism for Korea: 1967–1986

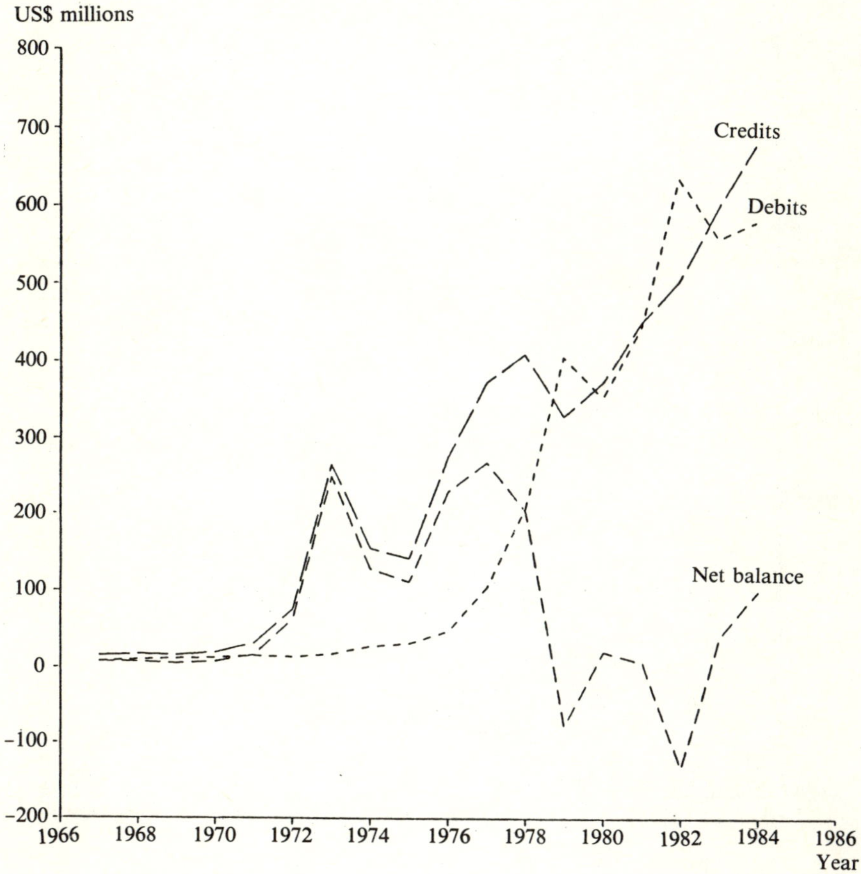

Figure 6.4 International Account for Tourism for Philippines: 1967–1986

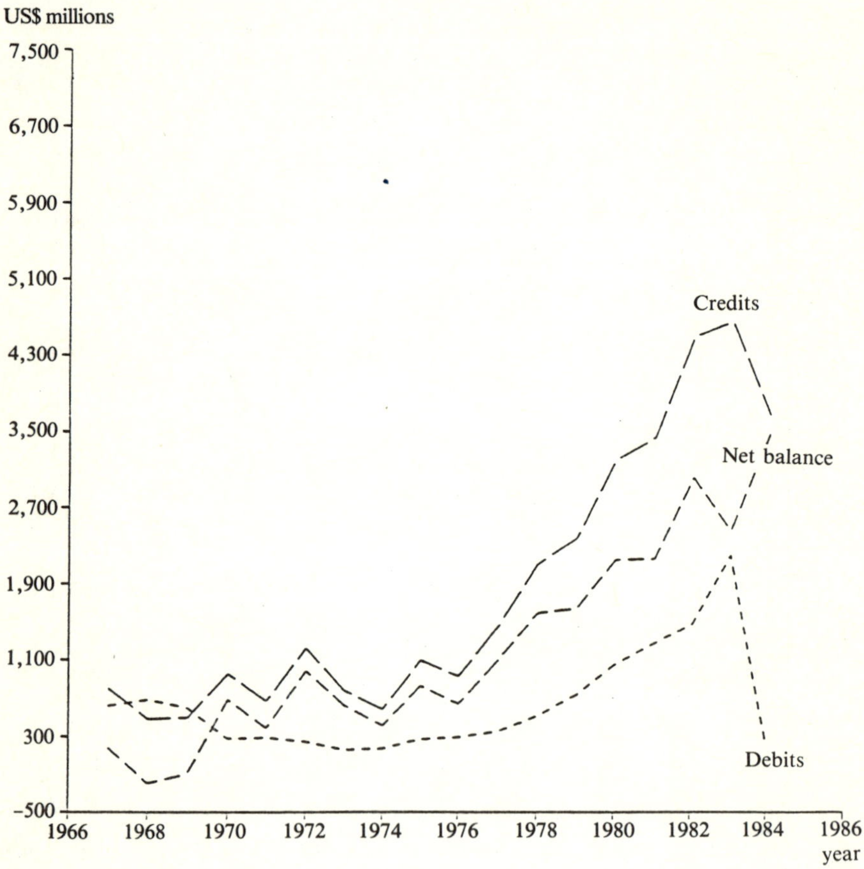

Figure 6.5 International Account for Tourism for Thailand: 1967–1986

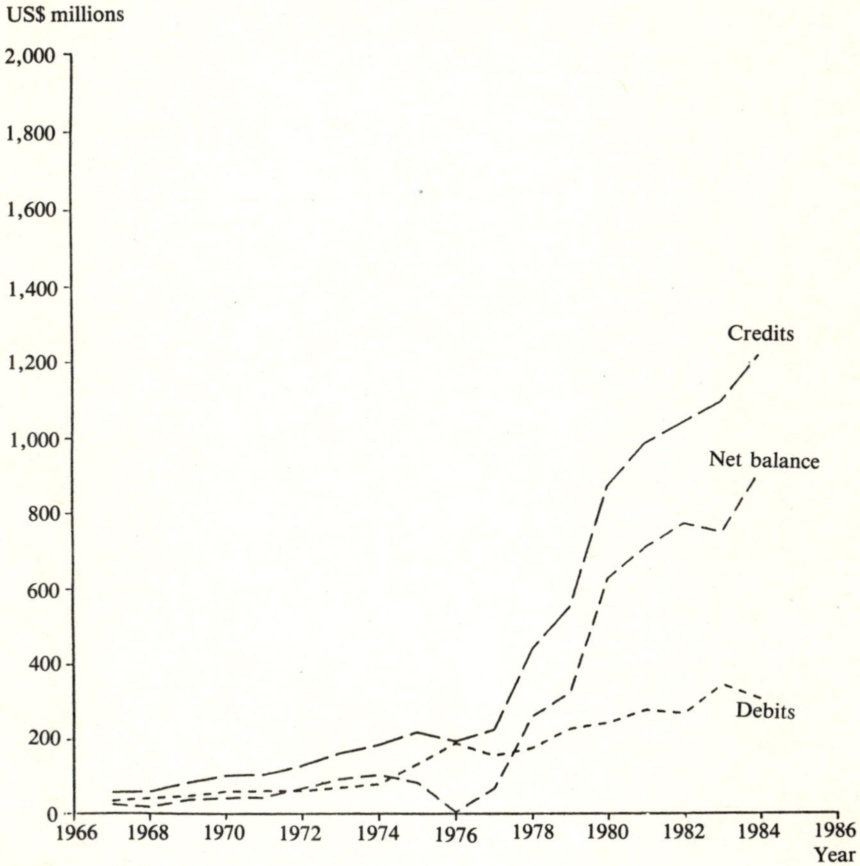

Figure 6.6 International Account for Tourism for Australia: 1967–1986

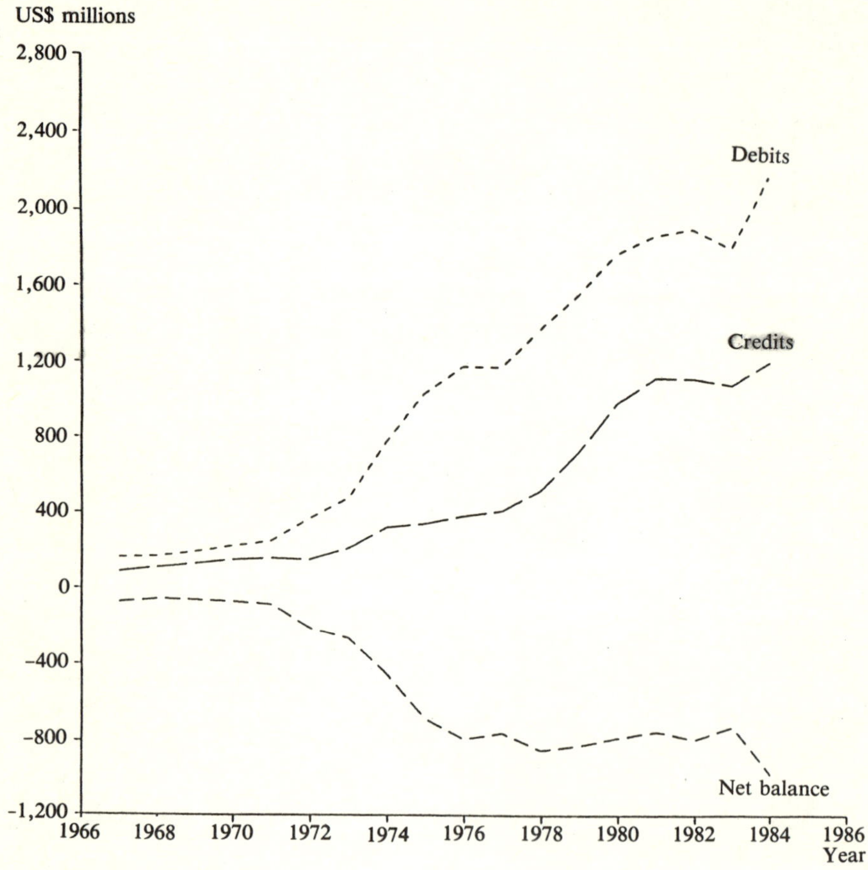

Figure 6.7 International Account for Tourism for New Zealand: 1967–1986

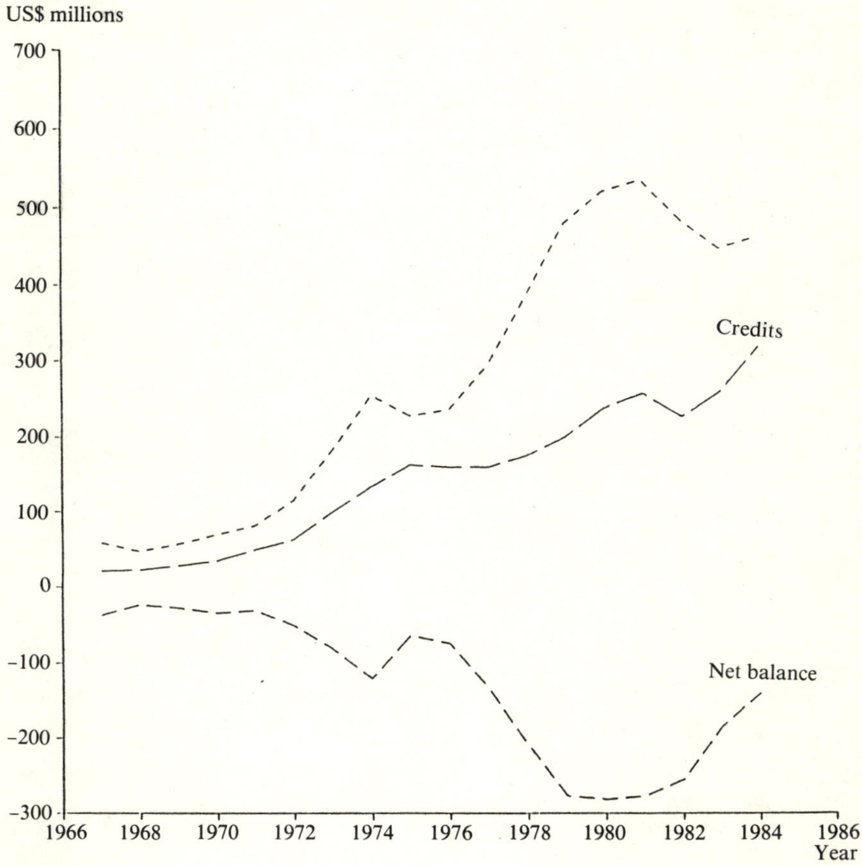

Figure 6.8 International Account for Tourism for Indonesia: 1967–1986

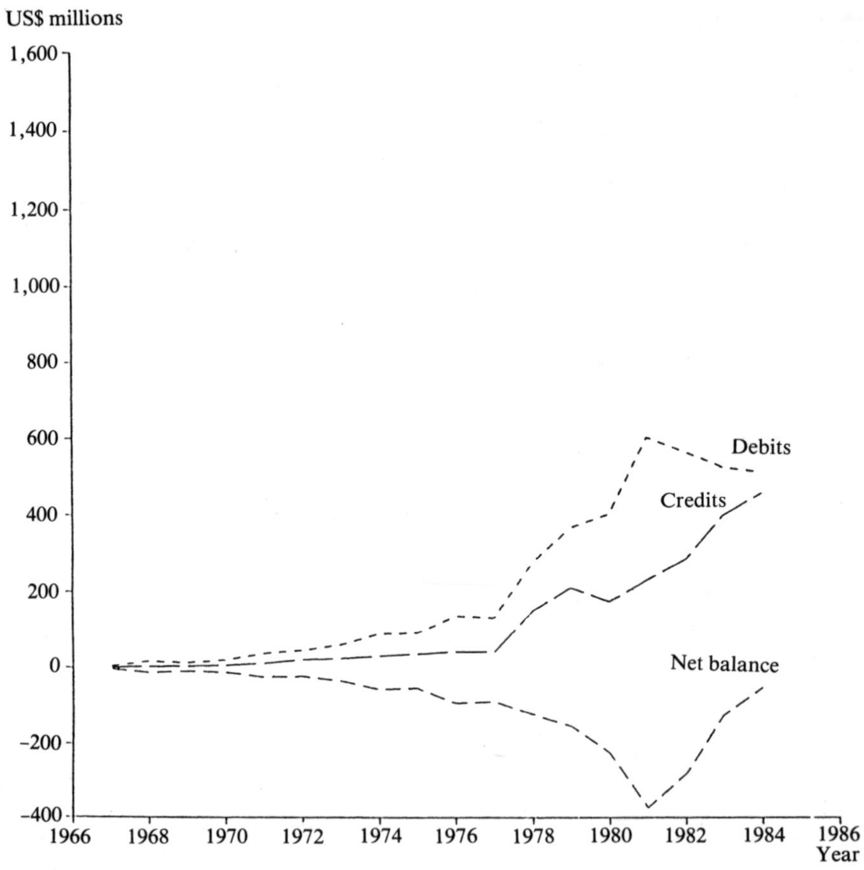

Figure 6.9 International Account for Tourism for Malaysia: 1967–1986

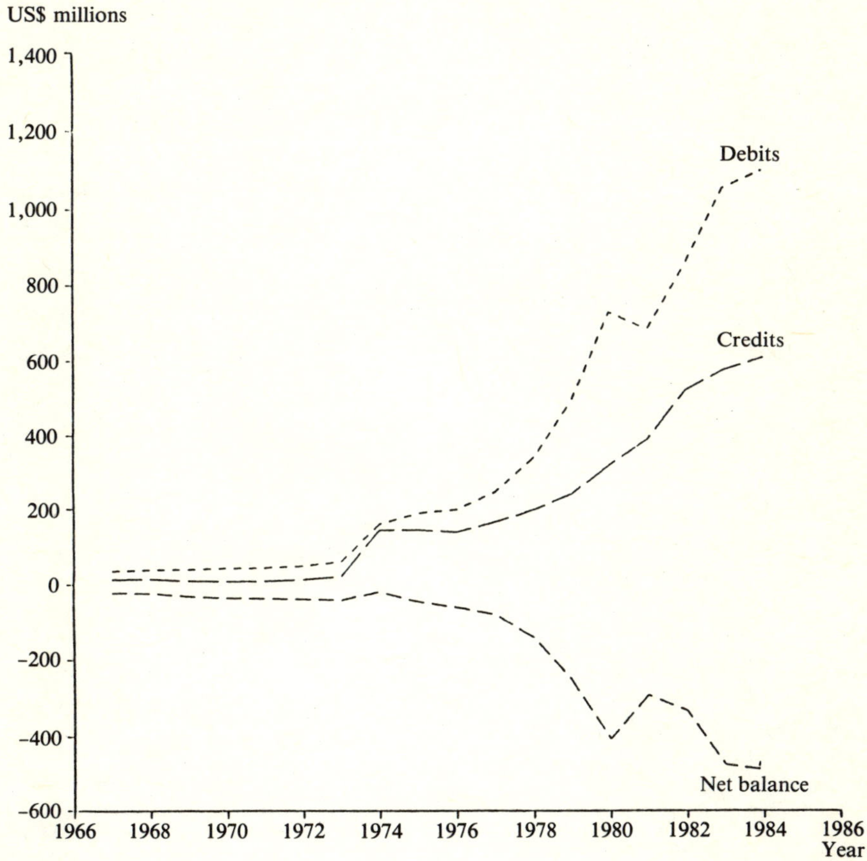

Figure 6.10 International Account for Tourism for Taiwan: 1967–1986

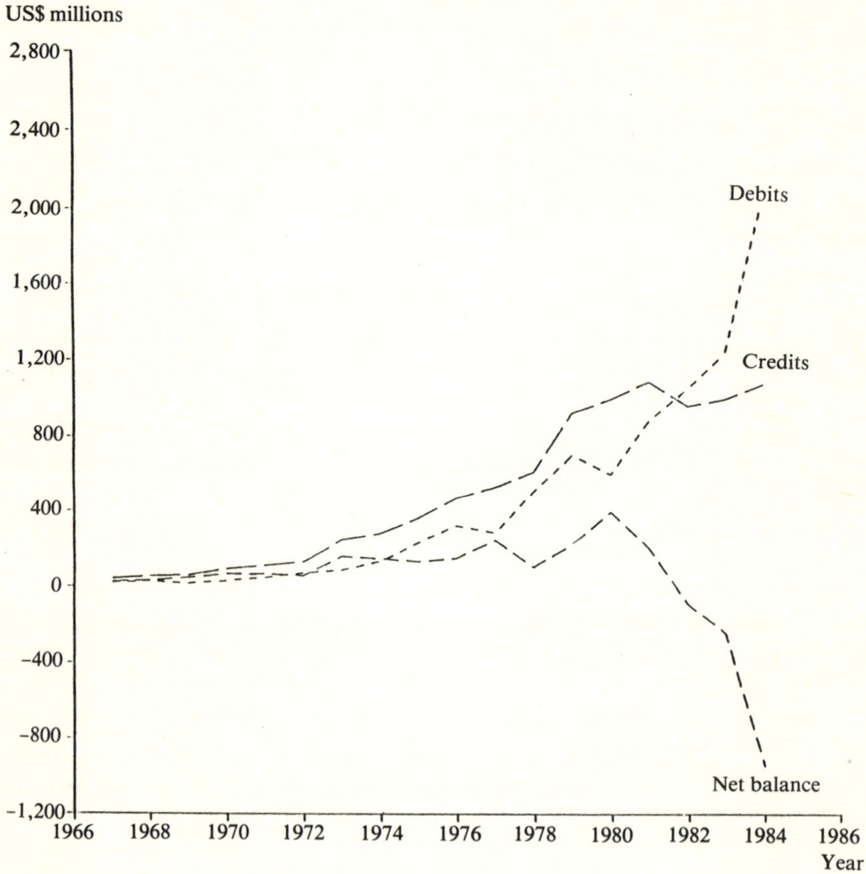

sought U.S. tourists. Currency devaluations have made travel to both countries much cheaper for Americans, and if airfares were to fall as they have on Atlantic routes, it is conceivable the present deficits could be reversed for both countries.

It is more difficult to explain the travel account deficits for Indonesia and Malaysia. Because both are Moslem countries, the underlying reasons for their travel deficits must include a substantial amount of travel for pilgrimages. For Malaysia, 38.4 percent of the travel payments in 1985 went for higher education abroad.

In November 1982 Indonesia imposed a stiff exit tax of Rp 150,000 (about US$140) on residents traveling abroad. In the following year, Indonesian arrivals in Singapore fell from 455,000 to 296,000. Although this has helped reduce Indonesia's travel account deficit, it has correspondingly reduced Singapore's travel earnings from abroad.

Taiwan, a country with persistent travel account surpluses through the 1970s, now has a deficit. With a healthy trade surplus in 1979, Taiwan eased some restrictions on resident overseas travel. However, due to the concern over accelerating overseas travel expenditures, it quickly reimposed a prohibition against Taiwanese travel in which Hong Kong and Macau were the first destinations on pleasure trips. As a result, Manila became the usual first destination before travelers continued on to Hong Kong.

Despite the eased travel restrictions, Taiwanese males of military age are still prohibited from making overseas pleasure trips. Another obstacle to overseas travel is the growing political isolation of Taiwan, which has made it difficult for Taiwan passport holders to gain entry visas to many countries. Foreign nationals also have difficulty obtaining the mandatory visas to visit Taiwan. Nevertheless, there was a sharp rise in overseas travel expenditures in the 1980s, causing a growing travel-account deficit. The opening of China to international tourism in 1978 has also contributed to this deficit by diverting tourist traffic away from Taiwan.

Among the countries enjoying travel account surpluses, Korea and the Philippines face considerable uncertainty. In the case of the Philippines, travel receipts and arrivals as well as expenditures have fallen since 1980 as a result of the political turmoil.

Korea's travel account has shown an erratic pattern, which is only partially explained by its occasional political disturbances. Because of rapid growth in travel to Korea, which was initiated by the normalization of relations with Japan in the early 1960s and restrictions imposed by the Korean government against nationals' traveling abroad for leisure, Korea experienced hefty travel surpluses through the 1960s and early 1970s. Due to the assassination of its president in 1979 and the ensuing imposition of martial law with the attendant negative publicity, which reduced foreign demand for travel to Korea, the surpluses have vanished.

In 1983 the Korean government began allowing exit tourist (i.e., pleasure trip) visas to be issued to those 50 years of age or older. However, applicants must deposit 2 million won (over US$2,200) that can only be withdrawn after one year in a local bank, and travel is restricted to one trip per year. Despite this liberalization, only one-half of 1 percent of Korean travel abroad in 1984 (2,576 travelers) was for pleasure, whereas 36 percent was for employment. By contrast, more than 80 percent of Japanese travel abroad is for pleasure. As the Korean trade position improves, it might be expected that the increased prosperity would permit Korea to follow the path of Japan in international travel. However, further liberalization is not foreseen until the 1988 Olympics at the earliest. Until then, there will be no repeat of the Japanese saga in Korean international tourism.

From a balance of payments perspective, the success stories are Singapore, Thailand, Hong Kong, and China. All four countries depend heavily on their tourist industries to generate much-needed foreign exchange. Among the Asia-Pacific countries, Singapore has the highest level of travel receipts, exceeding US$2 billion in 1984. Nearly 3 million visitor arrivals were recorded in 1984 (excluding Malaysian citizens arriving by land), against only 480,000 Singapore residents traveling abroad. Nevertheless, with no travel restrictions imposed on its residents (as in Hong Kong), Singapore has one of the highest departure rates for residents of any Asia-Pacific country, with one departure per six residents. This ratio is exceeded only by Hong Kong, which has a departure rate of one for every five residents (excluding visits to China). Singapore's high departure rate is almost certainly due, as with Hong Kong, to its small size, and its proximity to neighboring countries.

In sum, our survey finds that since the 1970s the Asia-Pacific region has experienced the fastest rate of tourism growth in the world. Much of this can be traced to the growing number of Asia-Pacific residents visiting other Asia-Pacific destinations. The usual explanations can be offered for this development: rapid regional economic growth, which has stimulated demand for both business and pleasure travel; an increase in leisure time available to Asia-Pacific residents; the advent of jet travel in the Pacific, which has reduced both the money and time cost of travel, particularly for insular countries such as Japan, Taiwan, Hong Kong, the Philippines, Australia, New Zealand, and the South Pacific island nations; and the introduction of the wide-body jet in the

1970s, which led to the development of the mass-marketed package tours demanded by Japanese travelers. Another key factor was the easing of various travel restrictions among the Asia-Pacific countries. Two events were particularly important in stimulating tourism in the region. One was the decision made by China in 1978 to open its doors to international tourism; the other was the series of decisions made by Japan to ease monetary restrictions on overseas travel by its nationals beginning in 1964, which produced a flood of Japanese travel abroad.

Japan in Asia-Pacific Tourism

After lifting restrictions on overseas travel in 1964, the Japanese government began raising the limit on the amount of currency that could be taken abroad. Between 1964 and 1968, the government allowed each Japanese traveler to take out US$500 for tourism. In 1969 the allowance was raised to US$700 and in 1970 to US$1,000.

At approximately the same time, from 1965 until 1973, when the first energy crisis dampened the demand for tourism, the rate of growth of Japanese outbound travel averaged 40 percent per year, rising from 160,000 to nearly 2.3 million (table 6.8). In 1965, 28 percent of total Japanese travel abroad was for pleasure. By 1969 the proportion of pleasure travel to total travel exceeded one-half (52 percent). The peak was reached in 1973, when 89 percent of all Japanese travel overseas was for pleasure.

The rapid growth in outbound travel was not entirely due to the easing of monetary restrictions; growth of income and leisure time were also important. The introduction of wide-body jets in 1970 made discounted fares for group travel available, and by the early 1970s tour costs to most destinations were reduced to nearly half their 1965 prices. Moreover, the greater buying power resulting from the revaluation of the yen in 1971 increased the Japanese demand for leisure travel. But it was primarily the lifting of monetary restraints that enabled the Japanese to satisfy their demand for overseas travel.

Although the rate of growth of departures slowed after 1973, further easing of monetary restrictions in 1975, 1976, and 1978 fueled the growth of travel expenditures. The easing of restrictions in the 1970s was clearly seen as the preferred response to the mounting external pressure to revalue the yen upward to stem the widening trade deficit between Japan and its major trading partners, especially the United States. In 1975 the government raised the currency limit for international travel to ¥30,000 and US$1,500. In the following year the limit

Table 6.8 Japan Tourism Data, 1964–1984

Year	Arrivals	Departures	Receipts (US$ millions)	Expen-ditures (US$ millions)	Balance (US$ millions)
1964	352,832	127,749	62	78	-16
1965	366,649	158,827	70	87	-17
1966	432,937	212,409	77	117	-40
1967	476,771	267,538	92	147	-55
1968	519,004	343,542	126	167	-41
1969	608,744	492,880	148	241	-93
1970	854,419[a]	663,467	232[a]	315	-83
1971	660,715	961,135	172	310	-337
1972	723,744	1,392,045	201	775	-573
1973	784,691	2,288,966	209	1,251	-1,043
1974	764,246	2,335,530	235	1,358	-1,123
1975	811,672	2,466,326	252	1,367	-1,115
1976	914,772	2,852,584	313	1,664	-1,351
1977	1,028,140	3,152,431	425	2,152	-1,727
1978	1,038,875	3,525,110	470	3,717	-3,247
1979	1,112,606	4,038,298	554	4,810	-4,256
1980	1,316,632	3,909,333	644	4,593	-3,949
1981	1,583,043	4,006,388	735	4,616	-3,883
1982	1,793,164	4,086,138	754	4,116	-3,362
1983	1,968,461	4,232,246	825	4,428	-3,603
1984	2,110,346	4,658,833	970	4,608	-3,638

Note: a. Osaka Exposition.
Source: Japan Ministry of Transportation, 1985a.

was raised again to ¥100,000 and US$3,000. By 1978 Japanese overseas travelers could take out an unlimited amount of foreign bank notes and traveler's checks. In table 6.8, the big jump seen in the travel account deficit between 1977 and 1978 can be attributed to the government's elimination of foreign exchange restrictions on travel. Japanese travel expenditures quickly exceeded half of all international travel expenditures by residents of Asia-Pacific countries, excluding overseas transportation payments.

However, a broader view must be taken of the definition of overseas travel expenditures by Japanese residents. For example, throughout 1986 a number of hotels in Hawaii were purchased by Japanese interests. Earlier acquisitions included major golf courses. Thus it is clear that a significant portion of Japanese tourist expenditures in

Hawaii may flow back to Japan and appear as a credit in the current account. In fact, the Japanese owners of these hotels and golf courses also receive a substantial amount of their business from American tourists. Japanese investments in Hawaii have lately gone beyond the hotel and golfing businesses. A Japanese company recently announced the purchase of the entire Burger King franchise in Hawaii.

No detailed data are readily available as to the amount of money Japanese travelers spend in each country. Data on the destinations of Japanese travelers indicate that in 1966 about 40 percent of overseas visits were to Asia (including South Asia) and the Pacific, increasing to 46 percent by 1984.[4]

On the receiving end, Japan's travel receipts compare favorably with other Asia-Pacific countries (table 6.7). In Japan's case, arrivals and receipts grew much more slowly than departures and travel expenditures. The principal reason is the relatively high cost of travel to Japan. In 1968 nearly half of all foreign arrivals were high-income Americans (accounting for 56 percent of total travel receipts); Asia-Pacific residents constituted less than 30 percent of the total. By 1983 the percentages had reversed.

Despite the large number of Japanese traveling abroad, the proportion of the Japanese population traveling internationally remains surprisingly small compared to the other Asia-Pacific countries. In 1984 Japan recorded one departure for every 26 residents (table 6.9), a rate that is roughly equal to that of Taiwan. However, Taiwan has a per capita income that is only one-third the size of Japan's, and Taiwan continues to impose restrictions on its nationals desiring to travel abroad. Two other countries with incomes comparable to that of Japan, Australia and New Zealand, have rates of departure two to three times as high as Japan's. This comparison suggests that, with some encouragement, there is little reason to doubt that Japan could easily raise (and perhaps even double) its rate of overseas travel in the near future.

What about the other countries in the region? There is considerable room for the expansion of leisure travel from the other East and Southeast Asian countries. For Japan and Hong Kong, more than 80 percent of overseas travel at present is undertaken for pleasure; for Singapore, the percentage is 55 percent (1984), with another 26 percent traveling for business and pleasure. For the remaining countries, the share of pleasure travel is significantly less than 50 percent: Taiwan recorded 42

4. The 46 percent is based on destinations visited, not the number of travelers. Statistics compiled by the Ministry of Justice showed that 52.7 percent of Japanese travelers went to Asia (including South Asia) and the Pacific in 1984 (Japan 1985a:8).

Table 6.9 Departures Among Selected Asia-Pacific Countries

Country	GNP per capita (US$)	1984 population (millions)	Number of departures in 1984	Ratio of departures to population
Japan	10,474	120.02	4,660,000	1:25.8
Hong Kong	5,937	5.36	1,140,000	1:4.7
Taiwan	3,042	19.01	750,000	1:25.3
Philippines	607	53.17	703,000	1:75.6
Korea	1,999	40.58	470,000	1:86.3
Singapore	705	2.52	450,000	1:5.2
Thailand	806	50.40	508,000	1:99.2
Malaysia	2,088	15.19	—	—
Indonesia	506	159.85	297,000	1:538.2
Australia	11,078	15.54	1,400,000	1:11.1
New Zealand	7,076	3.23	380,000	1:8.5

Sources: GNP and population data were obtained from the IMF. See notes to table 6.7 for data on visitor departures.

percent (1983), the Philippines had 23 percent (1983), and Korea had only 0.5 percent (1984). Comparable statistics are unavailable for Indonesia, Malaysia, Thailand, and China, but it is likely they also lie well below the 50-percent mark. For Korea and Taiwan, the easing of travel restrictions would undoubtedly help increase leisure travel abroad. Nonetheless, we suspect that the principal deterrent to increased leisure travel by residents of most East and Southeast Asian countries is their low income rather than the restrictions many governments impose in some form on outbound travel.

Obstacles and Restrictions on International Tourism

In 1979 the OECD made a decision to examine the general subject of trade in services in order to identify and analyze the existing obstacles to the liberalization of trade in a number of services. As part of its review, a tourism committee was established to examine the existing obstacles to international tourism within the OECD (OECD 1984). The examination was governed by two main principles: First, international travel, whether it be for business or pleasure, should be considered a right, and not a privilege. This right was enunciated in the Universal Declaration of Human Rights and reaffirmed in the Declarations of the World Tourism Conferences in Manila (1980) and Acapulco (1982).

Second, the provision of services to the tourist before, during, and after arrival should be governed by the normal rules of commercial competition in accordance with the philosophy behind the OECD's two Codes of Liberalization. Any measure that gives advantage to the nationals or national enterprises of one country over another should be considered an obstacle, even if it does not have the effect of discouraging the tourist from traveling.

The Tourism Committee examined 40 different types of possible obstacles (see appendix A) and solicited responses from the 24 members of the OECD as well as Yugoslavia. In 19 cases, responses indicated that at least one country has created obstacles that at least one respondent rated as a substantial obstacle or distortion to competition, and 12 such obstacles were reported in more than two countries. (The responses were not individually reported for each country.)

The areas of greatest concern appear to be those relating to entry and exit restrictions imposed on visitors. The most important of these are (1) entry visa requirements for specific nationals that are intended to limit the growth of asylum applicants or illegal immigrant workers, and (2) currency restrictions on residents for balance of payments reasons. Currency restrictions on visitors was less frequently cited as a serious problem. This issue concerns restrictions on the importation and exportation of domestic currency even though no rationale has been provided to justify such restrictions.

Transportation—particularly by air—is one of the areas rated "high" in obstacles. All the OECD countries limit equity participation in their domestic airlines, partly because of the public utility aspect of air transportation and partly because of the security implications of national air carriers. Other concerns in air transportation include discriminatory landing rights and access to reservations systems. The last is often justified on the ground that these systems are the property of private enterprises, and as such are subject to commercial negotiation between private parties.

Finally, in a number of countries obstacles are placed on the employment of nonnationals (often justified on grounds of high national unemployment) and on the right of foreigners to establish and operate tourist businesses.

Overall, the OECD Tourism Committee came to the following conclusions:

> International tourism within the OECD area does not suffer excessively from discriminating obstacles, at least by comparison with other sectors....

> On the other hand, the sector covering the "facilitation categories"...[5] is still subject to substantial restrictions.
>
> Tourism, in spite of its importance, is still regarded as an adjunct and is affected by restrictions which are imposed upon it for the benefit of other spheres of governmental activities such as immigration control and labour policy, balance of payments improvements, etc. The image of tourism and its low position in the priorities of governments need to be substantially improved (p. 70).

It should be pointed out that the ratings of degrees of severity in the OECD study were subjective, and no formal analyses have been conducted to determine the extent to which any of the obstacles cited restricts travel or distorts economic efficiency in the OECD member countries.

No comparable survey exists for the Asia-Pacific countries, although the WTO regularly publishes a world directory of frontier formalities for a selected number of countries that focuses on those restrictions affecting the individual traveler—that is, passport and visa requirements; customs, health, and currency regulations; and transportation facilities (WTO 1986b). A survey among the Asia-Pacific countries similar to the OECD survey would probably reveal the presence of more serious obstacles among them than among the OECD member countries.

Prospects for Continued Growth in Tourism

During the past two decades, international tourism in the Asia-Pacific region has grown rapidly. Most of the growth can be traced to the increase in intraregional travel among residents of the Asia-Pacific countries. High rates of economic growth in the region, reduced travel costs brought about by the use of jet aircraft, and the increase in leisure time have combined to fuel the demand for international travel. Faced with a strong demand and healthy trade surpluses, a number of countries have eased exit travel and currency restrictions imposed on their own residents. The most notable case has been Japan, which now is the major tourism generator in the region. In addition, many of the developing countries in the region have seen tourism as a potential major source of foreign exchange earnings and have sought to increase their tourist trade by expanding tourist facilities and by easing and

5. See Cheklist of Types of Obstacles to International Tourism.

streamlining entry formalities. The salient case here is China, which opened its doors to international tourism in the late 1970s and now accounts for 40 percent of all visitor arrivals and more than 10 percent of the gross earnings in the entire region. The continued development of tourism in the Asia-Pacific region will depend on (1) the willingness of area governments to allow their nationals to travel freely abroad, (2) the continued growth of their respective economies, and (3) a more competitive airfare structure in the region.

Appendix

Checklist of Types of Obstacles to International Tourism

Obstacles affecting the individual intending to travel

Imposed by the home country:
- Currency restrictions imposed upon residents.
- Conditions and procedures for issue of travel documents.
- Customs allowances for returning residents.
- Restrictions on overseas travel.

Imposed by the host country:
- Currency restrictions imposed upon visitors.
- Entry visas, identity documents, limitations on duration of stay.
- Formalities concerning entry of motor vehicles, pleasure boats, or other craft.
- Formalities concerning applicability of drivers licenses, car insurance, and so on.
- Restrictions on acquisition of property by nonnationals (e.g., holiday flats).
- Taxes on international travelers.

Obstacles affecting companies providing services to facilitate travel (e.g., travel agents, tour operators)

- Limitations on foreign investment and equity participation.
- Restrictions on the establishment of foreign-owned entities (branches and subsidiaries).
- Requirements for qualifications for operating professionally that are either directly discriminatory or more difficult for non-nationals to meet.
- Restrictions on nonnational personnel and employment (e.g., visas, work permits).
- Difficulties in obtaining licenses to operate.
- Relevant restrictions on transfer of funds in and out of the country
- Restrictions on the ability of nonestablished foreign companies to solicit customers, advertise, or sell directly to clients without locally established intermediaries.
- Distinction in EEC countries between EEC and non-EEC nationals

with regard to the preceding items.

Obstacles affecting companies providing transportation
(e.g., airlines, railways, coach operators, cruise liners)

All obstacles listed earlier that affect companies providing services to facilitate travel.
Restrictions on nonnational airlines, coach operators, or cruise liners.
Limitations on movements of passengers by foreign airlines or cruise ships.
Discriminatory landing dues, taxes, or port charges.
Lack of reciprocal recognition of qualifications (e.g., for air crew, site guides, coach drivers).
Requirements for government employees to use national airlines and ferry services.
Discriminatory access to special terms from state enterprises (e.g., airlines, railways), including differential commissions.
Limitations on access to reservation systems.

Obstacles affecting companies providing reception facilities
(e.g., hotels, resorts, car-hire firms)

All obstacles listed previously that affect companies providing services to facilitate travel.
Restrictions on imports of essential goods.
Requirements for placing of contracts (e.g., for site development) with local enterprises.
Discriminatory tax regimes for foreign entrants (including tax holidays not available to nationals).
Restrictions on ownership by nonnationals (e.g., leasing only permitted) and problems related to security of tenure or repatriation of investments.
Limitation on access to reservations systems.

Other obstacles

Discriminatory regulations on health inspection and consumer protection.
Compulsory use of centralized governmental or municipal organizations or middlemen.

Source: OECD, 1984b.

PART III
NATIONAL ISSUES

OVERVIEW

CHAPTER 7
Sazanami on Japan's Trade and Investment in Services

Professor Sazanami discusses the recent internationalization of three Japanese service industries (finance, information and communication, and business services), impediments to trade and investment in services, and the factors accounting for their removal or reduction.

Although Japan experienced a steady annual deficit in its overall service account between 1980 and 1985, its trade in management and technology increased significantly during the same period. According to Sazanami, this reflects the rapid internationalization of Japanese business activities, Japan's increasing demand for technology from its U.S. suppliers, and its increasing role as a supplier of technology to the developing countries in Asia.

In analyzing the liberalization process of the service industries, she points out the importance of foreign pressure. But, she adds, the process proceeded more rapidly when there were strong domestic forces favoring deregulation of the industries concerned. Interestingly, such forces arose in industries that contained a number of firms with experience in less regulated markets abroad. The effect of this foreign experience, which is usually overlooked in the analysis of the effects of open economies, may be as important for the country's economic growth and welfare as the commonly specified effects of trade, investment, and technology transfer.

Sazanami sees Japan's export of services steadily increasing over time as its financial resources accumulate further and as technological innovations continue in the information and communications industry.

She also sees increasing liberalization of service industries throughout the region, as other countries draw lessons from the experiences of Japan.

CHAPTER 8
Chung on the Liberalization of the Korean Capital Market

Chung presents a history of capital-market liberalization in Korea and reviews various arguments in favor of and against the liberalization.

The "Long-Range Internationalization Plan for Securities Market" announced by the Korean government in January 1981 stipulates a four-step reform over a ten-year period. The government has already implemented the first step of the reform, allowing indirect foreign investment through international investment trusts, and according to its plan the capital market should be completely liberalized by the end of the ten-year period. Chung argues that capital-market liberalization has been forced by the United States, which he claims is losing its comparative advantage in manufacturing industries, and by such internal factors as the necessity to finance Korea's huge external debt service payment and attempts by business firms to reduce their high debt-equity ratio.

Chung advocates a slow pace of liberalization on the grounds that Korea lacks the prerequisites for liberalization. He points out that in Korea foreign exchange transactions are restricted and the domestic financial market has yet to be fully liberalized. He questions the wisdom of liberalizing the capital market when foreign exchange and financial transactions are not yet completely liberalized. However, he argues that active measures should be taken to satisfy these prerequisites in a timely manner.

CHAPTER 7
Japan's Trade and Investment in Finance, Information, Communications, and Business Services

Yoko Sazanami

In the past three decades the service sector in the Japanese economy has expanded rapidly.[1] Although there was a minor setback in 1974, the rate of increase in the index of service production has continued to grow, exceeding that in the index of industrial production. Thus, by 1982 the service sector accounted for 59.4 percent of the gross domestic product and 57.7 percent of total employment. Although the two oil crises of the 1970s brought about an actual decline in the index of industrial production, they merely slowed down the rate of growth in the index of service production (table 7.1 and figure 7.1). Contributing to this sustained growth, especially after the second oil crisis, were finance and insurance, communications, and business services.

Faced with a depressed demand for manufactured products after the two oil crises, Japanese firms refrained from investing in real capital equipment and instead put their funds into the financial market. In addition, the change in the age composition of the Japanese population, which showed a rapid increase in the proportion of elderly citizens (reflecting greater life expectancy), affected the financial market in two ways. First, there was growth in pension funds that required banking services. Second, there was a growing demand for insurance to cover postretirement needs. This increasing flow of funds to financial markets was the primary force stimulating the growth of the finance and insurance industries. Furthermore, the decline in the cost of financial operations brought about by the introduction of computerized office equipment and the liberalization of financial markets increased business opportunities. The opportunity

1. Service industries include public utilities, transportation and communications, wholesale and retail trade, restaurants, finance and insurance, real estate, public services, and other services.

Table 7.1 Weighted Averages of Industrial Activity in Services

	Indices of industrial activity[a]		Rate of growth
Service Industry	1979	1985	1979/1985
Finance and insurance	90.3	157.3	74.2
Business services[b]	93.1	138.4	48.7
Communications	95.8	126.9	32.5
Public utilities	98.3	120.1	22.2
Wholesale and retail trade	96.5	115.8	20.0
Public services	97.2	115.6	18.9
Personal services	97.9	116.4	18.9
Real estate	99.9	111.0	15.3
Transportation	98.1	113.1	11.1
Total services	96.3	119.5	24.1

Notes: a. 1980 = 100.
b. Includes leasing, broadcasting, and advertising.

Source: Japan, MITI, 1986. "Daisanji Sangyo Katsudo Shisu" (Trends in Industrial Activity in Services).

to invest in foreign high-yield financial assets also stimulated the business of security and insurance companies and banks.

In communications there was a rapid introduction of new information services, for example, on-line systems such as Value Added Network (VAN). The emergence of these services, together with technological advances that decreased their cost, expanded demand for communications services. Indeed, as mentioned earlier, the increase in demand for financial services was brought about in large measure by the use of advanced communications networks that enabled the swift transfer of funds at low cost. Another industry that expanded significantly was business services, that is, leasing, broadcasting, and advertising (figure 7.1), whose development is also closely tied to improvements in communications systems technology.

Technological change in communications systems and the increase in the supply of funds to financial markets boosted demand for financial services and for new business services. These factors all contributed to the sustained growth of these service industries in recent years even when the manufacturing sector was slow in recovering from the second oil crisis.

Figure 7.1 Index of Industrial Activity in Services (1980 = 100)

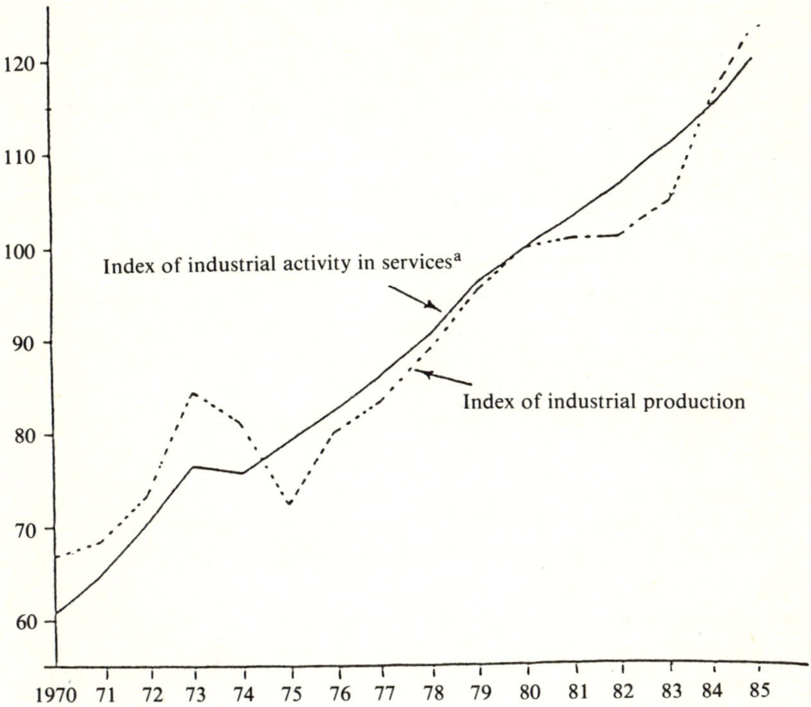

Note: a. Increase in industrial activity index between 1979 and 1985.
Source: Table 7.1.

Japan as an Exporter and Importer of Services

The amount of Japan's trade in services is about one-fifth its trade in merchandise.[2] Unlike trade in merchandise, in which the surplus has increased from US$2.1 billion to US$56 billion between 1980 and 1985, trade in services has shown a stable annual deficit of around US$12 billion during this period (table 7.2). In other words, while Japan was becoming a large net exporter of merchandise, it remained a stable net importer of services through the mid-1980s. The only area in services showing a surplus was official services; most of the other areas showed deficits.

2. Based on export and import totals.

Although the total deficit in services remained almost unchanged between 1980 and 1985, there was a change in the composition of services traded. A decline occurred in both exports and imports of transportation, reflecting the depressed demand for ocean shipping, whereas the trade in other private services increased substantially. Among the private services that increased in both exports and imports were management fees and patent licensing fees and royalties. In other items, such as agent fees, advertising, and tourism, Japan remained a stable net importer.

Causes of the Increase in the Receipt and Payment of Management Fees

The rapid internationalization of Japanese business activities was the primary cause for increased payment and receipt of management fees. The active involvement of Japanese firms in direct investment in manufacturing as well as in financial markets is reflected in the rise in investment income shown in table 7.2.

Net receipts of direct investment income increased from US$0.81 billion in 1980 to US$1.71 billion in 1985. Moreover, net receipts of interest on trade credit, loans, and bonds reached US$2.06 billion in the same year. The increase in the importance of investment income suggests that the role of Japan in international transactions is gradually shifting from that of a net supplier of merchandise to a supplier of capital, managerial skills, and technology. Since trade in services more frequently accompanies direct investment than trade in merchandise, the increase in Japan's investment in the 1980s is likely related to the increase in the importance of service transactions during this period.

The accumulated total of Japanese direct investment almost doubled from March 1981 to March 1985 (table 7.3). There was a sharp decline in investment directed to primary industry after 1981 and a rise in investment in services, construction, and real estate. Concurrently, investment in manufacturing continued to expand, with approximately US$2.5 billion being invested every year.

The most notable changes taking place in Japanese direct investment in the early 1980s were the increased investment in finance and insurance and the sharp decline in investment in primary industry. Faced with a sudden rise in crude oil prices in 1973 and a subsequent increase in energy prices, there was a strong inclination in Japanese business circles to invest in resource development. Japanese managers also sought to shift resource processing to foreign locations where energy prices were low.

Table 7.2 Japanese Exports and Imports of Services, Investment Income and Merchandise (US$ billions)

Items	1980			1981			1982			1983			1984			1985		
	Export	Import	Balance	Export	Import	Balance	Export	Import	Balance	Export	Import	Balance	Export	Import	Balance	Export	Import	Balance
Transportation[a]	13.0	17.3	-4.3	15.4	18.5	-3.1	13.3	16.7	-3.4	12.2	15.5	-3.3	12.9	15.9	-3.0	12.4	15.1	-2.7
Travel	0.6	4.6	-4.0	0.7	4.6	-3.9	0.8	4.1	-3.3	0.8	4.4	-3.6	1.0	4.6	-3.6	1.1	4.8	-3.7
Other private services[b]	5.3	10.4	-5.1	6.0	13.4	-7.4	6.4	13.2	-6.8	6.7	13.9	-7.2	7.1	14.5	-7.4	7.2	15.1	-7.9
Official services	1.5	0.3	1.2	2.0	0.3	1.7	2.3	0.3	2.0	2.3	0.3	2.0	2.5	0.3	2.2	2.7	0.4	2.3
Services total	20.4	32.5	-12.1	24.0	36.9	-12.9	22.8	34.3	-11.5	22.0	34.2	-12.2	23.4	35.4	-12.0	23.4	35.4	-12.0
Merchandise total	126.7	124.6	2.1	149.5	129.6	19.9	137.7	119.6	18.1	145.5	114.0	31.5	168.3	124.0	44.3	174.0	118.0	56.0
Investment income	11.1	10.3	0.8	15.8	16.5	-0.7	18.3	16.6	1.7	15.6	12.5	3.1	18.8	14.5	4.3	22.1	15.3	6.8

Notes: Direct investment is based on reports to the Ministry of Finance and does not coincide with the balance of payments figures.

a. Includes freight, insurance on international shipment, port disbursements, passenger fares, time charters, ocean vessels, and aircraft.

b. Includes management fees, patent and royalties fees, agents' fees, nonmerchandise, insurance, advertising, and film rentals.

c. Includes direct investment income, interest on trade credits, and interest on loans and bonds.

Source: Bank of Japan, "Monthly Balance of Payments."

Table 7.3 Japanese Direct Investment in Primary, Manufacturing, and Service Industries in Fiscal Years (April-March) 1981 and 1985[a]

	World total				North America				Europe				Asia			
	FY 1981 total		FY 1985 total		FY 1981 total		FY 1985 total		FY 1981 total		FY 1985 total		FY 1981 total		FY 1985 total	
Sector	US$	%	US$	%	US$	%	US$	%	US$	%	US$	%	US$	%	US$	%
Primary[b]	7,981	21.8	12,859	18.0	832	8.4	1,236	5.7	861	19.2	865	9.5	3,309	33.6	6,219	34.4
Manufacturing	12,573	34.4	22,048	30.8	2,428	24.7	6,483	30.1	844	18.8	1,765	19.4	4,571	46.5	7,057	39.1
Service	13,643	37.4	26,863	37.6	5,846	59.6	10,376	48.3	2,622	58.6	4,965	54.7	1,752	17.8	3,410	18.9
Commerce	5,409	14.8	11,128	15.9	3,493	35.6	6,645	30.9	817	18.2	2,076	22.8	401	4.0	922	5.1
Finance and insurance	2,426	6.6	7,054	9.8	951	9.7	2,729	12.7	822	18.3	2,742	30.2	286	2.7	613	3.4
Other services[c]	5,808	15.9	4,021	5.6	1,402	14.3	958	4.4	988	22.0	141	1.5	1,085	11.0	1,707	9.4
Transportation	—		4,660	6.5	—		44	0.2	—		6	0.0	—		168	0.9
Construction and real estate[d]	2,300	8.3	9,661	13.5	692	7.0	3,374	15.7	144	3.2	1,477	10.2	198	2.0	1,341	7.1
Total	36,497	100	71,431	100	9,798	100	21,469	100	4,471	100	9,072	100	9,830	100	18,027	100

Table 7.3 Continues on the following page.

Table 7.3 Continued

Sector	Latin America				Middle East				Africa				Oceania			
	FY 1981 total		FY 1985 total		FY 1981 total		FY 1985 total		FY 1981 total		FY 1985 total		FY 1981 total		FY 1985 total	
	US$	%	US$	%	US$	%	US$	%	US$	%	US$	%	US$	%	US$	%
Primary[b]	1,385	22.4	1,678	12.8	42	1.8	190	6.4	529	36.6	657	20.5	1,023	40.5	1,480	39.8
Manufacturing	2,781	45.0	4,236	32.5	1,064	47,1	1,257	42.9	96	6.6	211	8.5	789	31.2	1,040	27.9
Service	1,819	29.4	5,729	44.0	112	5.0	112	3.8	798	55.2	1,530	47.8	688	27.2	741	19.9
Commerce	437	7.0	957	7.3	10	0.4	15	0.5	3	0.2	7	0.2	248	9.8	506	13.6
Finance and insurance	298	4.7	781	5.9	25	1.1	91	3.1	2	0.1	3	0.0	62	2.4	96	2.5
Other services[c]	1,084	17.5	461	3.5	77	3.4	4	0.1	793	54.8	619	19.3	378	14.9	130	3.4
Transportation	—		3,530	27.1	—		2	0.0	—		901	28.1	—		9	0.2
Construction and real estate[d]	162	2.6	1,377	10.5	1,041	48.0	1,368	46.7	22	1.5	800	25.0	25	0.9	457	12.2
Total	6,167	100	13,020	100	2,259	100	2,927	100	1,445	100	3,198	100	2,525	100	3,718	100

Notes: Patent and royalty figures are from the prime minister's office and do not coincide with the balance of payment figures in table 4.2. The former are based on the total amount of payments and receipts reported by firms under patent, expertise and technological guidance. The data cover manufacturing. The balance of payment figure represents foreign exchange used for patent and royalty purposes.

a. US$ millions.

b. Primary industries include agriculture, forestry, fisheries, and mining.

c. Other services include personal service, leasing, car rental, broadcasting, advertising, hotels, movies, legal services, construction services, medical service, education, and academic research.

d. Also includes DFI not classified elsewhere.

Source: Figures on direct investment are based on reports to the Ministry of Finance and do not coincide with the balance of payment figures. Ministry of Finance "Monthly Fiscal and Monetary Statistics."

This trend continued until OPEC lost its grip on the market and oil prices began falling in the early 1980s. There was also a decline in the prices of other primary commodities, a sign of the slow recovery of industrial activity in developed countries during this period. Because of these changes, Japanese firms rapidly lost interest in investing in resource-related projects. Instead they turned to the financial markets, in which advances in computerized information and communications systems were creating a worldwide market for high-yield bonds.

Because of the growing demand for international financial services, Japanese banks and security companies found it necessary to open branches and subsidiaries to actively participate in foreign markets. The construction and real estate industries were also forced to invest abroad due to the sluggish activity in domestic construction and real estate markets during this period.

Direct investment in primary industry, which amounted to US$2.64 billion in 1981, dropped to US$747 million in 1982 and to US$417 million in 1983.[3] However, direct investment in finance and insurance doubled from US$533 million in 1982 to US$1.16 billion in 1983 and almost doubled again to US$2.08 billion in 1984. Direct investment in construction and real estate increased from US$619 million in 1981 to US$1.21 billion in 1985.

These changes in the industrial composition of Japan's direct investment in the early 1980s altered the regional distribution of business activities and the types of services offered. Japan's business activity decreased in goods production—primary commodities plus manufacturing—while it increased in the services sector.

Because the United States and other industrialized countries have more highly developed financial markets than do developing countries, almost 80 percent of direct investment in finance and insurance between 1981 and 1984 was made in North America and Europe. Consequently, the expansion in service-related business activities by Japanese firms increased direct investment to developed countries.

Elsewhere, the increase in investment in construction and real estate supported the continued expansion of direct investment to Asia.[4] The locational advantage for the development of resorts and hotels to meet Japanese tourist demand made these investments attractive. Thus, construction and real estate investment was related in part to the desire to increase the supply of hotel service in these countries in the future.

3. All direct investment figures in this section refer to the fiscal years 1981–1985.

4. This is particulary true in the cases of Hong Kong and Singapore. See JETRO, "White Paper on Direct Investment-1985" for details.

In the 1980s Japan paid and received more management fees because Japanese firms were actively joining the international markets, not only in merchandise trade but also in trade and investment in financial and other services. The active participation of Japanese firms in foreign financial markets and other service fields accelerated the liberalization of Japan's service markets in two ways. First, their experience in undertaking business in less regulated foreign markets made Japanese managers more keenly aware that domestic regulation was burdensome and prompted them to support deregulation. Secondly, foreign firms that saw Japanese firms profiting in less regulated markets while retaining vested interests at home began raising the reciprocity issue in an effort to open Japan's market in services, particularly financial services and communications. As liberalization proceeded in the 1980s an increase in foreign branch offices and subsidiaries in Japan generated a higher volume of management fees.

Table 7.4 Regional and Industrial Composition of Japan's Technology Exports (US$ millions)

	1978 Technology Exports[a]		
Industry	Asia	North America	World total
Chemicals	27.62	38.77	115.90
	(15.10)	(48.40)	(19.90)
Electrical equipment	27.62	12.34	50.56
	(15.10)	(15.40)	(8.70)
Machinery	—	6.97	6.97
		(8.70)	(1.20)
Transportation equipment	27.44	8.81	88.64
	(15.00)	(11.00)	(15.30)
Iron and steel	26.89	—	76.90
	(14.70)		(18.50)
Construction	15.18	—	132.09
	(8.30)		(26.70)
Ceramics	15.18	—	15.18
	(8.30)		(2.60)
Publishing and printing	15.18	—	15.18
	(8.30)		(2.60)
Other	27.80	13.22	79.59
	(15.20)	(16.50)	(13.70)
Regional totals	182.90	80.10	581.00[b]
	(100.00)	(100.00)	(100.00)

(*Table 7.4 continues on the following page.*)

	1983 Technology Exports[a]		
Chemicals	36.12	45.34	130.66
	(8.40)	(17.90)	(12.86)
Electrical equipment	75.68	48.89	131.11
	(17.60)	(19.30)	(12.90)
Machinery	25.37	10.90	39.97
	(5.90)	(4.30)	(3.93)
Transportation equipment	46.01	32.68	121.85
	(10.70)	(12.90)	(12.00)
Iron and steel	58.48	16.00	169.30
	(13.60)	(6.30)	(16.66)
Construction	50.74	—	114.48
	(11.80)		(11.26)
Ceramics	—	—	6.42
			(0.01)
Publishing and printing	—	—	—
Other	137.60	99.54	302.48
	(32.00)	(39.30)	(29.76)
Regional totals	430.0	253.3	1,016.30[b]
	(100.00)	(100.00)	(100.00)

Notes: a. Percentage of column total in parentheses.
b. Does not equal column total due to rounding.

Table 7.5 Regional and Industrial Composition of Japan's Technology Imports (US$ millions)

	1978 Technology Imports[a]	
Industry	North America	World total
Chemicals	73.94	133.40
	(12.40)	(14.60)
Electrical equipment	168.72	224.38
	(28.30)	(24.50)
Machinery	72.15	105.05
	(12.10)	(11.50)
Transportation equipment	141.92	199.78
	(23.80)	(21.80)
Iron and steel	29.22	29.66
	(4.90)	(3.20)
Ceramics	—	19.29
		(2.10)
Food	—	42.06
		(4.50)

(*Table 7.5 continues on the following page.*)

Nonferrous metals	—	.32
		(0.00)
Other	115.68	165.77
	(19.40)	(18.10)
Regional totals	596.30	914.40[b]
	(100.00)	(100.00)
	1983 Technology Imports[a]	
Chemicals	110.50	177.47
	(13.50)	(15.06)
Electrical equipment	304.48	387.69
	(37.20)	(32.90)
Machinery	78.58	119.93
	(9.60)	(10.18)
Transportation equipment	145.69	198.38
	(17.80)	(16.83)
Iron and steel	57.30	57.30
	(7.00)	(4.86)
Ceramics	—	—
Food	—	27.07
		(2.29)
Nonferrous metals	—	—
Other	121.96	210.17
	(14.90)	(17.84)
Regional totals	818.50	1,178.10[b]
	(100.00)	(100.00)

Notes: a. Percentage of column total in parentheses.
b. Does not equal column total due to rounding.

Causes of Increased Payments and Sales in Patent Licensing Fees and Royalties

Japan's technology exports almost doubled from US$578 million in 1978 to US$1.02 billion in 1983, and imports increased from US$915 million to US$1.18 billion during tnis period. As a result Japan decreased its trade deficit in technology trade in the early 1980s (tables 7.4 and 7.5).

The largest trading partners in Japan's technology trade were the United States in imports and Asia in exports. In 1978 Japan paid 65 percent of its patent licensing fees and royalties to the United States, and 28 percent of such payments were related to electrical machinery. The tendency to depend on the United States as the major supplier of technology, particularly in electrical machinery, became more pronounced in 1983, when almost 70 percent of patent fees and royalties were directed to the United States, and 37 percent of these payments were for electrical machinery. On the export side, Asia continued to be the major recipient of Japanese technology. In 1978, 40 percent of patent and royalty payments to Japan were from Asia, and the proportion increased to 49 percent in 1983. In 1983 Japan exported many types of industrial technologies, such as electrical machinery (17.6 percent), iron and steel (13.6 percent), and construction (11.8 percent) to Asia (excluding West Asia).

In the early 1980s Japan held an intermediary position in the field of technology trade, exporting technology to Asia and importing technology from the United States. Indeed, the heavy reliance of Asian countries on Japanese technology is evident from the fact that as much as 56.3 percent of the technology contracts made in Korea during the 1962–1983 period were with Japan, as were 65.5 percent of the contracts made in Taiwan between 1952 and 1983.[5] Only 23.1 percent and 21.4 percent of the technology contracts made in Korea and Taiwan respectively were with the United States during the same period.

Liberalization Issues in Japanese Trade and Investment in Services

The active participation of Japanese firms in a broad range of international markets, extending from investing in primary industries and manufacturing to services, resulted in calls for Japan to liberalize its own service industries. The firms and governments of other nations, particularly the United States, demanded the liberalization of services in Japan on the grounds that they should be allowed the same opportunities in Japan's service market as those enjoyed by Japanese firms at home and in the United States. These calls for liberalization, known in Japan as *gaiatsu* (foreign pressure), seem to be a historically necessary element in any liberalization process in Japan and have helped tip the balance in favor of deregulation. However, as in the

5. Technology contracts include management, joint ventures, technical services, patent fees, royalties, and engineering. See "Nihon to Hatten Tojo Koku to no Aida no Gijutsu Masatsu, Boeki Masatsu Mondai," Asia Development Institute, 1985.

liberalization of other industries, it was the strength of domestic forces—both in the public and in the affected service industries—that supported the change that determined how swiftly the liberalization process would proceed.

Japanese service industries such as banking and securities, communications, transportation, and legal services were highly regulated by various ministries and professional groups until the late 1970s (Alexander and Tan 1984). When foreign firms tried to enter the Japanese service market, they found that these regulations and informal business rules were a major impediment.

In most service industries Japan's liberalization of service trade came along with deregulation. Furthermore, the process of liberalization proceeded more rapidly in service industries that had a strong group supporting the deregulation. Although the government and sometimes the press frequently claimed that *gaiatsu* was the primary agent forcing Japan's service market to change, it was only one of the forces leading to deregulation and thus liberalization. A major domestic force favoring liberalization was exerted by the firms with operating experience in less regulated markets, such as banking and securities. Eventually these firms concluded that regulations were also limiting their own opportunities, not just those of the foreign competition.

In communications, the demand for new media made the old regulations obsolete and therefore led to deregulation and liberalization. In legal services, because the domestic institutions were firmly rooted in traditional legal philosophies favoring social consensus rather than court settlement, changes came more slowly.

Liberalization Issues in Financial Services

The liberalization issues in Japan's financial services involve three different but closely related problems: (1) the question of equal treatment for foreign financial institutions and their domestic counterparts (i.e., national treatment); (2) the issue of whether foreign financial institutions are given the same opportunities Japanese firms have in foreign markets (reciprocity); and (3) the claim that the closed state of the Japanese capital market impedes the flow of funds and the internationalization of the yen. This claim is based on the argument that the yen does not reflect the potential strength of the Japanese economy, a situation that leads to undervaluation of the yen (market efficiency).

The first issues were dealt with swiftly, and by the early 1980s national treatment problems had been largely eliminated. However, because the second and third issues are related to the alteration of

Table 7.6 Liberalization Issues in Japan's Financial Services

Type of trade	Forms of trade	Liberalization issues raised[a]	Type of issue
Transborder service trade	Holding accounts at foreign banks; foreign lending of domestic banks deposit and loan, trade-related settlements, and remittance.		
Direct investment-related service trade	Establishment of agents, subsidiaries, and branch offices.	Approval of issuance of bank debentures by commercial banks.	Market access
	Offering financial services, e.g., deposits and loans, foreign remittance, and other services.	Relaxation of conditions for issuing domestic certificates of deposit. Deregulation of interest rates on deposits.	National treatment
	Capital investment in domestic banks; takeovers and mergers.	Additional memberships to the Tokyo Stock Exchange. Relaxation of conditions for issuing yen-denominated foreign bonds.	Reciprocity
		Establishment and expansion of treasury bill market. Establishment of a market for bankers' acceptances.	Deregulation
		Relaxation of standards for qualification to issue Euroyen bonds. Establishment of an offshore market.	Market efficiency
Commercial presence-related service trade	Bank officers and staffs working in Japan. Specialists on foreign exchange dealings and other activities working in Japan.	Visas and work permits.	

Note: a. Mainly issues raised by foreign bank officials, U.S. government and EEC officials, as of 1988.
Sources: Alexander and Tan, 1984a, Japan Economic Research Institute 1984; various newspaper articles.

regulatory practices in Japan's financial system, the changes in these areas have been more gradual. As with any change in regulatory practice there was strong opposition from the groups that would lose their advantage. External pressure, such as the establishment of the Working Group of the Japan–United States Yen-Dollar Committee in 1983, helped focus attention on the issues and accelerated the liberalization process. Such issues as approval of certificates of deposit (May 1979), removal of the rule prohibiting membership in the Tokyo stock exchange (April 1982), and admittance of foreign banks to trust banking (May 1984) were gradually resolved. The issues remaining to be dealt with either involve relaxing the conditions of regulations or establishing systems that promote the efficiency of the financial market (table 7.6). Resolution of both issues will require alterations in the Japanese financial system, a task made formidable by the system's long history as well as public resistance to change. Any alterations will surely cause further discussion and require negotiations among domestic groups before liberalization can proceed.

The Japanese financial market in the postwar period was highly regulated with respect to interest rate determination, foreign exchange transactions, and services provided by different types of financial institutions. The primary purpose of these regulations was to ensure the supply of low-cost funds to a rapidly growing industrial sector. The regulatory protection offered to financial institutions, particularly to banks, insured the safety of bank deposits and attracted more personal savings in spite of low interest rates. The free play of market forces in financial services was severely restricted to promote saving and to direct needed funds to key industrial sectors during the period of high growth.

The economic conditions supporting the regulatory practices rapidly faded in the 1970s. As the rate of economic growth slowed after the first oil crisis, government had to finance the stimulation of the business recovery at a time when tax revenue was reduced by the slump. The government relied heavily on its own bond issues to replace lost tax revenues. Although the government lacked funds, the corporate sector was enjoying a surplus because of restrained investment in capital equipment due to the overcapacity caused by slow growth. Excess corporate funds were directed to the bond market, which was subsequently deregulated, allowing market forces to determine yields.

In the 1970s deregulation of financial markets, conventionally termed "financial innovation," was proceeding rapidly in the United States and in European countries. The computerization of financial transactions enabled the transmission of funds swiftly and at reduced cost between markets. It therefore became possible to incorporate certain bonds into high-yield assets. The increase in opportunities to trade in the financial markets abroad induced Japanese financial institutions to participate in international financial transactions.

Beginning in the late 1970s, profits of the international sections of Japanese banks grew at higher rates than those in their domestic sections.[6] The active participation of Japanese banks and security companies in deregulated financial markets abroad had a pronounced influence on the liberalization and deregulation of Japan's financial services. Japanese financial institutions gradually accumulated managerial skills and gained competitive strength by operating in deregulated markets and thus were prepared for the liberalization of their home market. As mentioned before, they even concluded that regulations limiting financial services provided by banks and security companies and foreign exchange controls restricting external capital flows were burdensome to their own business operations. In 1980 security companies were allowed to introduce a medium-term government bond fund that provided a service similar to bank deposits. The enactment of a new bank law in 1982 allowed commercial banks to deal in the government bonds. In this manner the regulations dividing the financial services provided by banks from those provided by security companies were gradually lessened. Foreign exchange restraints on capital flows were also relaxed by the end of 1980 and again in 1984 when the "real" demand rule was removed.[7]

Although deregulation and liberalization of Japan's financial markets has proceeded steadily, complaints are still heard from foreign financial institutions on the issue of reciprocity. Moreover, the large surplus in the Japanese current account has raised the question of undervaluation of the yen caused by restrictions on its use as an international currency.

The complaints of non-Japanese financial institutions have focused on international transactions, for example, the conditions necessary for issuing yen-denominated foreign bonds or the qualifications for Euroyen bonds issued by both residents and nonresidents. However, since domestic corporate bonds have a long tradition of being issued under the principle of secured bonds, the relaxation of the conditions in Euroyen bond issue implies the eventual alteration of the domestic

6. Appendix to Ministry of Finance "Kinyu no Jiyuka to sono Kankyo Seibi" (1985).

7. Foreign exchange transactions were only permitted for "real" demand, such as trade settlements and refunds of foreign currency deposits and excluded "speculation" demand.

financial system as well. This is also true of the requests from other nations and their firms to lift controls on interest rates on deposits. This change would affect the fundamental structure of the Japanese flow of funds, including postal savings.[8] Though the interest rates on call money and the discount market were deregulated and liberalized by the early 1980s, and guidelines for interest rates on large deposits are expected to be removed soon, deregulation of small deposits will probably occur last. This is not only because such deregulation will affect the large mass of depositors, but also because it involves changes in institutional arrangements between ministries, between ministries and banks, and between banks themselves.[9] Also causing heated discussion on the domestic front on the question of the continued effectiveness of monetary policy are the establishment or expansion of a treasury bill market or banker's acceptance market and, particularly, the establishment of a Tokyo offshore market.[10]

It may be true that Japanese investors—the majority of savers—are accustomed to the government-protected financial market and are not prepared to take the risks involved in obtaining higher returns. Nevertheless, it is also true that other considerations, such as the accumulation of their financial assets and the development of the bond market in the 1970s, are gradually causing them to become more concerned with the future yields of their financial assets. Opening this market will also intensify the competition among financial institutions and accelerate the process of deregulation. The foreign financial institutions that have already acquired managerial skills and experience in coping with financial innovations will have the advantage in the deregulated Japanese market. The total number of branch offices of the 76 foreign banks in Japan reached 108 as of March 1985. Their collective interest in liberalization will be a strong force for deregulating Japan's financial services and promoting efficiency in Japan's financial market.

Liberalization Issues in Information and Communications Services

Until the enactment of the new telecommunications law (Denki

8. Postal savings constituted 37 percent of total savings in deposits as of September 1984 and are regulated by the Ministry of Post and Telecommunications.

9. The Ministry of Finance opposed the Ministry of Post and Telecommunications in the postal savings case. Disputes between the two ministries are discussed in detail in Alexander and Tan (1984a).

10. The Tokyo offshore market is scheduled to open in October 1986. For details on the discussion see *Nihon Keizai Shinbun*, 11 May 1986.

Tsushinho) in April 1985, telecommunications services in Japan were basically monopolized by two giant operating companies, Nippon Telegraph and Telephone Corporation (NTT) and Overseas Telegraph and Telephone Company (KDD). Indeed, until the late 1970s strong regulatory practices through government-supported monopoly and surveillance were considered indispensable for providing inexpensive and efficient communications services. However, the condition that necessitated this government-supported monopoly and regulation faded rapidly as the introduction of computers and digital techniques reduced the merit of economies of scale in providing such services. It even became clear that regulations prohibiting the use of leased circuits by third parties and restrictions on message switching and data transfer were impeding the growth potential of telecommunications services in Japan.

The domestic forces that pushed for the removal of outmoded restrictions on telecommunications were client firms—namely, banks, trading companies, and others that would benefit from the use of cheaper on-line data communications services. The software and systems information service industries that depended on the use of circuits were also potential beneficiaries of deregulation. Producers of telecommunications equipment in general supported deregulation that would expand the market for their products. Foreign forces—mainly from the United States—joined these domestic forces in promoting deregulation and liberalization.

The liberalization of Japan's information and communications services involves three issues that are different from the issues facing other service industries.

First, since limitations on the use of communications networks are based on a public policy that gave the monopoly position to two operating companies (NTT and KDD) foreign penetration into information and communications services requires a change in public policy as well as industrial organization.

Second, because the supply of information and communications services is closely linked with communications equipment, the discriminatory government procurement practices or regulatory standards on imports limit the use of foreign equipment and, consequently, limit services. Thus liberalization issues regarding information and communications services extend into commodity-related trade issues, such as government procurement policy on satellites, technical standards on telephone equipment, and the validity of technical examination schemes used by business organizations (table 7.7).

Table 7.7 Liberalization Issues in Japan's Information and Communications Services

Type of trade	Forms of trade	Liberalization issues raised[a]	Type of issue
Transborder service trade	International communications services, e.g., communication satellite, cable communication, international VAN.	Registration requirement for type II special service.	Market access
		Ambiguity in difference between general and type II special services.	Reciprocity
Direct investment-related service trade	Establishment of communications networks, e.g., telephone and telegraph, TV and radio, VAN, point of sale.	Same as those in transborder service trade.	Market access
		Entry barrier to foreign subsidiary with foreign holdings exceeding one-third of total capital in type I services.	Reciprocity National treatment
		Participation of foreign firm officials on the telecommunications council.	Transparency
		Opening the hearings to foreign firms' opinions on the process of determining technical standards rules.	Standards
Commercial presence-related service trade	Consultants and various communication operators working in Japan.	Working permits and visa status.	
		License limitation on foreigners (wireless radio operators).	
Commodity-related trade	Imports of communications apparatus, e.g., satellites, computers, semiconductors, integrated circuits and others.	Ambiguity in the procurement policy of communications satellites.	Government procurement
		Business practices that may affect trade in communications apparatus.	
		Relaxing technical standards rules.	Transparency
		Consolidating the technical examination organizations.	Standards

Note: a. Mainly issues raised in U.S.–Japan talks on information and communications service, as of 1986.
Sources: Alexander and Tan, 1984a; Nihon Sogo Kenkyujo, 1985; various newspaper articles.

Table 7.8 Liberalization Issues in Japan's Legal Services

Type of trade	Forms of trade	Liberalization issues raised[a]	Type of issue
Transborder service trade	Legal advice and consultation from overseas.		
Direct investment-related service trade	Establishment of law firms offering legal services, e.g., court activity, real estate and testamentary services, consultation on domestic law, consultation on international law.	Limitations on establishment of law firms. Limitations on employment and joint management with Japanese attorneys. Limitations on legal services in general.	National treatment
		Permission for legal consultation on international law by foreign attorneys.	Reciprocity
Commercial presence-related service trade	Foreign attorneys practicing in Japan.	Visas and work permits. Licensing of foreign attorneys.	Reciprocity

Note: a. Mainly issues raised between U.S. and Japan, as of 1986.
Sources: Alexander and Tan, 1984a; Nihon Sogo Kenkyujo 1985; various newspaper articles.

Third, since information and telecommunications represents an area in which the future prospects for technological advances are enormous, government assistance provided to technical research raises the issue of government subsidies to specific industries. For example, the United States-NTT procurement issue of 1979 clearly illustrates the complicated interrelationships between these three issues. The United States has argued that the Japanese are in effect using their protected home market to improve their communications technology while aggressively pushing it into the open American market.

Barriers to the use of public communications systems were reduced substantially when liberalization measures were introduced by the partial amendment of the public telecommunications law in 1982. The major revisions were (1) to permit the use of data circuit systems for data processing, (2) to improve the utilization scheme of the digital data exchange service provided by NTT, (3) to enable connections between intra-building telephone lines or private branch exchanges and computers, and (4) to extend the use of value-added networks to medium- and small-sized firms. Moreover, it had become clear by then that further liberalization and deregulation required a new law that would cover the entire telecommunications system, including the problem of making NTT a private enterprise.

In December 1984 three related bills concerning telecommunications were passed in the Diet, were enacted, and took effect beginning in April 1985, resulting in further liberalization of information and communications systems. The changes from the former regulation scheme were that restrictions on the use of circuits were essentially abolished, and as a result information services—such as sales inventory management services, data processing, and computing services—were liberalized. Under this new law, telecommunications firms were divided into two categories: type I carriers, which own their circuits, and type II telecommunications businesses, which use circuits leased by type I firms. The type II group is subdivided into special and general services.

Although the enactment of this new law has promoted the liberalization of information and communications services in Japan, a number of problems still exist regarding questions of national treatment and reciprocity. On the grounds that type I services are basically related to public policy, foreign establishments with foreign holdings exceeding one-third of total capital are still restricted from entering into this category of services.

The U.S. information and communications industry experienced its own rapid deregulation in the 1970s, and by 1980 the only restrictions left were those on such basic communications services as telephone and telegraph, circuit transmission, and simple pocket transmission. Thus, U.S. industry requests for reciprocity meant further deregulating entry and simplifying regulatory practices, especially in those areas where the United States had a competitive edge over Japan.

The competitive position of U.S. firms in the fields of information and communications, including communications equipment, affected the liberalization issues in several ways. Communications-related equipment includes such items as computers, switchboards, exchangers, communication cables, and communication satellites. The United States holds a predominant technological advantage in such products as digital exchangers and satellites. However, the technological gap between the two countries has narrowed in recent years, and in some products, such as telephone receivers, Japanese goods now have a price advantage over those produced in the United States.

Liberalization measures that will increase the transparency in determining the standards of such equipment will help to increase imports. However, the most important impact of the deregulation and liberalization of Japan's information and communications services on its commodity trade will come from the expansion of domestic demand in information services caused by the introduction of competition in less regulated markets. When there is a greater demand for information services, import demand for high-technology communications equipment will increase. In the field of information services, such as computer software, databases, and VAN service, U.S. firms evidently have a substantial competitive edge. They have accumulated both the technological skills and experience in developing the networks necessary to provide such services. The fact that the United States holds approximately a 55- percent share of world production in databases is evidence of American competitive strength in this field. In the case of Japan, as much as 80 percent of the database used at present is provided by foreign firms, mainly those from the United States (Johosabisu Kyokai 1986:79). Furthermore, in VAN services U.S. firms have provided a variety of services since the mid-1970s, and their competitive edge over Japanese firms is apparent.

The recent deregulation and liberalization of the communications industry will undoubtedly expand the opportunities for U.S. firms to do business in Japan. Many plans for joint ventures, such as those involving AT&T, IBM, and GTE Telenet Communications joining with Japanese partners to provide various VAN services, have already been announced. In the field of communications satellites, American companies have plans for joint ventures and sales cooperation with

Japanese firms. This type of active participation by foreign firms in Japan's information and communications services will no doubt increase domestic demand for such services and expand service trade.

Liberalization Issues in Business: Legal and Advertising Services

The active involvement of Japanese firms in business abroad has increased the demand for consulting services related to international transactions. In the area of legal services, it became clear that domestic supply could not meet the new demand. As Japanese firms increased their business activities in foreign markets, they encountered various problems requiring the assistance of lawyers experienced in transborder disputes. There was a demand for lawyers who could conduct international financial negotiations, help establish transnational projects, and provide advice on international contracts. This demand could not be satisfied by Japanese attorneys, who provided legal services that were restricted to court activity and settlement and who were not prepared to deal with international economic disputes. In order to meet this new demand, it was necessary to import services, which required a change in the legal system.

To be a licensed attorney in Japan, a lawyer has to register and become a member of the Japanese Federation of Bar Associations. A license is only given to those who have passed the national examination and have completed a two-year training program. This system made it impossible to meet the demand for new legal services through imports of services. However, legal services were in fact imported by assigning foreign lawyers a trainee status in Japanese firms or by opening legal sections in foreign subsidiaries. These lawyers came mainly from the United States, where they had accumulated substantial experience in handling international economic disputes.

In 1974 New York State allowed foreign attorneys to engage in consulting services on the basis of foreign certification. And in recent years resentment has been growing among U.S. lawyers, who feel that on the grounds of reciprocity Japan should permit American attorneys to provide consultation on matters of international law. The issue of liberalizing Japan's legal services was discussed in several U.S.–Japan talks dealing with opening Japanese service markets (table 7.8). Eventually it was included as a major service area to be liberalized in the Action Program for Market Access (July 1985).

In the spring of 1986 the law permitting legal services activities by foreign lawyers on the grounds of reciprocity passed in the Diet. According to this law, a foreign attorney may engage in legal activities related to the law of the country or state in which the attorney's license was issued or as permitted by the Minister of Justice. However, foreign attorneys will be under the surveillance and guidance of the Japanese Federation of Bar Associations.

One of the major law firms in New York was reportedly preparing to open a branch office in Tokyo in April 1987 (*Nihon Keizai Shinbun* 24 April 1986). They are expected to concentrate their legal services in the areas of consultation and mediation of Japanese direct investment in the United States; mediation of joint venture projects in construction and real estate; and analysis and information concerning the U.S. government and the Congress. Their legal services, therefore, are dictated by the needs of Japanese firms.

The case of liberalization in legal services shows that even in an area such as the Japanese legal system, in which tacit public support to maintain the system is strong, business interests are inducing change. Thus, a shortage in the domestic supply of particular legal services caused a change in legal services regulation, despite the fact that the public in general still preferred out-of-court settlements through negotiations and mutual consent and did not necessarily see the need for the change.

In contrast to legal services issues, which caused heated discussion between the United States and Japan, there were actually no disputes in opening Japan's market to foreign advertising companies. The major problem for them probably is the practice of Japanese businesses of maintaining strong ties between specific advertising companies and the mass media—television, radio, and newspapers. To overcome differences in consumer tastes, which requires understanding the traditions and culture of prospective consumers, leading U.S. advertising companies preferred to establish joint ventures.

Japanese advertising companies hold a competitive advantage in developing sales campaigns using television, newspapers, or outdoor advertising, whereas U.S. firms lead in the areas of market research and marketing strategy. The primary role of Japanese advertising firms abroad is to assist in promoting the sales of Japanese subsidiaries abroad. Per contra, U.S. multinational advertising companies have a significant lead in establishing international advertising networks. The internationalization of Japan's business activity will therefore increase the demand for the services of U.S. advertising firms.

It appears, then that even in the field of business services such as legal services and advertising, in which social tradition and culture play an important role, barriers have been gradually removed—by strong business interests in the case of legal services, and by foreign firms choosing Japanese partners in the case of advertising.

After Liberalization—The Role of Japan in Trade and Investment in Services in the Asia-Pacific Region

The growth of Japan's service activity accelerated after the first oil crisis and the increased importance of service transactions has affected Japan's trade and investment in various ways. In service trade, receipt and payment of management fees has increased, reflecting the internationalization of Japanese business activities, particularly in the financial services area, in which strong domestic demand has stimulated external transactions. Between 1981 and 1985, direct investment in finance and insurance increased more than in all other industries, and as Japanese financial institutions accumulated the managerial skills needed to provide international financial services in less regulated markets, a move began to deregulate the domestic market.

At present the deregulation and liberalization of Japan's financial market is proceeding rapidly. This trend will undoubtedly continue in the future, since growth of Japanese capital assets abroad will increase the need for financial institutions to participate in the international capital market. And in order to promote the internationalization of the yen, a link between the domestic market and the world's financial centers must be forged. In this manner Japan can establish its role as a supplier of international capital flows as well as financial services. If Japan can play such a role, it will improve the efficiency of international capital flows, especially in the Asia-Pacific region, where Japan has already built strong economic ties through merchandise trade and direct investment. The establishment of international information and communications networks is necessary for the swift transfer of funds and for the development of an efficient capital market.

In the field of information and communications, Japan as a major supplier can contribute to the development of the countries in the Asia-Pacific region by providing the necessary communications equipment, such as computers, exchangers, communication cables, and telephone receivers. In 1984, 7.5 percent of the economic aid and 6.9 percent of the government loans from Japan were in the area of communications. NTT and KDD have contracts for technological cooperation with telecommunications establishments in such Asian countries as China, Thailand, Korea, Malaysia, Singapore, and Sri Lanka. In 1985 the Asia Telecommunications Organization (Ajia Denki Tsushin

Kyoryoku Kiko) was established to promote technological cooperation and research in the Asia-Pacific region.

The importance of Japan as a major supplier of communications technology to countries in the Asia-Pacific region should increase in the future, since the establishment of communications networks will benefit all countries involved. Japanese businesses will benefit from the establishment of regional communications networks that enable the swift transfer of business information between countries. As for the other countries in the region, industrialization is only possible when information can be swiftly transmitted internally as well as abroad at low cost.

Currently, service industries such as finance, insurance, and communications are commonly operated either as government monopolies or subject to strict government regulations in the Asia-Pacific region. Although government provision of basic social services may be necessary at the initial stage of development, policies assuring control of the domestic market by a particular service supplier create vested interests. These vested interests often become major impediments to technological progress and to the development of strong service industries.

The lesson to be learned from liberalization in Japan's trade and investment in services is that internationalization of business activities has rendered obsolete the reasons for regulating service industries. Although demands by outside forces to open markets for financial, communications, and information services contributed to liberalization, the primary reason for change was that Japanese firms favored deregulation. Those domestic firms that foresaw the opportunities created by expanding their business activities abroad supported deregulation. Even in legal services, which had a long tradition of providing services primarily in legal settlement and court activity, the system has recently been amended to allow foreign attorneys to provide legal services in the area of international business, for which Japan's demand has grown rapidly.

The deregulation of services undoubtedly will intensify the competition in financial as well as communications and information services and will contribute to the further growth of service activities in Japan. Indeed, as was pointed out in the introduction to this chapter, finance and insurance, business services, and communications were the industries that experienced both the highest rate of growth in the 1980s and the most rapid deregulation and liberalization.

The liberalization of trade in services is often considered more difficult than that in merchandise, because demand for services is more closely related to culture and tradition. Consequently, the supply of services more frequently requires commercial presence and direct investment. In advertising services, for instance, U.S. firms chose Japanese partners for joint ventures in order to overcome deficiencies in knowledge of cultural differences. Then U.S. and Japanese advertising firms jointly supplied services using their respective strengths—U.S. firms in planning market research and Japanese firms in media sales campaigns. As a result, Japanese consumers and businesses alike benefited by getting better information about products and markets through the efficient supply of advertising services. However, because it involves the issue of work permits, which affect employment and thus the income of domestic groups, solving the problem of commercial presence will be more complex. Nevertheless, the liberalization of Japan's legal services, based on reciprocity with the United States, shows that gradual changes are possible if a sufficient domestic demand for such services exists.

The Tokyo Economic Declaration (6 May 1986) stated "the new round [of GATT] should, *inter alia*, address the issues of trade in services and trade-related aspects of intellectual property rights and foreign direct investment." The Japanese plan submitted to the GATT secretariat in early 1986 also included the establishment of international rules for trade in services among the items to be taken up in the coming GATT negotiations. Because service transactions are rapidly increasing their importance in the Japanese economy, Japan as well as its trading partners—including the countries in the Asia-Pacific region—will benefit greatly if the new round of GATT negotiations succeeds in establishing a trading system that can assure the freer transmission of such service activities throughout the world.

CHAPTER 8
Capital Liberalization in Korea

Un-Chan Chung

A strong trend toward capital liberalization is growing in the securities industry of the Republic of Korea (Korea). There is a sizable demand abroad for the stock issued by various Korean trusts (such as the Korea Trust and the Korea International Trust) and for all beneficial certificates issued exclusively to foreigners. The Korea Fund is also enjoying immense popularity abroad. Moreover, U.S. and Japanese securities companies interested in entering the Korean securities industry are pressuring the Korean government to further relax the regulations controlling the securities market. They are demanding that non-Koreans be given access to securities transactions and that the securities companies of other countries receive the same treatment as their Korean counterparts.

Three arguments have been offered in favor of opening up Korea's capital market: (1) the irreversible dependency of the Korean economy on external forces has already made its internationalization inevitable; (2) imports of foreign capital must be continued in order to pay interest and principal on foreign debts; and (3) it is necessary to diversify the sources of such capital imports.

It is argued that the ensuing inflow of foreign capital will strengthen the securities market and the infusion of advanced managerial technology will contribute to qualitative improvements. Furthermore, capital liberalization will transform the Korean securities market into a reliable and efficient one for financial investment and for securing funds, thereby making security financing easier for business firms. The greatest benefit from liberalization would be improved corporate financial structure due to increased equity financing. Finally, it is often pointed out that the presence of foreign capital in the securities market will help secure political and military stability for Korea. Accordingly, the government has permitted leading industrial groups to float convertible bonds in Europe and to sell depository receipts in foreign capital markets.

The History of the Capital Liberalization Movement

What are the origins of the movement toward capital liberalization? Externally the impetus comes from current developments in the U.S. economy; internally it has been generated by recent changes in the Korean economy.

The United States is currently undergoing a transformation of its industrial structure that has been called the "third industrial revolution." In this phase of economic development, propelled by the dynamic growth of its information and communications technology, the U.S. economy's comparative advantage is shifting away from traditional manufacturing industries toward service industries. In April 1982, the work force employed in nongovernment U.S. service industries exceeded for the first time the number of workers employed by the entire goods-producing sector (manufacturing, construction, and mining). Today, if the government sector is included, approximately one in 10 Americans is employed in the service sector. The contribution of services to the U.S. gross national product has progressed at a similar rate, a trend that is directly reflected in the U.S. balance of payments. In the years from 1970 through 1983, the United States experienced an increasing deficit in its merchandise account. In contrast, its balance in private services showed an increasing surplus over the same period. As seen in table 8.1, these surpluses constitute a significant offsetting item against the deficits in the merchandise account.

Despite such recent developments, however, it appears that U.S. service industries have yet to achieve the degree of internationalization found in the manufacturing sector. One reason for this may be that the shift in the comparative advantage of the United States to service industries has occurred only recently, and the United States has not yet learned how to fully exploit this new-found competitive edge. Another reason may be that the trading partners of the United States impose various restrictions on trade and investment in services. Thus it is not surprising that in the new round of negotiations at GATT, the United States is pushing for free trade in service industries and that is demanding that Korea and Japan open their service markets, especially those in the financial industry.

What then is the state of the Korean economy? Virtually nothing seems to be wrong if a macro- or flow-oriented view is taken. A high rate of growth is being sustained despite the global recession; inflation is under control; and the balance-of-payments deficit, which was shrinking gradually, even became a surplus in 1986.

Table 8.1 U.S. Balance of Trade in Merchandise and Services, 1970–1983 (US$ millions)

Year	Balance in merchandise trade	Balance in private services trade[a]	Sum
1970	2,603	535	3,128
1971	-2,260	549	-1,711
1972	-6,416	-4,866	-11,282
1973	911	487	1,398
1974	-5,505	1,350	-4,155
1975	8,903	2,404	11,307
1976	-9,483	2,891	-6,592
1977	-31,091	2,690	-28,401
1978	-33,966	3,539	-30,427
1979	-27,555	4,036	-23,519
1980	-25,544	7,283	-18,261
1981	-28,067	8,968	-19,099
1982	-36,389	7,583	-28,806
1983	-61,055	5,683	-55,372

Note: a. Private services are travel, passenger fares, transportation, royalties and miscellaneous private services.
Sources: Diluilo, 1981; various other issues.

However, the micro- or stock-oriented view gives an entirely different picture. Encouraged by the government's growth-first policy, Korean firms have grown at a spectacular rate over the past two decades. However, this rapid growth has not been without its costs. Duplication of investment in production facilities has resulted in an inefficient allocation of resources, and because investment funds were mainly secured from outside sources rather than through accumulation of capital, the financial structure of certain firms has steadily deteriorated (see table 8.2). Korean firms have recently shown markedly low profitability despite strong government support in the form of tax incentives and low-dividend-payment guidelines. A favorable business environment created by the steady global and domestic economic recovery, stable raw material prices, and repeated reductions in domestic interest rates have also failed to alleviate this problem.

The profitability problem can be traced to the large debts acquired by Korean firms that relied on loans to finance their rapid expansion in the 1970s. The sharp rise in interest rates in the international market in the early 1980s severely affected these firms, causing huge increases in their nonoperating expenses (table 8.3).

Table 8.2 Corporate Financial Structures in Korea's Manufacturing Sector

Year	Debt-equity ratio
1961	135.9
1962	153.5
1963	92.2
1964	100.5
1965	93.7
1966	117.7
1967	151.2
1968	201.3
1969	270.0
1970	328.4
1971	394.2
1972	313.4
1973	272.7
1974	316.0
1975	339.5
1976	364.6
1977	350.7
1978	366.8
1979	377.1
1980	487.9
1981	451.5
1982	385.8
1983	360.3

Source: Bank of Korea, personal communication.

Table 8.3 Comparison of Profit Margins in Manufacturing Sectors (average annual percentage)

	Korea			Japan	Taiwan
	1970–1974	1975–1979	1980–1984	1980–1984	1980–1983
Gross profits less interest expense to total sales ratio	4.1	3.5	1.2	3.3	3.7
Gross profits to total sales ratio	9.4	7.3	7.5	4.6	6.0

Source: Same as table 8.2.

Although gross profits remain at a healthy 7 percent of total sales, before-tax profits net of interest expenses have dropped sharply since 1980 to approximately 1 percent, about one-third those of Japan or Taiwan.

On the national level, after an export-oriented strategy was adopted in the early stages of economic development, rapid growth became possible. However, this was only achieved by overcoming low domestic savings rates through active import and utilization of foreign capital and by maintaining a high rate of investment. This dependence on foreign capital has led to an accumulation of foreign debts, which steadily increased through the two oil crises to reach US$46.7 billion by the end of 1985. The Korean economy was left struggling under US$4 billion in annual interest payments. Worse, the composition of Korea's foreign debt continues to shift toward loans with shorter maturities, and the terms of the loans become more burdensome. Successful debt management has kept the foreign debt issue from becoming an even more crippling problem. However, it must be remembered that debt crises are inherently unpredictable.

Why Liberalize the Capital Market?

A more active capital market is regarded as one way to put the Korean economy on a stable growth path. Firms would improve their financial structures by being able to raise capital in the equity market, and increased domestic savings should lessen dependency on foreign capital. Furthermore, if an active market were to gain international credibility, it would attract foreign capital.

The government's plans for capital liberalization may be examined in other contexts. Despite vigorous economic growth over the past 20 years, the Korean economy faces many structural problems. Rigid institutions and inefficient decision-making processes frequently result in the wasteful use of resources. An awareness of such problems in the economy has spurred the reform of various institutions and the adoption of more efficient management practices over the past few years.

The recent history of the financial sector reveals the government's policies on reform. Prior to 1980 the Korean government had intervened to an extreme degree in determining loan and deposit interest rates and credit allocation, believing that credit would not be allocated according to government social and economic priorities without its guidance. Thus, through its annual financial stabilization plans, the government allocated 50 to 70 percent of total domestic credit each year as command loans or policy loans to specified sectors, industries, and purposes. Moreover, the government built an increasingly complicated interest rate structure in its attempt to more effectively make priority loans. This regulatory regime was effective during the early phase of development, but its limitations became obvious as a more complex economic structure emerged. The inefficient allocation of resources and the chronic excess demand for funds resulting from such excessive intervention eventually led to sustained inflation and a flourishing curb market for funds.

Accordingly, beginning in 1980 the government enacted a series of measures designed to increase the autonomy of the financial sector. The management of commercial banks was restored to the private sector, and money and banking policy was only controlled indirectly from that point. Market forces were allowed a large role in determining certain interest rates, and strong government support was given to the introduction of new financial instruments (e.g., certificates of deposit, credit cards) to the market. The internationalization of finance is another government-enacted measure and is intended to facilitate the introduction of advanced financial technology and to raise the economy's international credit standing. Capital liberalization is a parallel process in this move toward financial internationalization.

In sum, the movement toward capital liberalization in Korea is the combined result of pressures from the U.S. financial industry as it aims for the expansion of its overseas markets, attempts by Korean firms to improve their financial structure, difficulties in Korea's foreign debt management, and the spillover effects of financial internationalization in Korea.

Plans for and Current Progress of Capital Liberalization

Until 1980, investment in domestic securities by foreigners was limited to government-guaranteed bonds denominated in foreign currencies and issued by the Korea Development Bank. However, in January 1981, the government, in its Long-Range Internationalization Plan for the Securities Market, disclosed its intention to gradually open domestic securities investment to foreigners. The plan involved a four-step reform process over a 10-year period, by which Koreans as well as foreigners would be able to invest in domestic securities.

The first phase of the plan, which has been successfully carried out, allowed indirect foreign investment through international investment trusts. This phase also allowed domestic securities companies to prepare themselves for the internationalization of the securities market in 1984. The second phase, in progress at this writing, opens direct acquisition of securities to foreigners, although investment methods, volume, and the types of industries may still be restricted. Also in the second phase, Korean corporate securities are being issued and listed in overseas exchanges. The third phase will widen the extent of liberalization after 1988, giving foreign securities investors equal status with local investors and permitting foreign securities companies to provide limited services in Korea on a reciprocal basis. The fourth and final phase will allow foreign securities investment for Koreans and will completely liberalize the securities business.

In the first stage of its plan, the government on several occasions instructed Korean trust companies to float various trusts and issue exclusive beneficial certificates for foreigners in foreign markets. These trusts and certificates now amount to a total of more than US$200 million. The portfolio management principle of these beneficial certificates is that more than 90 percent of the net asset value must be invested in domestic listed stocks. Other than this, the same restrictions governing domestic investment companies also apply. The trusts are popular among foreigners, who have demanded extra stock issuance. This popularity can be attributed to the high regard in which foreigners hold the long-term prospects of the Korean economy.

The government also promoted the establishment of the Korea Fund, a U.S. investment company with investment in Korean securities as its primary objective. It began to float its stocks in August 1984 in the United States and European markets. Because it is a closed-end investment company, the Korea Fund's equity capital is fixed, its shareholders receive dividends, and its shares may be transacted only in predesignated stock exchanges. Although the public offering of the fund's equities amounted to US$60 million, the net asset value after deducting subscription expenses is said to be US$56 million. The fund's portfolio management principle is to invest more than 80 percent of its net assets in the listed securities (primarily stocks) of Korean companies. It is prohibited from dealing in real estate, lending and borrowing funds, investing more than 5 percent of its assets in a single issue of securities, or investing more than 25 percent of its assets or more than US$15 million in a single industry.

The fund's great popularity apparently stems from faith in the potential for Korea's economic growth and from the fact that Korean stock prices are generally undervalued. The price-earnings ratio in

Table 8.4 Comparison of Price-Earnings Ratios

	1973	1975	1978	1980	1982	1983
Korea	15.7	5.3	5.9	2.6	3.4	3.8
United States	15.9	10.2	8.7	7.9	8.2	11.2
Japan	13.3	27.0	34.3	20.4	25.8	34.7

Source: Same as table 8.2.

Korea is low relative to past periods of economic expansion or concurrent figures in the United States and Japan (table 8.4), a fact that suggests a promising future for the Korean stock market.

In addition to this type of securities offering, the government has been pursuing bilateral agreements with other countries under which one country's securities companies will be allowed to operate in the other's market. The government's objective is to have Korean securities companies prepare themselves for the internationalization of the securities market by giving them some experience in competing with foreign companies. As a result, four major Japanese companies (Nomura, Yamaichi, Daiwa, and Nikko) have had branches in Seoul since December 1980, and Korean securities companies, mainly the large ones, have had branch offices in New York, London, and Tokyo since 1984. Moreover, Korean securities companies have subscribed to Korean securities issued overseas since 1980 and have bought the Korea Development Bank's foreign currency bonds, beneficial certificates for foreigners, and equity shares of the Korea Fund. More activity of this type has been observed since foreign issuance of private corporate securities was permitted.

In another government measure designed to support and reinforce the securities industry in its move toward internationalization, the government revised the Securities and Exchange Law in April 1982 to provide the basis for (1) foreign securities companies to operate in Korea, (2) Korean securities companies to operate in overseas markets, (3) limiting acquisition of securities by foreigners, and (4) the registration and control of such acquisitions by foreigners. In addition, in August 1984 the Securities Supervisory Board established the rules for managing and regulating securities investments by the Korea Fund. Since July 1983, the government has allowed stock issuance at market value and foreign equity participation in Korean securities companies, while encouraging large-scale expansion of securities companies to develop a strong securities industry and to better prepare it for internationalization.

As mentioned before, the government has already established various trusts in order to increase indirect acquisition of securities from abroad. Furthermore, several big financial conglomerates have been floating convertible bonds and depository receipts in foreign markets. This could be a step toward direct foreign securities investment.

Some Reservations on Capital Liberalization

The pace of capital liberalization in Korea is increasing. Although the capital market does eventually need to be liberalized, the process of liberalization should, in my view, be slowed and even postponed until certain preparations have been made.

In Korea, foreign exchange transactions are not yet completely free. Korea's foreign exchange law explicitly specifies which currencies are to be used in transactions with other countries and designates the U.S. dollar as the sole vehicle currency. The law also stipulates that, in the case of capital transactions, payments to other countries be authorized only within the limit set for total capital outflows in Korea's plans for its capital account transactions and that each payment be approved by the government and a foreign exchange bank. Government approval is also required in the case of payments for goods and services. Thus exchange rates are not freely determined in the market, foreign exchange transactions are under the centralized control of the government (the central bank), and the Korean won is not allowed to be used as a means of payment to other countries. In short, foreign exchange transactions (payments) have not been liberalized. What effect capital liberalization would have on the economy when its foreign exchange transactions are not free has not been carefully analyzed. It therefore seems that capital liberalization should be carried out gradually and only after preconditions such as liberalization of trade and foreign exchange transactions have been met.

One of the preconditions should be the liberalization of domestic financial markets. But they have until now been controlled by the government, and, to make matters worse, they have been badly shaken by sporadic and impractical reforms. For example, the interest rate policy, from the time of the decree of 3 August 1972 until the interest rate increase in 1980, was so rigid that it kept real interest rates negative throughout this entire period (table 8.5). And the interest rate reforms in 1965, 1972, 1980, and 1982 were so drastic that interest

Table 8.5 Interest Rates in Korea, 1972–1979

		GNP deflator		Real interest rate	
	Nominal interest rate	Actual rate of increase	Expected rate of increase	Based on actual rate	Based on expected rate
1972	12.0	15.6	14.7	-3.6	-2.7
1973	12.0	13.2	14.3	-1.2	-2.3
1974	15.0	29.6	14.1	-14.6	0.9
1975	15.0	24.7	17.3	-9.7	-2.3
1976	16.2	17.7	21.7	-1.5	-5.5
1977	14.4	16.3	22.7	-1.9	-8.3
1978	18.6	20.6	21.2	-2.0	-2.6
1979	18.6	20.6	18.8	-2.0	-0.2

Source: East Asian and Pacific Regional Office, 1980.

rate changes ranged from 17.5 percent to 100 percent of previous levels (table 8.6), which severely disrupted the flow of funds in the financial market.

In view of these macroeconomic considerations, Korea does not appear to fully meet the economic prerequisites for capital liberalization. Before or while internationalizing the securities market, Korea must strive to satisfy these prerequisites. It has been said that Korea's trade volume and overall economic strength exceed those of Japan in its early stages of partial capital liberalization. The argument that the Korean economy at present is comparable to the Japanese economy in its transition to an open economic system in the early 1960s is not persuasive. Such a contention must be supported by a more detailed analysis that takes into account the synchronous international and domestic economic circumstances and the reasons for liberalizing capital transactions in each country.

It may be helpful for Korea to consider the experiences of other countries. Japan and West Germany used conservative methods to successfully bring about capital liberalization, even though both had strong economies. In contrast, capital liberalization caused severe economic problems in Brazil and Mexico that have yet to be corrected. The latter countries radically liberalized their capital markets in pursuit of short-term benefits despite structurally weak economies. There is a lesson for Korea in the experience of each group.

Practical considerations should also discourage hasty capital liberalization. The argument that capital liberalization is urgently needed to induce larger capital inflows cannot be justified; the Korean securities market is too small. It is unreasonable to expect large capital inflows

Table 8.6 Fluctuation of Interest Rates in Relation to Financial Reforms

Date of reform	Interest rates on time deposits				Interest rates on loans			
	Before	After	Interest rate change in percentage points	Rate of change	Before	After	Interest rate change in percentage points	Rate of change
9/30/65	15.0	30.0	+15.0	+100.0	16.0	26.0	+10.0	+62.5
8/03/72	17.3	12.6	-4.7	-27.6	20.0	16.5	-3.5	-17.5
1/12/80	18.6	24.0	+5.4	+29.0	18.5	24.0	+5.5	+29.7
6/28/82	12.6	8.0	-4.6	-36.5	14.0	10.0	-4.0	-28.5

Source: Same as table 8.2.

when the total market value of listed stocks falls short of US$8 billion.

A more serious problem is the combination of low stock prices and high yields. The price-earnings ratio in Korea is low relative to the high yield on bonds (table 8.4). Whatever the reason for this, it is commonly believed that the price-earnings ratio can be raised considerably. If this is true, it would be advisable to sell securities to foreigners after raising stock prices rather than to make haste with capital liberalization and sell cheaply. However, raising stock prices without disturbing the securities market requires time. For this reason, it would be best to delay the internationalization of the securities market.

The safest way to carry out capital liberalization would be to wait until all the prerequisites for success have been satisfied. The basic direction to be followed in Korea's capital liberalization, however, is to seek to satisfy the necessary conditions and proceed cautiously as circumstances permit. This is obviously a more positive approach to liberalization than simply waiting for the right moment to come.

Strategies for Accommodating Capital Liberalization

Measures to upgrade and expand the domestic securities industry need to be taken before carrying out capital liberalization. First, equity financing must be encouraged. There is a marked tendency among Korean firms to avoid equity financing in the securities market, for two major reasons.

First, majority shareholders are afraid that corporate disclosure or issuing new shares could threaten their control of management. They have therefore avoided going public or have done so only if they controlled more than 50 percent of total shares issued. A survey shows that among the unlisted companies, at least 100 sound companies are capable of going public, and this figure is expected to rise sharply. In order to encourage corporate disclosure, Korea needs to educate large shareholders concerning the eventual benefits of going public and to make them aware of measures that will protect their managerial control even after going public.

Second, there are many easier and more attractive methods of financing than issuing stocks. Business firms can get bank loans at less than the real interest rate, issue guaranteed bonds with payment guaranteed by financial intermediaries, or go to a short-term financing company or the curb market.

On the demand side in the securities market, there are approximately

700,000 individual shareholders in Korea, which is about 6 percent of the economically active population. This figure represents a drastic decrease from the 960,000 shareholders in 1978. Two fundamental reasons can be cited.

First, there is a deep-rooted distrust of the securities market, notably the stock market, among the general public. It is hard to see any difference between the market and a gambling house when one considers the history of the Korean stock market. Transactions by the large investors and insiders have been an important factor in causing sudden and large fluctuations in stock prices. Therefore, rules prescribing ethical conduct in securities transactions must be established in order to attract investors to a more stable stock market.

Second, a general mistrust of business firms by the public decreases the demand for securities. Among other things, the business ethics of entrepreneurs, abnormal corporate financial structures, and stock price manipulation by business firms account for this lack of confidence. Means of restoring trust do not seem to be readily available. All sectors of the economy should strive for an environment that discourages unsavory economic activities.

Anticipatory measures to upgrade the securities market for capital liberalization should also be enacted with regard to institutional investors. Institutional investors currently hold less than 30 percent of aggregate stocks in Korea, and if the shares held by the three investment trusts are excluded, the amount of institutional investment in stocks is negligible. This contrasts sharply with the role of institutional investors in the securities market in the economically advanced countries, where they hold 70 to 80 percent of total shares. Institutional investors provide a stable supply of funds to the securities market, attract long-term investments by stabilizing the market, and provide more scientific evaluations of investments. More participation by institutional investors in the securities market will be required to foster growth in the Korean market.

Contributors

Yale Braunstein is Associate Professor at the School of Information and Library Science at the University of California at Berkeley. His research and publications are concerned with the economics of mass communications industries and their regulation as well as the economics of information.

Un-Chan Chung is Associate Professor of Economics at Seoul National University. He has taught at Columbia University and is currently engaged in research on monetary economics and the financial policies of Korea.

Herbert G. Grubel is Professor of Economics at Simon Fraser University and Director of the Services Industries Project, the Fraser Institute, Vancouver, British Columbia. He has contributed extensively to the fields of international finance, trade, and employment.

Bernard M. Hoekman is a Ph.D. candidate at the University of Michigan. He has done research on the effects of the Tokyo Round Codes.

Meheroo Jussawalla is Research Associate at the Institute of Culture and Communication, East-West Center. She was dean of the university and Professor of Economics at Osmania University. She has published extensively in the area of communications policy and planning for developing countries.

Chung H. Lee is Chairman of the Department of Economics at the University of Hawaii at Manoa and Research Associate at the Resource Systems Institute, East-West Center. He has done research in the areas of international capital movements, direct foreign investment, and technology transfer. Currently he is engaged in research on international transactions in services and the economic development of the Asian NICs.

James Mak is Professor of Economics at the University of Hawaii at Manoa. He has done research in regional and urban economics. He is a leading scholar in the economics of tourism and travel.

Walter Miklius is Professor of Economics at the University of Hawaii at Manoa. He has served as senior staff economist in the U.S. Department of Transportation and has published extensively on the economics of transportation.

Seiji Naya is Director of the Resource Systems Institute at the East-West Center and Professor of Economics at the University of Hawaii at Manoa. He has worked at the National Bureau of Economic Research and was chief economist at the Asian Development Bank. He has done research in trade policy and economic integration and is a leading expert on the ASEAN economies.

Yoko K. Sazanami is Professor of Economics at Keio University, Tokyo. She was economic affairs officer at United Nations Headquarters and has served in various capacities in the Japanese government. She has published numerous articles and books on the subjects of international economics and trade policy.

Marcellus S. Snow is Professor of Economics at the University of Hawaii at Manoa and Researcher at the Social Science Research Institute at the University of Hawaii at Manoa. His areas of research are econometric testing and industrial organization. He is a leading scholar in the economics of telecommunications.

Robert M. Stern is Professor of Economics and Public Policy at the University of Michigan at Ann Arbor. He is a leading scholar in international economics and trade policy and has published a number of articles and books in those fields.

Kenneth J. White is Associate Professor of Economics at the University of British Columbia. His extensive contributions are in the fields of econometric computation, telecommunications, and tourism.

Bibliography

Agmon, T., and C.P. Kindlebergen, 1977. *Multinationals from Small Countries,* Cambridge, MA: MIT Press.

Alexander, A., and H.W. Tan, 1984a. *Barriers to U.S. Service Trade in Japan*. Santa Monica, CA: Rand Corporation.

________, 1984b. *Case Studies of U.S. Service Trade in Japan*. Santa Monica, CA: Rand Corporation.

Allgeier, P.F., 11 August 1986. Testimony before the Special Subcommittee on U.S.-Pacific Rim Trade, Committee on Energy and Commerce, U.S. Trade Representative Press Release.

Aronson, J.D., 1986. "Trade in Services: An Agenda for International Trade Negotiations," Mimeo.

Aronson, J.D., and C.M. Aho, 14 September, 1986. "Let's Settle Nagging Trade Issues, Not Postpone Them," *Los Angeles Times.*

Asia Travel Trade, 1978-1986. Various Issues.

ASMAL Pacific Report, 1985, 1986. Various Issues.

Australia, Department of Sport, Recreation and Tourism, 1985. *Australian Tourism Trends, An Overview*. Canberra: Australian Government Publishing Service.

Bailey, E.E., and A. Friedlander, 1982. "Market Structure and Multi-product Industries," *Journal of Economic Literature*, Vol. 20, No. 3 (September), pp. 1024-48.

Balassa, B., 1983. "Comments," in W.R. Cline (ed.), *Trade Policies in the 1980s*. Cambridge, MA: MIT Press.

Baldwin, R.E., 1979. "Determinants of Trade and Foreign Investment: Further Evidence," *Review of Economics and Statistics*, Vol. 61, No. 1 (February), pp. 40-48.

Bank Negara Malaysia, *Annual Report*, 1985.

Baughcum, A., 1986. "Deregulation, Divestiture, and Competition in U.S. Telecommunications: Lessons for Other Countries," in M.S. Snow (ed.), *Marketplace for Telecommunications: Regulation and Deregulation in Industrialized Democracies.* New York: Longman, pp. 69-105.

Baumol, W.J., and Y.M. Braunstein, 1977. "An Empirical Study of Scale Economies and Production Complementarity: The Case of Journal Production," *Journal of Political Economy*, Vol. 85, No. 5 (October), pp. 1037-48.

Baumol, W.J., E.E. Bailey, and R.D. Willig, 1977. "Weak Invisible Hand Theorems on Sustainability of Multiproduct Natural Monopoly," *American Economic Review*, Vol. 67, No. 3 (June), pp. 350-65.

Baumol, W.J., J.C. Panzar, and R.D. Willig, 1982. *Contestable Markets and the Theory of Industry Structure*. New York: Harcourt Brace Jovanovich.

Bhagwati, J.N., 1984a. "Splintering and Disembodiment of Services and Developing Nations," *The World Economy*, Vol. 7, No. 2 (June), pp. 133-44.

________, 1984b. "Why Are Services Cheaper in Poor Countries?" *Economic Journal*, Vol. 94, No. 374 (June), pp. 279-86.

________, 10 November 1985. "Opening Up Trade in Services: U.S. Should Heed Third World Demands," *The New York Times*.

________, 1985. "Trade in Services and Developing Countries," Xth Annual Geneva Lecture at London School of Economics, Mimeo.

Bigelow, R.P., 1986. "Legal Protection of Computer Software," *Transnational Data Report* (March), pp. 19-21.

Brock, W.A., 1983. "Contestable Markets and the Theory of Industry Structure: A Review Article," *Journal of Political Economy*, Vol. 91, No. 6 (December), pp. 1055-66.

Bock, W.E., 1982. "A Simple Plan for Negotiating Trade in Services," *The World Economy*, Vol. 5, No. 3 (November), pp. 229-40.

Brooks, M.R., 1985. "Fleet Development and the Control of Shipping in Southeast Asia," Occasional Paper No. 77. Singapore: Institute of Southeast Asian Studies.

Campbell, N., 1986. "Service Sector Costs and their Effect on the International Competitiveness of Traded Industries," Discussion Paper. Industries Assistance Commission, Australia.

Canada, Task Force on Trade in Services, 1982. *Background Report* (October). Ottawa: Unpublished.

________, Statistics Canada, 1983a. *Historical Statistics of Canada,* Second edition. Ottawa: Statistics Canada.

________, Statistics Canada, 1983b. *Historical Statistics of Canada*, Series D9-55, Ottawa: Statistics Canada.

________, Statistics Canada, 1985. "Features 40th Anniversary of the Labour Force Survey," *The Labour Force* (November), Ottawa: Statistics Canada.

________, *Bank of Canada Review*, May 1986. Table J-2, Series D60501 and D60502. Ottawa: Statistics Canada.

________, Statistics Canada, Various Issues. Catalogue 13531, Table 6, *National Income and Expenditure Accounts*, Vol. I, Catalogue

13-001, Quarterly. Ottawa: Statistics Canada.

________, Statistics Canada, Various Issues, *Gross Domestic Product by Industry*, Catalogue 61-213. Ottawa: Statistics Canada.

Canadian-U.S. Conference on Communications Policy, 1984. *Cultures in Collison*. New York: Praeger Special Studies.

Carlson, S., 1977. "Company Policies for International Expansion: The Swedish Experience," in T. Agmon and C.P. Kindleberger (eds.), *Multinationals from Small Countries*. Cambridge, MA: MIT Press.

Choy, D.J.L., and C.Y. Gee, 1983. "Tourism in the PRC—Five Years after China Opens Its Gates," *Tourism Management* (June), pp. 85-93.

Chung, U.C., 1985. "Financial Internationalization" (in Korean), *Banker* (January).

Coase, R.H., 1937. "The Nature of the Firm," *Economica*, Vol. 4 (November).

Davlantes, N., 15 September 1986. "Japanese Insurance Firm Joins as Owners of Mauna Lani Hotel," *Pacific Business News*, p. 1.

________, 10 November 1986. "Japanese Firm Adds Quality Inn to Its Hawaii Hotel Portfolio," *Pacific Business News*, p. 1.

________, 8 December 1986. "Japan Firm buys Pentagram: Burger King Franchise Sold for Cash," *Pacific Business News*, p. 1.

Deardorff, A.V., 1980. "The General Validity of the Law of Comparative Advantage," *Journal of Political Economy*, Vol. 88, No. 5 (October), pp. 941-57.

________, 1984. "Comparative Advantage and International Trade and Investment in Services," Institute of Public Policy Studies Discussion Paper No. 210. Ann Arbor: University of Michigan.

________, 1985. "Comparative Advantage and International Trade and Investment in Services," in R.M. Stern (ed.), *Trade and Investment in Services: Canada/U.S. Perspectives*. Toronto: University of Toronto Press (for the Ontario Economic Council).

Deardorff, A.V., and R.M. Stern, 1986. "Current Issues in Trade Policy: An Overview," in R.M. Stern (ed.), *U.S. Trade Policies in a Changing World Economy*. Cambridge, MA: MIT Press.

Derthick, M., and P.J. Quirk, 1985. *The Politics of Deregulation*. Washington, D.C.: Brookings Institute.

Diluilo, A.J., 1981. "Service Transactions in the U.S. International Accounts, 1977-1980," *Survey of Current Business* (November), pp. 29-46.

Dixit, A.K., 1986. "How Should the U.S. Respond to Other Countries' Trade Policies?" in R.M. Stern (ed.), *U.S. Trade Policies in a Changing World Economy*. Cambridge, MA: MIT Press.

Djacic, S., and H. Kierzkowski, 1986. "Goods, Services, and Trade," Mimeo.

Dunning, J.H., and A.M. Rugman, 1985. "The Influence of Hymer's Dissertation on the Theory of Foreign Direct Investment," *American Economic Review* (May), pp. 228-32.

East Asian and Pacific Regional Office 1980. Korea: *Financial Sector Report*.

E.G. Frankel, Inc., 1981a. "Review of Existing Agreements and Potential Cargo Sharing Arrangements," *Impact of Cargo Sharing on U.S. Liner Trade with Countries in the Far East and South East Asia*, Vol. I. Report prepared for the Federal Maritime Commission.

________, 1981b. "Liner Services and Operational Impacts of Cargo Sharing," *Impact of Cargo Sharing on U.S. Liner Trade with Countries in the Far East and South East Asia*, Vol. II. Report prepared for the Federal Maritime Commission.

________, 1981c. "Economic Impacts of Cargo Sharing," *Impact of Cargo Sharing on U.S. Liner Trade with Countries in the Far East and South East Asia*, Vol. III. Report prepared for the Federal Maritime Commission.

Ebel, R., and J. Mak, 1974. *Current Issues in Hawaii's Economy*. Honolulu: Crossroads Press.

Economic Consulting Services, Inc., 1981. *The International Operation of U.S. Service Industries: Current Data Collection and Analysis*. Prepared for the U.S. Departments of State and Commerce and the Office of the U.S. Trade Representative, Washington, D.C.

Ethier, W.J., and L.E.O. Svensson, 1986. "The Theorems of International Trade with Factor Mobility," *Journal of International Economics*, Vol. 20, No. 1/2 (February), pp. 21-42.

Evans, D.S., and J.J. Heckman, 1983. "Multiproduct Cost Function Estimates and Natural Monopoly Tests for the Bell Systems," in D.S. Evans (ed.), *Breaking Up Bell: Essays on Industrial Organization and Regulation*. New York: Elsevier, pp. 252-83.

________, 1984. "A Test for Subadditivity of the Cost Function with an Application to the Bell System," *American Economic Review*, Vol. 74, No. 4 (September), pp. 615-23.

Far Eastern Economic Review, 1985. "Travel Trade Asia," *Far Eastern Economic Review* (September 12), pp. 56-84.

________, Various Issues.

Feketekuty, G., and J.D. Aronson, 1984. "Meeting the Challenges of the World Information Economy," *The World Economy*, Vol. 7,

No. 1 (March), pp. 63-86.

Feketekuty, G., and L.B. Krause, 1986. "Service and High Technology Goods in the New GATT Round," Paper presented at the First Pacific Trade Policy Forum (20-22 March), San Francisco.

Feldman, R.A., and A.J. Proctor, 1983. "U.S. International Trade in Services," *Federal Reserve Bank of New York Quarterly Review* (Spring), pp. 30-36.

Findlay, C., 1985. "A Framework for Services Trade Policy Questions," Pacific Economic Papers No. 126. Canberra: Australian National University.

Fuchs, V.R., 1968. *The Service Economy*. New York: National Bureau of Economic Research.

Gallant, P., 1985. *Electronic Treasury Management*. Wolfeboro, NH: Woodhead-Faulkner Publications.

Garrod, P.V., and W. Miklius, 1983. "Estimated Value of Improvements in Transport Services," *Transportation Research*, (A), Vol. 17A, No. 1 (January), pp. 33-37.

Gershuny, J.I., and I.D. Miles, 1983. *The New Service Economy*. London:Frances Pinter.

Gomez-Ibanez, J.A., and I.P. Morgan, 1984. "Deregulating International Markets: The Examples of Aviation and Ocean Shipping," *Yale Journal on Regulation*, Vol. 2, No. 1, pp. 107-44.

Gray, H.P., 1967. "Tourism as an Export Industry in Southeast Asia: A Long-Run Prognostication," *The Philippines Economic Journal*, Vol. I, No. 2, pp. 155-69.

Grey, R. deC., 1985. "Negotiating about Trade and Investment in Services," in R.M. Stern (ed.), *Trade and Investment Services: Canada/U.S. Perspectives*. Toronto: University of Toronto Press (for the Ontario Economic Council).

Grossman, G.M., and C. Shapiro, 1985. "Normative Issues Raised by International Trade in Technology Services," in R.M. Stern (ed.), *Trade and Investment in Services: Canada/U.S. Perspectives*. Toronto: University of Toronto Press (for the Ontario Economic Council).

Grubel, H.G., and D.L. Hammes, 1986. "A Note on the Importance of Monetization in the Growth of Market Service Consumption," Discussion Paper. Vancouver, BC: The Fraser Institute.

Grubel, H.G., and A.D. Scott, 1977. *The Brain Drain: Determinants, Measurement and Welfare Effects*. Waterloo, Ontario: Wilfred Laurier University Press.

Hawaii, State of, Department of Planning and Economic Development (DPED), International Services Branch, 1986. "A Listing of Foreign Investments in Hawaii'' (September 4), Honolulu: DPED, International Services Branch.

Herman, B., and B. van Holst, 1981. ''Toward a Theory of International Trade in Services.'' Netherlands Economic Institute, Mimeo.

Hill, T.P., 1977. ''On Goods and Services,'' *Review of Income and Wealth*, Vol. 23, No. 4 (December), pp. 315-38.

Hindley, B., and A. Smith, 1984. ''Comparative Advantage and Trade in Services,'' *The World Economy*, Vol. 7, No. 4 (December), pp. 369-90.

Hong Kong Tourist Association, Annual Issues 1977-1985. *A Statistical Review of Tourism, Hong Kong*. Hong Kong: Hong Kong Tourist Association.

Inman, R.F. (ed.), 1985. *Managing the Service Economy: Prospects and Problems*. Cambridge, England: Cambridge University Press.

International Monetary Fund (IMF), 1985. *Balance of Payments Statistics*, Vol. 36, Yearbook, Part I. Washington, D.C.: IMF.

———, 1984. *Balance of Payments Statistics*, Vol. 35, Yearbook, Part I. Washington, D.C.: IMF.

———, Various Annual Issues. *Balance of Payments Statistics*, Washington, D.C.: IMF.

International Tourism Reports, 1986. ''National Report Number 111: South Korea,'' No. 1, pp. 57-71.

———, 1986. ''National Report Number 115: Taiwan,'' No. 2, pp. 52-68.

International Tourism Quarterly, 1973. ''National Report Number 12: Japan,'' No. 4, pp. 30-46.

———, 1983. ''National Report Number 81: Japan,'' No. 3, pp. 18-35.

———, 1984. ''National Report Number 92: Thailand,'' No. 2, pp. 12-30.

Ito, Y., 1986. ''Telecommunications and Industrial Policies in Japan: Recent Developments,'' in M.S. Snow (ed.), *Marketplace for Telecommunications: Regulation and Deregulation in Industrialized Democracies*. New York: Longman, pp. 210-30.

Jansson, J.O., 1979. ''Marginal Cost Pricing on Scheduled Transport Services,'' *Journal of Transport Economics & Policy*, Vol. 13, No. 3 (September), pp. 268-94.

Japan Economic Research Institute, 1984. *Analysis of the Degree of Openness of the Japanese Market*.

Japan, Ministry of Finance, 1981. Monthly Statistical Review of Public Finance and Money, No. 356 (December).

________, Ministry of Transportation, 1985a. *Tourism in Japan, 1969–1985.*

________, Ministry of Transportation (ed.), 1985b. *The Current Situation of Japanese Shipping.* Tokyo: Japan Maritime Development Association.

Joho Sabisu Kyokai, 1986. "Whitepaper on Information Service Industry," (in Japanese).

Jones, R.W., 1985. "Comments" on A.V. Deardorff, "Comparative Advantage and International Trade and Investment in Services," in R.M. Stern (ed.), *Trade and Investment in Services: Canada/U.S. Perspectives.* Toronto: University of Toronto Press (for the Ontario Economic Council).

Jonscher, C., 1986. "Telecommunications Liberalization in the United Kingdom," in M.S. Snow (ed.), *Marketplace for Telecommunications: Regulation and Deregulation in Industrialized Democracies.* New York: Longman, pp. 153-72.

Jussawalla, M., 1985. "Constraints on Economic Analysis of Transborder Data Flow," *Media, Culture and Society*, Vol. 7, pp. 297-312.

Knieps, Gunter, Jurgen Muller, and C.C. Von Weizsacker, 1981. *Die Rolle des Wettbewerbs im Fernmeldebereich* (The Role of Competition in the Telecommunications Sector). Baden-Baden: Nomos.

Korea, Bureau of Tourism, Ministry of Tourism, 1974. *Tourism and Statistics.* Seoul: Ministry of Tourism.

________, Korean Securities Exchange Commission, 1982. "A Study on Capital Liberalization" (in Korean). Seoul: Korean Securities Exchange Commission.

________, Ministry of Transportation, 1985. *Korean Tourism, Annual Report, 1983-1985.*

Korea Research and Development, Inc., 1982. *Study of Potential Korean Holiday Travel Market with Specific Reference to the Pacific Area.* Seoul: Korea Tourism Research and Development, Inc.

Kravis, I.B., 1983. "Services in the Domestic Economy and in World Transactions," National Bureau of Economic Research (NBER) Working Paper 1124. New York: NBER.

________, 1985a. "Comments," IN R.M. Stern (ed.), *Trade and Investment in Services: Canada/U.S. Perspectives,* Toronto: University of Toronto Press (for the Ontario Economic Council).

________, 1985b. "Services in the Domestic Economy and World Transactions," in R.P. Inman (ed.), *Managing the Service Economy: Prospects and Problems.* New York: Cambridge University Press.

Kravis, I.B., A.W. Heston, and R. Summers, 1982. *World Product and Income: International Comparisons of Real Gross Product*. Baltimore: Johns Hopkins University Press.

———, 1983. "The Share of Services in Economic Growth," in F.G. Adams and B.G. Hickman (eds.), *Global Econometrics*. Cambridge, MA: MIT Press.

Krugman, P., 1986. "Strategic Sectors and International Competition," in R.M. Stern (ed.), *U.S. Trade Policies in a Changing World Economy*. Cambridge, MA: MIT Press.

Kumar, K., and M.G. McLeod, 1981. *Multinationals from Developing Countries*. Lexington: C.D. Heath & Co.

Kyle, R., 1984. *Review and Evaluation of Analyses on the Economic Impact and Service Cooperation by Ocean Liner Conferences* (March). Washington, D.C.: U.S. Department of Transportation.

Kyle, R., and L.T. Phillips, 1983. "Maritime Protections: A New Call for Cargo Preference," *Transportation Research Forum, Proceedings of the 24th Meeting*, pp. 700-05.

Lamberton, D.M., 1986. "Australian Regulatory Policy," in M.S. Snow (ed.), *Marketplace for Telecommunications: Regulation and Deregulation in Industrialized Democracies*. New York: Longman, pp. 231-52.

Lederer, E.P., W. Lederer, and R.L. Sammons, 1982. "International Services Transactions of the United States: Proposals for Improvement in Data Collection" (January). Prepared for the Departments of State and Commerce and the Office of the United States Trade Representative, unpublished.

Lee, C.H., and S. Naya, "The Internationalization of U.S. Service Industries and Its Implications for Developing Countries," *Journal of International Economic Integration* (forthcoming).

Lipsey, R.E., and I.B. Kravis, 1985. "The Competitive Position of U.S. Manufacturing Firms," *Banca Nazionale del Lavoro Quarterly Review* (June), pp. 127-54.

Lloyd's Register of Shipping, 1985. Statistics Tables, Register of Ships. London: Lloyd's Register of Shipping.

Madec, A., 1980. "The Political Economy of Information Flows," Intermedia, Vol. 9, No. 2.

Malmgren, H.B., 1985. "Negotiating International Rules for Trade in Services," *The World Economy*, Vol. 8, No. 1 (March), pp. 11-26.

Marcus, H.S., 1986. "Trends in U.S. Liner Shipping: Past, Present, and Future," Paper presented at the Fourth World Transportation Research Conference, 11-15 May, Vancouver, B.C., Canada.

McCulloch, R., 1985. "Comments" on G.M. Grossman and C.

Shapiro, "Normative Issues Raised by International Trade in Technology Services," in R.M. Stern (ed.), *Trade and Investment in Services: Canada/U.S. Perspectives*. Toronto: University of Toronto Press (for the Ontario Economic Council).

McIntyre, A.S., 1985. *Asia/Pacific Travel Markets and Their Potential for Hawaii Tourism* (April 24), Hawaii Visitors Bureau, Market Research Department, Honolulu, Mimeo.

Melvin, J.R., 1985. "Comments," in R.M. Stern (ed.), *Trade and Investment in Services: Canada/U.S. Perspectives*. Toronto: University of Toronto Press (for the Ontario Economic Council).

Mizoguchi, M., 1986. "Japan, the Pacific and the New Road," Paper presented to the First Pacific Trade Policy Forum held in March.

Mohring, H., 1972. "Optimization and Scale Economies in Urban Bus Transportation," *American Economic Review*, Vol. 62, No. 4 (September), pp. 591-604.

Momigliano, F., and D. Siniscalco, 1982. "The Growth of Service Employment: A Reappraisal," *Banca Nazionale del Lavoro Quarterly Review* (September), pp. 269-306.

Mundell, R.A., 1957. "International Trade and Factor Mobility," *American Economic Review*, Vol. 47, No. 3 (June), pp. 321-35.

Neumann, K.H., 1986. "Economic Policy Toward Telecommunications, Information and the Media in West Germany," In M.S. Snow (ed.), *Marketplace for Telecommunications: Regulation and Deregulation in Industrialized Democracies*. New York: Longman, pp. 131-52.

Neumann, K.H., U. Schweizer, and C.C. Von Weizsacker, 1983. "Welfare Analysis of Telecommunications Tariffs in Germany," in Finnsinger (ed.), *Public Sector Economics*. New York: St. Martin's Press, pp. 65-85.

Neumann, K.H., and B. Wieland, 1985. "Competition and Social Objectives: The Case of West German Telecommunications," Diskussionsbeitrage zur Telekommunikationsforschung, No. 14, Deutsche Bundespost, Wissenschaftlickes Institut fur Kommunikations dienste, Bonn.

Noam, E.M., 1986. "Telecommunications Policy on the Two Sides of the Atlantic: Divergence and Outlook," in M.S. Snow (ed.), *Marketplace for Telecommunications: Regulation and Deregulation in Industrialized Democracies*. New York: Longman, pp. 255-74.

Noll, R.G., 1983. "The Political Foundations of Regulatory Policy," *Zeitschriff fur die gesamte Staatswissenschaft*, Vol. 139, No. 3 (November), pp. 377-404.

———, 1986. "The Political and Institutional Context of Communications Policy," in M.S. Snow (ed.), *Marketplace for Telecommunications: Regulation and Deregulation in Industrialized Democracies*. New York: Longman, pp. 42-65.

Noll, R.G., and B.M. Owen, 1983. *The Political Economy of Deregulation: Interest Groups in the Regulatory Process*. Washington, D.C.: American Enterprise Institute.

Organization for Economic Cooperation and Development (OECD), 1983. *International Trade in Services: Insurance*. Paris: OECD.

________, 1984a. *International Trade in Services: Banking*. Paris: OECD.

________, 1984b. *Tourism Policy and International Tourism in OECD Member Countries*. Paris: OECD.

________, 1985. *Maritime Transport 1984*, Paris: OECD.

Olson, M., 1982. *The Rise and Decline of Nations: Economic Growth, Stagflation and Social Rigidities*. New Haven, CT: Yale University Press.

Oum, B., 1984. *Capital Liberalization and Internationalization of Securities Markets* (in Korean). Seoul: Korean Development Institute.

Pacific Area Travel Association, 1984. *Study of Overseas Holiday Travel from Hong Kong to the Pacific Area*, San Francisco: Pacific Area Travel Association.

Petit, P., 1986. *Slow Growth and the Service Economy*. New York: St. Martin's Press.

Philippines, 1983. *Philippine Yearbook, 1983*, Manila: PNEDA.

________, Philippines National Economic and Development Authority (PNEDA), 1985. *Philippine Yearbook, 1985*, Manila: National Economic and Development Authority (PNEDA).

Praet, P., 1985. "EEC and ASEAN in the International Exchange of Services: A European Perspective," in J. Waelbroeck, P. Praet, and H.C. Rieger (eds.), *ASEAN-EEC Trade in Services*. Singapore: Institute of Southeast Asian Studies.

Republic of China (ROC), 1985. *Statistical Yearbook of the Republic of China, 1985*. Taipei: Directorate General of Budget, Accounting, and Statistics, the Republic of China.

Riddle, D.I., 1986. Service-Led Growth: The Role of the Service Sector in World Development. New York: Praeger.

Robinson, S., 1986. "Analyzing the Information Economy: Tools and Techniques," *Information Processing and Management*, Vol. 22, No. 3, pp. 183-202.

Royama, Asano, and Ueno, 1986. "Sabisu Boeki Masatsu: Dai San no Jiyuka ni Mukete" (Trade Friction in Services: Toward the Third Liberalization), Nihon Keizai Shihbun Sha.

Rubin, M.R., and E. Taylor, 1981. "The U.S. Information Sector and GNT: An Input-Output Study," *International Processing and Management*, Vol. 17, No. 4, pp. 163-94.

Rubin, M.R., and M.E. Sapp, 1981. "Selected Roles of Information Goods and Services in the U.S. National Economy," *Information Processing and Management*, Vol. 17, No. 4, pp. 195-213.

Sampson, G.P., and R.H. Snape, 1985. "Identifying Issues in Trade in Services," *The World Economy*, Vol. 8, No. 2 (June), pp. 171-82.

Sapir, A., 1981. "Determinants of Trade in Services," CEME Discussion Paper No. 8104. Brussels: Universite Libre de Bruxelles.

Sapir, A., and E. Lutz, 1980. "Trade in Non-Factor Services: Past Trends and Current Issues," World Bank Staff Working Paper No. 410. Washington, D.C.: World Bank.

________, 1981. "Trade in Services: Economic Determinants and Development-Related Issues," World Bank Staff Working Paper, No. 480. Washington, D.C.: World Bank.

Sapir, A., and D. Schumacher, 1984. "The Employment Impact of Shifts in the Composition of Commodity and Services Trade," OECD Intergovernmental Conference on Employment Growth in the Context of Structural Change. Paris: OECD.

Sauvant, K.P., 1983. "Transborder Data Flows and the Developing Countries," *International Organization*, Vol. 37, No. 2, pp. 359-71.

Saxonhouse, G.R., 1985. "Services in the Japanese Economy," in R.P. Inman (ed.), *Managing the Service Economy: Prospects and Problems*. New York: Cambridge University Press.

Sharkey, W.W., 1982. *The Theory of Natural Monopoly*. New York: Cambridge University Press.

Shelp, R.K., 1981. *Beyond Industrialization*. New York: Praeger Publishers.

Shepherd, W.G., 1983. "Concepts of Competition and Efficient Policy in the Telecommunications Sector," in E.M. Noam (ed.), *Telecommunications Regulation Today and Tomorrow*, New York: Harcourt Brace Jovanovich, pp. 79-120.

________, 1984. "Contestability vs. Competition," *American Economic Review*, Vol. 74, No. 4 (September), pp. 572-87.

Shneerson, D., 1986. "Efficiency and Competition in Liner Shipping," Paper presented at the Fourth World Transportation Research Conference, 11-15 May, Vancouver, B.C., Canada.

Singapore Tourist Association, Annual Publications 1982-1984, *Annual Statistical Report of Visitor Arrival to Singapore*.

Snow, M.S., 1976. *International Commercial Satellite Communications:*

Economic and Political Issues of the First Decade of INTELSAT. New York: Praeger.

________, 1982. "Telecommunications and Media Policy in West Germany: Recent Developments," *Journal of Communication*, Vol. 32, No. 3 (Summer), pp. 20-32.

________, 1983. "Telecommunications Deregulation in the Federal Republic of Germany," Columbia Journal of World Business, Vol. 18, No. 1 (Spring), pp. 53-61.

________, 1985. "Arguments for and against Competition in International Satellite Facilities and Services: A U.S. Perspective," *Journal of Communication*, Vol. 35, No. 3 (Summer), pp. 51-79.

________, 1986. "An Economic Issue in International Telecommunications: Natural Monopoly in Commercial Satellite Systems." Paper presented at the "Explorations in Space Policy" Symposium held in Washington, D.C. by Resources for the Future and National Academy of Engineering.

________, (forthcoming). "The State as Stopgap: Social Economy and Sustainability of Monopoly in the Telecommunications Sector," *Review of Social Economy*.

Snowberger, V.C., 1978. "Sustainability Theory: Its Implications for Governmental Preservation of a Regulated Monopoly," *Quarterly Review of Economics and Business*, Vol. 18, No. 4 (Winter), pp. 81-89.

Spence, A.M., 1983. "Contestable Markets and the Theory of Industry Structure: A Review Article," *Journal of Economic Literature,* Vol. 21, No. 3 (September), pp. 981-90.

Ssangyong Investment & Securities Co., Ltd., Research Department, 1984. "Capital Liberalization and Strategies of Korean Firms" (in Korean), Seoul: Ssangyong Investment and Securities Co., Ltd.

Stanbeck, T.M., Jr., 1979. *Understanding the Service Economy*. Baltimore: The Johns Hopkins University Press.

Stern, R.M., 1984. "Current Issues in Trade and Investment in Service Industries," Paper presented at the Third Annual Workshop on U.S.-Canadian Relations.

________ (ed.), 1985a. *Trade and Investment in Services: Canada/U.S. Perspectives.* Toronto: The Univeristy of Toronto Press (for the Ontario Economic Council).

________, 1985b. "Global Dimensions and Determinants of International Trade and Investment in Services," in R.M. Stern (ed.), *Trade and Investment in Services: Canada/U.S. Perspectives*. Toronto: University of Toronto Press (for the Ontario Economic Council).

Stern, R.M., and B.M. Hoekman, 1986. "Data Needs for Trade Negotiations in Services," Paper presented at the National Bureau of Economic Research (NBER) Conference on Data Needs for U.S. Bilateral and Multilateral Trade Negotiations, held 19 September in Washington, D.C.

Summers, R., 1985. "Services in the International Economy," in R.F. Inman (ed.), *Managing the Service Economy: Prospects and Problems*. Cambridge, England: Cambridge University Press.

Taplin, J.H.E., 1983. "Regulation, Deregulation, and the Sustainability of Transport Monopolies," *The Logistics and Transportation Review*, Vol. 19, No. 1 (March), pp. 31-44.

Temple, Barker & Sloane, Inc., 1984. "Strategic Options for U.S. Liner Operations" (July), Report prepared for DOT/Transportation Systems Center.

Thailand, Tourism Authority of Thailand, 1985. *Annual Statistical Report on Tourism in Thailand, 1984*, Bangkok.

Thiemeyer, T., 1983. "Deregulation in the Perspective of the German *Gemeinwirtschaftelehre*," *Zeitschrift fur die gesamte Staatswissenschaft*, Vol. 139, No. 3 (November), pp. 405-18.

Turvey, R., and H. Mohring, 1975. "Optimal Bus Fares," *Journal of Transport Economics & Policy,* Vol. 9, No. 3 (September), pp. 280-86.

Tustin, W.J., 1984. "The Logistics of the Falklands War," *The Army Quarterly and Defence Journal*, Vol. 114, No. 3/4 (July).

Tyler, C., 15 July 1986a. "Developing Countries Dig in for Services Battle," *Financial Times*.

________, 23 June 1986b. "GATT and World Trade: A Suitable Case for Salvage," *Financial Times*.

United States, United States International Trade Commission (USITC) 1982. *The Relationship of Exports in Selected U.S. Service Industries to U.S. Merchandise Exports*. Publication 1290 (September), Washington, D.C.: USITC.

________, USITC, 1983a. *U.S. National Study on Trade in Services.* A Submission by the United States Government to the General Agreement on Tariffs and Trade (December). Washington, D.C.: Office of the U.S. Trade Representative.

________, Office of the United States Trade Representative, 1983b. *U.S. National Study on Trade in Services*, Washington, D.C.

________, U.S. Department of Commerce, Various Issues, *Survey of Current Business*.

Vestal, J.E., 1985. *An Analysis of the Determinants and Commodity Trade Effects of Japanese Technology Trade*. Ph.D. diss.,

The University of Michigan.

Voge, J.P., 1986. "A Survey of French Regulatory Policy," in M.S. Snow (ed.), Marketplace for Telecommunications: Regulation and Deregulation in Industrialized Democracies. New York: Longman.

Von Weizsacker, C.C., 1986. "Free Entry Into Telecommunications?" in M.S. Snow (ed.), *Marketplace for Telecommunications: Regulation and Deregulation in Industrialized Democracies*. New York: Longman, pp. 20-41.

Voss, B., 23 December 1985. "Hong Kong Group Buys Tropical Rent-A-Car," *Pacific Business News*.

Whichard, O.G., 1984. "U.S. International Trade and Investment in Services: Data Needs and Availability," Bureau of Economic Analysis Staff Paper 41 (September). Washington, D.C.: U.S. Department of Commerce.

Whichard, O.G., and A. Shea, 1985. "1982 Benchmark Survey of U.S. Direct Investment Abroad," *Survey of Current Business*, Vol. 65, No. 12 (December).

White, K.J., and M.B. Walker, 1982. "Trouble in the Travel Account," *Annals of Tourism Research*, Vol. 9, No. 1 (Spring), pp. 37-56.

World Bank, 1985. *World Development Report 1985*, Washington, D.C.: World Bank.

World Tourism Organization (WTO), 1980, *Economic Review of World Tourism*, Madrid: WTO. 1985a. *Regional Breakdown of World Travel and Tourism Statistics, 1980-1984*, Madrid: WTO.

________, 1985b. *Traveller Destinations and Main Destinations, 1980-1984*, Madrid: WTO.

________, 1986a. *Economic Review of World Tourism, 1980-1986*, Madrid: WTO.

________, 1986b. *Travel Abroad, Frontier Formalities*, Madrid: WTO.

Index